Transgender Studies Quarterly

Volume 4 ★ Number 1 ★ February 2017

Trans- Political Economy

Edited by Dan Irving and Vek Lewis

T0313409

General Editors' Introduction

PAISLEY CURRAH and SUSAN STRYKER

June 2016 saw the US-based multinational bank Goldman Sachs flying the pink, white, and blue transgender flag outside its Manhattan headquarters. It saw the United Nations Human Rights Council passing a resolution to appoint an "Independent Expert" to study violence and discrimination based on sexual orientation and gender identity. It saw Pentagon officials announcing the end of the ban on transgender people serving in the US armed forces. No longer occupying a position on the margins of civic and economic life, transgender people, it would seem, are increasingly valued as employees, as consumers, as victims in need of saving, and now in the United States, as potential warriors.

Valued is right. The recognition of transgender as a source of value, not only for corporations but also for nonprofit sectors that have embraced the rhetoric of the market, has become a popular theme for the ideologues of the current capitalist moment. Whether rescuing trans "victims," profiting from the creativity of gender-diverse employees, or carving out new transgender-specific consumer markets, the neoliberal creed now presents discrimination against trans (and GLB) people as "an enormous waste of human potential, of talent, of creativity, of productivity, that weighs heavily on society and on the economy" (Park 2015: 1). As the head of the largest GLBT advocacy group in the United States explained at the Davos World Economic Forum, "Around the world, businesses have far outpaced lawmakers in embracing the basic premise that the hard work and talents of all their employees—regardless of who they are or whom they love—are rewarded fairly in their workplaces. . . . No executive wants to lose the next brilliant employee to a competitor simply because the business has not caught up with the times in terms of inclusive policies" (Griffin 2016).

Of course, precisely how transgender becomes a source of value depends on its location vis-à-vis the "coloniality of power," as guest editors Vek Lewis and Dan Irving point out in the introduction to this issue. Understanding "how contemporary 'architectures' of power differentially and unequally affect trans

TSQ: Transgender Studies Quarterly ∗ Volume 4, Number 1 ∗ February 2017
DOI 10.1215/23289252-3711481   © 2017 Duke University Press

and sex/gender-diverse people across the globe," they write, requires us to "grapple with the complexity of trans/gender capitalist and colonial relations, including the ways in which the transgender paradigm itself, which is of US origin, can be epistemologically and politically complicit." For example, an activist writing about the UN Human Rights Council's decision to appoint an expert on sexual orientation and gender identity suggests that "employing SOGI/LGBTI/queer/trans as a singular palatable thing, rather than a queer, feminist and anticolonial resistance," fails to "trouble the normativity of a human rights discourse that leaves colonialism, racism and global north exceptionalism largely unchallenged" (Hoosain Khan 2016). Directing our attention to particular identities in need of rescue masks the processes and structures that manufacture privilege and precarity alongside commodities. Such an approach also makes possible the emergence of a "*comprador* LGBT movement" (some of largest LGBT organizations doing international work are funded by the US State Department) that advances the interests of global capitalism, economic imperialism, and militarism (Long 2016). Indeed, as we were drafting this introduction, one of us received a fund-raising solicitation from a US-based international LGBTQ rights organization with "Fight ISIS" in its subject line.

This special issue of *TSQ* on what the authors call trans- political economy (TPE) provides a timely and necessary intervention in trans studies. In their extensive introduction, Lewis and Irving lay out the contours of TPE as it currently exists and map the field's relation to the feminist, antiracist, and decolonial work in political economy that made it possible. The articles that follow demonstrate how trans studies and political economy's reigning binaries, labor-capital and transgender-cisgender, obscure the centrality of racializing, colonizing, and gendering processes within the architectures of power they purport to interrogate. As Lewis and Irving point out, and as the contributors empirically demonstrate, the production of vulnerability in racialized and colonized gender-nonconforming populations is not accidental but *integral* to capitalism and the neoliberal political project—from the commodification of a legible minoritizing trans identity in asylum claims to the economic value attached to whiteness, able-bodiedness, and hegemonic gender, to the cultivation of trans entrepreneurship in the new sharing economy, to the affective yet marginalized labor demanded of some trans people in the Global South.

Far from inserting a conservatizing identity politics into the field of political economy, and far from simply asking that trans and sex/gender-diverse people be added to such already existing categories as worker and consumer, Lewis and Irving and the contributors to this issue reveal how the narrowly constructed "proper objects" of trans studies and political economy (e.g., gender, labor, class, the economy) have been "complicit in necropolitical devaluations of trans lives and actually existing strategies crafted for trans survival." Certainly the efforts of TPE scholars to remedy these exclusions are far from complete. But at a moment when "the main center of discontent within the capitalist dynamic is increasingly shifting [from production] to struggles over the realization of value" (Harvey 2016), the field's attention to "the ways that particular trans lives become imbued with (or stripped of) value," as Lewis and Irving put it, augurs well for its significance in the years to come.

Paisley Currah is professor of political science and women's and gender studies at Brooklyn College and the Graduate Center of the City University of New York, and general coeditor of *TSQ: Transgender Studies Quarterly*.

Susan Stryker is associate professor of gender and women's studies at the University of Arizona and general coeditor of *TSQ: Transgender Studies Quarterly*.

References

Griffin, Chad. 2016. "How Businesses Are Standing Up for LGBT Rights." *World Economic Forum*, January 7. www.weforum.org/agenda/2016/01/how-businesses-are-standing-up-for-lgbt -rights/.

Harvey, David. 2016. "Neoliberalism Is a Political Project." *Jacobin*, July 23. www.jacobinmag.com /2016/07/david-harvey-neoliberalism-capitalism-labor-crisis-resistance/.

Hoosain Khan, Gabriel. 2016. "The UN, Seen from Khayelitsha: Guest Post." *A Paper Bird: Sex, Rights, and the World* (blog), July 6. paper-bird.net/2016/07/06/the-un-seen-from -khayelitsha/.

Long. 2016. "Cairo, and Our Comprador Gay Movements." *A Paper Bird: Sex, Rights, and the World* (blog), June 22. paper-bird.net/2016/06/22/cairo-comprador-gay-movements/.

Park, Andrew. 2015. "The Price of Exclusion: A Research Guide to Accompany the *Price of Exclusion* Video by Free & Equal, Narrated by Zachary Quinto." Williams Institute. December 11. williamsinstitute.law.ucla.edu/wp-content/uploads/The-Price-of-Exclusion -Research-Guide.pdf.

Strange Alchemies
The Trans- Mutations of Power and Political Economy

VEK LEWIS and DAN IRVING

The Rebis, the early modern European alchemical symbol pictured on the cover of this issue, is a winged hermaphroditic figure — half woman, holding aloft a crown, half bearded man, brandishing a scepter — that stands on a dragon whose twin heads encircle the dual figure's legs. The Rebis represented the pinnacle of alchemical transformation: it conjoined the lower realms with the higher, the secular with the divine, the physical with the spiritual, mind with matter, and masculine with feminine to depict the perfect resolution of all dichotomies, dualities, and antinomies. The Rebis is also a figure of sovereignty; it bears symbols of authority, holds sway over the elements, and is capable of surveilling all directions simultaneously with its double-headed vision. As an emblem redolent of godlike mastery over the material transformations of bodies, lives, and worlds, the Rebis exemplifies a Eurocentric and implicitly colonizing fantasy about the nature of power. As such, it exemplifies as well the key vectors of analysis, central categories of thought, and principal forms of rhetoric and representation that we seek (in less mystical and magical modes) to explore, critique, and resist in this special issue of *TSQ* on trans- political economy.

Our chief concern is with how contemporary "architectures" of power differentially and unequally affect trans and sex/gender-diverse people across the globe — and how we all, from our different social and political locations, become implicated in those architectures through our everyday interactions with a variety of coordinated and contradictory institutions and rationalities that order our lives across different local and global geopolitical spaces and scales. The arrangements of power that concern us here are often rendered synonymous with modernity, itself a shorthand for contemporary industrial civilization, which we understand as an enterprise emanating from the Global North and which we can characterize with a single term: *capitalism*.

DOI 10.1215/23289252-3711493   © 2017 Duke University Press

Capitalist modernity is a dynamic social order composed of multiple sociopolitical, economic, and cultural institutions. It is defined broadly by a philosophical approach to the physical world whereby human intervention transforms nature through a competitive market economy, industrial production, sovereign nation-states, and mass democracies (Giddens and Pierson 1998). It is characterized by rationalization, objectivism, mechanization, alienation, secularism, hierarchization, commodification, individualism, subjectification, and decontextualization. As a set of processes with global reach, modernity is inextricably tied up with colonialism: first in constructing a Eurocentric world-system (Wallerstein 1979) by expropriating foreign lands and enslaving and co-opting Indigenous and African labor and knowledge, and second in promulgating Eurocentric modernity as the most desired outcome of socioeconomic developmentalism the whole world over. Taken up by elites on the so-called periphery of the Eurocentric world-system, the push toward capitalist modernity interacts with local cultures, political structures, and socioeconomic processes, giving rise to differential and contradictory modernities and relations of dependency to the Eurocentric core. As such, modernity and its effects provide an indispensable schematic for social-scientific theorizations of the existing world order and constitute the chief preoccupations and problems confronted by political economy in its dominant form.

Defining Political Economy

En route to propounding what we are calling trans- political economy (TPE), it is first necessary to explain what we mean by "political economy" itself. Political economy is grounded on the premise that economic activities are not isolated from political and social processes. This broad framework problematizes the intertwined relationship between economic systems, political environments, social organizations, familial structures, and informal networks. Beyond technical economic debates, one major arena of analysis probes economic doctrines such as classical liberal models of free market competitive capitalism — which have inspired contemporary neoliberal formations — "to disclose their sociological and political premises" (Maier 1987: 4). State institutions and strategies to control resources — which often reflect corporate interests — represent another aspect of political economy. Key questions in this domain address the dynamic and often contradictory governmental processes of integrating free market logic into domestic and international policies, and of engaging in a social and environmental calculus of costs and benefits to cultivate the ground for continuous economic growth.

Analysis of political economy can contribute to feminist, antiracist, and decolonial scholarship given the interconnectedness of capitalism with heteropatriarchy and colonialism. Feminist political economy (FPE) works to dislodge the "masculine mythology" (Ferber and Nelson 1993) underlying economic theorizations of modernity that devalue femininity by deploying objectivist, rationalist, and universalizing principles. Other FPE scholars emphasize the primacy for capital accumulation of women's unpaid work in the private sphere (e.g., child care, housework, and emotional labor) and the naturalization of this labor appropriation through gender- and sexuality-based subject formation and political mobilization (Bakker and Gill 2003; Bezanson and Luxton 2006; Brown 1995; Hennessy 2002). Antiracist FPE scholars in the North challenge the ways that white middle-class femininity can be privileged even within radical critiques of the gendered dimensions of social reproduction, while other debates shift focus to the implications for the Global South of the transnational circulation of Northern configurations of gender, sexuality, and race in neoliberal post-Fordist regimes of accumulation (Connell 1987). Still other scholars interrogate new demands for "immaterial" or "affective" work that supersedes conventional notions of labor and value, and that requires particular bodies to produce feelings of excitement, tranquility, hope, satisfaction, and legitimacy for themselves and others—work performed with increasing frequency by bodies designated as "transgender." Such concerns, however, lie far from the heart of orthodox political economy.

Trans- Political Economy as Existing Subfield

We take up a political economy analysis whose inspirations are found beyond the traditional reach of the field, in the deconstructive work of feminist, antiracist, and decolonial scholarship. A relatively new subfield in transgender studies, TPE is nevertheless a key area of scholarship and activism. From its inception in the early 1990s through the work of Sandy Stone (1991) and Susan Stryker (1994), transgender studies theorized sexed embodiment and gendered subjectivity as social phenomena. Especially influential was the concept of the de/construction of the sex/gender system through the instantiation of norms, and the generative in/coherencies in the production of sexed and gendered bodies. In contrast to this concern with sex/gender norms and the transgression of the sex/gender binary, TPE has highlighted the links between the exploitative logics of capitalism and trans/gender oppression (Feinberg 1992, 1996, 1998). TPE addressed issues such as employment discrimination (Broadus 2006; Namaste 2000; Schilt 2010), poverty (Gehi and Arkles 2007), and the lack of access to essential social services (Spade 2006a), as well as barriers to accessing shelters and housing, and the criminalization of trans women, particularly sex workers (Namaste 2011; Ross, c. 2005).

TPE scholarship has been particularly prominent in Latin America. Josefina Fernández (2004) focuses on the sociopolitical and economic dimensions of *travesti* lives in Buenos Aires, and documents how these lives are regulated via discourses of abnormality, control, observation, and juridical interpellation.

Leticia Sabsay (2011) shows how moral universes related to gender and sexuality impinge on notions of citizenship in Argentina, specifically in relation to the irruption of a *travesti* sex worker presence in the urban capital. Other social scientists — Daniel Hernández-Rosete Martínez (2008, Mexico), Joselí Maria Silva and Marcio Ornat (2015, Brazil), Antonio Agustín García García and Sara Oñate Martínez (2008, Ecuador), Katrin Vogel (2009, Venezuela) — focus on the matrix of violence, labor, and health care (particularly transition-related care and HIV/AIDS) for trans women and *travestis*. Giuseppe Campuzano (2009) in particular frames this violence as an inheritance of colonial legacies. Several of these scholars focus on trans migration, detailing the transnational economies of sex work through which many trans women and *travestis* both encounter and challenge local forms of racial discrimination and criminalization while managing to produce social and economic capital of benefit both to themselves and to their families back home. TPE work specifically on Latin American trans migration, together with other recent work on other parts of the Global South, gives us a newly sophisticated understanding of the transnational circuits of capital, labor, and consumption (David 2015; Aizura 2011), as well as the gendered politics of mobility and nation building within and across territorial and categorical borders.

Neoliberalism as a specific regime of capitalist accumulation has captivated the attention of TPE scholars and activists in both the North and the South. Influenced by Michel Foucault's (1991, 2007) theories of governmentality and biopower, these scholars have focused on discourses of self-sufficiency, personal responsibility and productivity, investment in the self, and consumer activities to demonstrate the "psychic life" (Butler 1997) of neoliberalism. They argue that political economy always depends on particular forms of sexed embodiment and gender performance, and that "transgender" becomes somehow functional in transnational neoliberal regimes. Neoliberalism constructs certain forms of trans subjectivity as "proper," "good," and "deserving" of access to life chances, human rights protections, and national belonging (Spade 2006b; Irving 2008; Aizura 2006). Such subjectivities are rendered intelligible precisely through their interactions with the state and other instruments of governmentality. Critical TPE scholarship unveils how the recognition of trans people's economic value hinges on their relationships to whiteness, hegemonic masculinity or normative femininity, able-bodiedness, and citizenship status. Such queer and trans of color critiques challenge the deprioritization of white supremacy, racialization, and colonization in transgender studies itself (Haritaworn, Kuntsman, and Posocco 2014).

TPE scholarship often reorients the focus of political economy away from biopolitics (the ways that neoliberal states, institutions, and organizations administer the lives of their populations) and, building on the work of Achille Mbembe, toward necropolitics (the ways certain categories of bodies are marked for premature death) to better understand the lives of racialized and colonized gender-nonconforming subjects, and to advance an interconnected analysis of the gender, sexual, capitalist, colonial, and national relations of power that can best be conceptualized as "a politics of war" waged against those deemed inimical to "life itself" in its privileged forms (Mbembe 2003). Queer and trans necropolitical analysis focuses, in part, on the ways that racialized trans* subjects are constructed as an enemy to be marginalized or cast out from heteronormative, homonormative, and trans-normative liberal capitalist, settler colonial, and seemingly postcolonial societies (Raha 2015).

Contemporary forms of neoliberal policy and governance, like the rationalities of modernity and capitalism on which they depend, have given rise to various neoliberal regimes in different parts of the current global order (Connell and Dados 2014). If we turn to the issue of capital accumulation, however, we can see how heavily dependent all such regimes have become on precarious, low-wage, part-time, and informal employment with few or no benefits. Vulnerability is not an exception to neoliberal capitalism but an integral mechanism for exploitative processes of wealth accumulation. Trans people of color, two-spirit people, and *travestis* are overrepresented among the swelling ranks of those deemed "existentially surplus" (Hong 2006; Carreras Sendra 2009). The lives of so many racialized trans people, especially trans women, are conceptualized as worthless lives unfit for living; they are devalued as "bare life" devoid of political significance (Agamben 1998). The exclusion of such lives from the domain of lives worth living exceeds the symbolic realm and results in the literal deaths of trans subjects through imprisonment or immigration detention, interpersonal violence, and stigmatization related to HIV/AIDS—to name but a few ways to eliminate the racialized and colonized others that make up the bulk of the "surplus" population. In this vein, key work in TPE has emerged on trans subject-formation, neoliberal governance (De Angelis 2005; Santos 2009), and the ways that particular trans lives become imbued with (or stripped of) value in relation to race, as well as discourses and policy concerning ethnic "minorities" (Thomas 2006; Juang 2006; Haritaworn, Kuntsman, and Posocco 2014).

TPE critiques a political economy orthodoxy that occupies a privileged position on the left, particularly in Northern-dominant spaces, such as world-systems approaches and singular Marxist approaches. TPE scholarship emphasizes "ghostly" phenomena (Roundtable, this issue) that are usually illegible within such orthodox approaches. TPE resists "additive" logics whereby trans*, two-spirit, gender-nonconforming, colonized, and racialized others are integrated into economic categories such as "the working class," "the precariat," "consumers," or "reproductive labor(ers)" that are naturalized as preexisting classifications. It emphasizes instead the specificity of activities undertaken by trans* women and men and trans* communities as integral to contemporary regimes of wealth accumulation. TPE points, however, to a more fundamental necessity for reformulating political economic analysis entirely. While it is important to ensure that gender-nonconforming subjects are understood as vital albeit typically unrecognized parts of existing economies, it is equally important to expand the definition of "economy," to move past imagining capitalism as the singular mode of production and reducing the entirety of the contemporary regime of wealth accumulation to neoliberalism. Such imaginative and critical failures may themselves become complicit in necropolitical devaluations of trans lives and actually existing strategies crafted for trans survival.

The Coloniality of Power and the Colonial Matrix

Theorists of the decolonial turn contend that modernity and coloniality cannot be perceived as two different processes (Quintero 2010; Mignolo 2000; Escobar 2005; Quijano 1992). Most of the Global South has not entered into any kind of postcoloniality and still exists within an asymmetrical global division of labor and geopolitical power. Decolonial theorists critique Eurocentrism as an ostensibly universal frame of knowledge that propounds a system of hierarchical racial/ethnic and gender/sexual classifications with the values of democracy and individualism, a belief in "progress" and rationality of culture, and capitalist economic relations (Escobar 2005). Aníbal Quijano (2000: 368) introduced the counter-Eurocentric concept of *colonialidad del poder* to signal how, since the colonization of the Americas, people have been classified within a power structure based on labor, race, and gender to control both resources and the reproduction of life. Similarly, Ramón Grosfoguel proposes that we see the present world-system as entailing a "system of heterarchic power," that is, a system compounded from multiple hierarchies of labor, ethnicity/race, gender, sex, epistemology, spirituality, aesthetics, pedagogy, and language (quoted in Montes Montoya and Busso 2007: 4–5).

The "coloniality of power" framework underpins all the contributions to this special issue of *TSQ*. It creates a space for uncovering logics of domination that frequently operate under the guise of freedom, progress, modernization, or development that are discursively posited as being for the good of all but which typically result in ecological devastation and the exploitation of Southern lives. The closely related concept of a "colonial matrix" also comes into play here (Mignolo 2000: 6–11). The matrix encompasses four major registers of power — economic, political, civic, and epistemic or subjective/personal. Colonial dominance in the economic realm is exercised through the seizure and privatization of resources, and the control of finance and the distribution of wealth; the political component involves the exercise of authority, while colonial control over the forms of civil society influence the social organization of gender and sexuality; the fourth aspect involves the control of knowledge that informs the construction of individual subjectivity. María Lugones (2007) takes this analysis further by conceptualizing the "coloniality of gender," which understands the gender orders inaugurated through colonialism as more than just an aspect of the coloniality of power. For Lugones, colonial gender systems installed new gender orders in colonized territories and transformed gender relations locally and translocally in ways every bit as substantive as transformations in the register of race. These racial and gender schema have histories that still affect the material and social conditions of human and nonhuman lives across the globe — including, significantly, sex/gender-diverse peoples. Emphasizing the coloniality of power and acknowledging the persistence of the colonial matrix lets us grapple with the complexity of trans/gender capitalist and colonial relations, including how the transgender paradigm itself, which is of US origin, can be epistemologically and politically complicit in the reiteration of capitalist/colonialist relations and effects.

Although capitalist exploitation and the genocidal logics of colonialism continue to configure most of the world's societies, there are spaces where subaltern knowledges are re/produced and distributed but nevertheless remain marginalized. Approaching TPE through the coloniality of power illuminates spaces where "border thinking" (Mignolo 2000) already takes place or where it could become a possibility. Global capitalism, cultural and economic imperialism, and Western exceptionalism cannot be understood as wholesale impositions that totally obliterate existing societies. Understanding the coloniality of power enables us to comprehend each aspect of the colonial matrix as a set of contested territories. Because competing understandings and practices coexist, aspects of global capitalist relations can be resisted and sometimes rejected or ignored; they can be adopted or adapted in ways that integrate aspects of both subaltern and dominant knowledges or approaches to the social order.

The Articles

The first article, Emmanuel David's "Capital T: Trans Visibility, Corporate Capitalism, and Commodity Culture," posits that a new value, symptomatic of the lures and maneuvers of neoliberal capital, is being generated at the three-fold juncture of trans consumption, production, and labor. In this age of the "Transgender Tipping Point," capital has become capable of the ultimate form of appropriation in the name of trans recognition: extending its sphere of influence into trans labor, desire, and political energy. David offers a "friendly critique" of Angelica Ross's TransTech Social Enterprises, which trains and hires trans and gender-diverse people as remote IT-support contract workers. Ross argues that her business model is community serving because it provides labor opportunities so often denied to trans people, promotes peer-to-peer empowerment, and offers a healthy workplace by distancing workers from immediate encounters with transphobia and racism. While the appeal of TransTech as social enterprise is clear, David argues that its workers are nevertheless exploited through the contractual burdens and conditions of dependence, surveillance, labor instability, and lower-economic-rung existence that typify the industry. He demonstrates how "trans value," created precisely by the recognition of trans people as marginalized yet recuperable minority subjects, hence becomes "an important site of recruitment and extraction." The point on capitalist value and extraction becomes more critical when considering TransTech's projections of contracting among sex/gender-diverse people in the Global South, on local wage scales, which could implicate its operations in economic imperialism.

In "The Afterlife of Data: Identity, Surveillance, and Capitalism in Trans Credit Reporting," Lars Mackenzie similarly explores the regulation of trans lives in the private sector. He details how the persistence of electronic records, particularly credit reports, creates an environment fraught with risk for trans people through the threat of inadvertent disclosure of their trans status and transition history, which can result in discrimination. However, to *not* link personal identity and financial information across a gender transition carries risks of its own, namely, becoming a person with no credit history in an economic system that uses debt and credit to regulate the life chances of a range of populations. These tensions, as well as the lack of standardization of electronic identity recognition practices across numerous institutional contexts, create a chaotic landscape that trans people must creatively navigate in a high-stakes game that could make or break the financial viability of their lives.

In the third article, "Categories and Queues: The Structural Realities of Gender and the South African Asylum System," B Camminga also focuses on the institutional creation and regulation of knowable gendered identities, through an ethnographic study of undocumented trans and nonbinary asylum seekers in South Africa—one of the few countries in the world that offers asylum to people based on their trans or gender-variant status. Camminga charts the problems encountered by refugees who seek to register with a Refugee Register Office by examining the risks of queuing in lines segregated by sex/gender. Gender-variant and trans refugees must perform a particular kind of gender labor to successfully navigate the asylum process, convince officers of their identities and experiences of persecution, and hence secure asylum. Visibility, once again, has two faces: it involves the risk of being seen as an incoherent subject, unworthy of asylum, as well as the potential benefit of accruing social capital as a recognized and recognizable trans refugee—and thus being able to work or study in South Africa.

An ethnographic attention to questions of recognition, capital, and nation similarly characterizes Benjamin Hegarty's "Value of Transgender: *Waria*

Affective Labor for Transnational Media Markets in Indonesia." *Waria* is an Indonesian portmanteau term for people on the male-to-female spectrum, derived from the words *wanita* (woman) and *pria* (man); Hegarty builds on a concept of affective labor derived from Antonio Negri, Michael Hardt, and feminist affect theory scholars to stress the importance of understanding *waria* labor within Indonesian histories of gender and sexuality. Hegarty observes and analyzes how *waria* have responded to foreign filmmakers who perpetuate a trope of *waria* as particularly marginalized and oppressed transgender sex workers, a trope that serves necropolitical ends by folding *waria* into a decontextualized, transnationally circulating "transgender" status. The *waria* themselves, however, typically consider participation in such documentary films as a form of *prestasi* (morally worthy achievement or accomplishment) that reflects a desire to secure recognition as a good subject of the nation, and thus the rightfulness of their belonging to and value in Indonesian society. *Waria* affective labor in transnational media markets therefore constitutes a mode of resistance to the devaluation of *waria* lives while reproducing and circulating an image of *waria* as profoundly socially marginal.

The fifth article, Anne Balay's "Sex and Surveillance on the Highway," explores the world of self-styled "T-Girl" truck drivers working in the heart of global capitalism in the United States. Balay offers a vivid ethnographic account of T-Girls who imagine themselves as outlaws: gender outlaws who defy normative gender, sexual outlaws who seek pleasure outside the bounds of bourgeois conventions, and economic outlaws whose literal mobility promises to keep them one step ahead of the authorities. At the same time, she details the often brutal, increasingly regulated, and highly monitored life that most truckers endure. As the neoliberal state expands its surveillance practices, and the trucking industry finds creative new ways to extract ever-greater amounts of value from a workforce that has become predominantly composed of immigrants, people of color, and trans people, the vision of independent, well-paying, self-directed work that enticed many truck drivers to take up their trade in the first place is increasingly illusory. And yet, as Balay demonstrates, T-Girl truckers and their coworkers are nevertheless capable of resistance to what they view as government overreach in the management of their working lives.

In the final article, "Staging the Trans Sex Worker," Nihils Rev and Fiona Maeve Geist challenge the investment many radical and critical trans scholars and activists make in the figure of the "trans prostitute" as a metaphor for social death. Influenced by Marcia Ochoa's research on *transformistas* in Venezuela, Rev and Geist argue that trans individuals engaging in sex work economies are agents navigating complex identities amid violent assemblages of social power relations. Rev and Geist call for an analysis of the complex material conditions that shape the lives of trans individuals who do sex work and insist on the necessity of comprehending participation in this criminalized economy as a form of agency, of escape from even "more profoundly violating social conditions," and as a site for the formation of vibrant and resistive social networks and communities.

Vek Lewis is senior lecturer in Latin American studies at the University of Sydney and the author of *Crossing Sex and Gender in Latin America* (2010).

Dan Irving is associate professor at the Institute of Interdisciplinary Studies at Carleton University. He is coeditor of *Trans Activism in Canada: A Reader* (2014).

References

Agamben, Giorgio. 1998. *Homo Sacer: Sovereign Power and Bare Life*. Stanford, CA: Stanford University Press.

Aizura, Aren Z. 2006. "Of Borders and Homes: The Imaginary Community of (Trans) Sexual Citizenship." *Inter-Asia Cultural Studies* 7, no. 2: 289–309.

———. 2011. "The Romance of the Amazing Scalpel: 'Race,' Labour, and Affect in Thai Gender Reassignment Clinics." In *Queer Bangkok: Twenty-First-Century Markets, Media, and Rights*. Hong Kong: Hong Kong University Press.

Bakker, Isabella, and Stephen Gill, eds. 2003. *Power, Production, and Social Reproduction: Human In/security in the Global Political Economy*. New York: Palgrave Macmillan.

Bezanson, Kate, and Meg Luxton, eds. 2006. *Social Reproduction: Feminist Political Economy Challenges Neo-Liberalism*. Montreal: McGill-Queen's University Press.

Broadus, Kylar W. 2006. "The Evolution of Employment Discrimination Protections for Transgender People." In *Transgender Rights*, edited by Paisley Currah, Richard M. Juang, and Shannon Price Minter, 93–101. Minneapolis: University of Minnesota Press.

Brown, Wendy. 1995. *States of Injury: Power and Freedom in Late Modernity*. Princeton, NJ: Princeton University Press.

Butler, Judith. 1997. *The Psychic Life of Power: Theories in Subjection*. New York: Routledge.

Campuzano, Giuseppe. 2009. "Contemporary Travesti Encounters with Gender and Sexuality in Latin America." *Development* 52, no. 1: 75–83.

Carreras Sendra, Natatxa. 2009. "Sexoservidores-homosexuales-vestidas en la ciudad de Puebla" ("Sex Workers-Homosexuals-*Vestidas* in the City of Puebla"). In *Sujetos neoliberales en México (Neoliberal Subjects in Mexico)*, edited by Ricardo Francisco Macip Ríos, 17–50. Puebla, Mexico: BUAP.

Connell, Raewyn. 1987. *Gender and Power: Society, the Person, and Sexual Politics*. Stanford, CA: Stanford University Press.

Connell, Raewyn, and Nour Dados. 2014. "Where in the World Does Neoliberalism Come From? The Market Agenda in Southern Perspective." *Theory and Society* 43, no. 2: 117–38.

David, Emmanuel. 2015. "Purple-Collar Labor: Transgender Workers and Queer Value at Global Call Centers in the Philippines." *Gender and Society* 29, no. 2: 169–94.

De Angelis, Massimo. 2005. "The Political Economy of Global Neoliberal Governance." *Review* 28, no. 3: 229–57.

Escobar, Árturo. 2005. *Más allá del tercer mundo: Globalización y diferencia* (*Beyond the Third World: Globalization and Difference*). Bogotá, Colombia: Instituto Colombiano de Antropología e Historia.

Feinberg, Leslie. 1992. "Transgender Liberation: A Movement Whose Time Has Come." In *The Transgender Studies Reader*, edited by Susan Stryker and Stephen Whittle, 205–20. New York: Routledge.

———. 1996. *Transgender Warriors: Making History from Joan of Arc to Dennis Rodman*. Boston: Beacon.

———. 1998. *Trans Liberation: Beyond Pink or Blue*. Boston: Beacon.

Ferber, Marianne A., and Julie A. Nelson, eds. 2009. *Beyond Economic Man: Feminist Theory and Economics*. Chicago: University of Chicago Press.

Fernández, Josefina. 2004. *Cuerpos desobedientes: Travestismo e identidad de género* (*Disobedient Bodies:* Travestismo *and Gender Identity*). Buenos Aires: Edhasa.

Foucault, Michel. 1991. "Governmentality." In *The Foucault Effect: Studies in Governmentality*, edited by Graham Burchell, Colin Gordon, and Peter Miller, 87–104. Hemel Hempstead, UK: Harvester Wheatsheaf.

———. 2007. *Security, Territory, Population: Lectures at the Collège de France, 1977–78*. New York: Palgrave.

García García, Antonio Agustín, and Sara Oñate Martínez. 2008. "Transexuales ecuatorianas: El viaje y el cuerpo" ("Ecuadorian Transsexuals: The Voyage and the Body"). In *América Latina migrante: Estado, familias, identidades* (*Migrant Latin America: State, Families, Identities*), edited by Gioconda Herrera and Jacques Ramírez, 343–60. Quito, Ecuador: FLACSO.

Gehi, Pooja S., and Gabriel Arkles. 2007. "Unraveling Injustice: Race and Class Impact of Medicaid Exclusions of Transition-Related Health Care for Transgender People." *Sexuality Research and Social Policy: Journal of NSRC* 4, no. 4: 7–35.

Giddens, Anthony, and Christopher Pierson. 1998. *Conversations with Anthony Giddens: Making Sense of Modernity*. Oxford: Polity.

Haritaworn, Jin, Adi Kuntsman, and Silvia Posocco. 2014. *Queer Necropolitics*. New York: Routledge.

Hennessy, Rosemary. 2002. *Profit and Pleasure: Sexual Identities in Late Capitalism*. New York: Routledge.

Hernández-Rosete Martínez, Daniel. 2008. "La otra migración: Historias de discriminación de personas que vivieron con VIH en México" ("The Other Migration: Histories of Discrimination of People That Lived with HIV in Mexico"). *Salud Mental* (*Mental Health*) 3, no. 4: 253–360.

Hong, Grace Kyungwon. 2006. *The Ruptures of American Capital*. Minneapolis: University of Minnesota Press.

Irving, Dan. 2008. "Normalized Transgressions: Legitimizing the Transsexual Body as Productive." *Radical History Review*, no. 100: 38–59.

Juang, Richard M. 2006. "Transgendering the Politics of Recognition." In *Transgender Rights*, edited by Paisley Currah, Richard M. Juang, and Shannon Price Minter, 242–61. Minneapolis: University of Minnesota Press.

Lugones, María. 2007. "Heterosexualism and the Colonial/Modern Gender System." *Hypatia* 22, no. 1: 186–219.

Maier, Charles S. 1987. *In Search of Stability: Explorations in Historical Political Economy*. New York: Cambridge University Press.

Mbembe, Achille. 2003. "Necropolitics." *Public Culture* 15, no. 1: 11–40.

Mignolo, Walter. 2000. *Local Histories / Global Designs*. Princeton, NJ: Princeton University Press.

Montes Montoya, Angélica, and Hugo Busso. 2007. "Entrevista a Ramón Grosfoguel" ("Interview with Ramón Grosfoguel"). *Polis*, 18. polis.revues.org/4040.

Namaste, Viviane. 2000. *Invisible Lives: The Erasure of Transsexual and Transgendered People*. Chicago: University of Chicago Press.

———. 2011. *Sex Change, Social Change: Reflections on Identity, Institutions, and Imperialism*. Toronto: Canadian Scholars' Press.

Quijano, Aníbal. 1992. "Colonialidad y modernidad/racionalidad" ("Coloniality and Modernity /Rationality"). *Perú Indígena* (*Indigenous Peru*) 13, no. 29: 11–20.

———. 2000. "Colonialidad del poder y clasificación social" ("Coloniality of Power and Social Classification"). *Journal of World-System Research* 5, no. 2: 342–86.

Quintero, Pablo. 2010. "Notas sobre la teoría de la colonialidad del poder y la estructuración de la sociedad en América Latina" ("Notes on the Theory of the Coloniality of Power and the Structuring of Society in Latin America"). *Papeles de Trabajo* (*Work Papers*) 9: 1–15.

Raha, Nat. 2015. "The Limits of Trans Liberalism." Verso Books Blog. September 21. www.verso books.com/blogs/2245-the-limits-of-trans-liberalism-by-nat-raha.

Ross, Mirha-Soleil. c. 2005. "Prostitution as Financially, Sexually, and Culturally Validating for French Working Class Transsexuals." Unpublished paper.

Sabsay, Leticia. 2011. "The Limits of Democracy: Transgender Sex Work and Citizenship." *Cultural Studies* 25, no. 2: 213–29.

Santos, Boaventura de Sousa. 2009. "Governance: Between Myth and Reality." *RCCS Annual Review* 1: 1–15.

Schilt, Kristen. 2010. *Just One of the Guys? Transgender Men and the Persistence of Gender Inequality*. Chicago: University of Chicago Press.

Silva, Joselí Maria, and Marcio Ornat. 2015. "Intersectionality and Transnational Mobility between Brazil and Spain in Travesti Prostitution Networks." *Gender, Place and Culture* 21, no. 8: 925–44.

Spade, Dean. 2006a. "Compliance Is Gendered: Struggling for Gender Self-Determination in a Hostile Economy." In *Transgender Rights*, edited by Paisley Currah, Richard M. Juang, and Shannon Minter Price, 217–41. Minneapolis: University of Minnesota Press.

———. 2006b. "Undermining Gender Regulation." In *Nobody Passes: Rejecting the Rules of Gender and Conformity*, edited by Mattilda Bernstein Sycamore, 64–70. Emeryville, CA: Seal.

Stone, Sandy. (1992) 2006. "The *Empire* Strikes Back: A Posttranssexual Manifesto." In *The Transgender Studies Reader*, edited by Susan Stryker and Stephen Whittle, 221–35. New York: Routledge.

Stryker, Susan. (1994) 2006. "My Words to Victor Frankenstein above the Village Chamounix: Performing Transgender Rage." In *The Transgender Studies Reader*, edited by Susan Stryker and Stephen Whittle, 244–56. New York: Routledge.

Thomas, Kendall. 2006. "Afterword: Are Transgender Rights Inhuman Rights?" In *Transgender Rights*, edited by Paisley Currah, Richard M. Juang, and Shannon Price Minter, 310–26. Minneapolis: University of Minnesota Press.

Vogel, Katrin. 2009. "The Mother, the Daughter, and the Cow: Venezuelan *Transformistas'* Migration to Europe." *Mobilities* 4, no. 3: 367–87.

Wallerstein, Immanuel. 1979. *The Capitalist World-Economy*. Vol. 2. Cambridge: Cambridge University Press.

Trans* Political Economy Deconstructed

A Roundtable Discussion

DAN IRVING, VEK LEWIS, NAEL BHANJI, RAEWYN CONNELL,
QWO-LI DRISKILL, and VIVIANE NAMASTE

Abstract This roundtable discussion took place January–July 2016 via e-mail after participants and special issue editors initially met in virtual mode online. The editors posed the initial questions, and participants e-mailed their responses. Two further rounds of questions and responses ensued, and participants also viewed the responses of their peers on the roundtable. The questions were intended to generate rigorous dialogue about the uses of and problems associated with political economy (PE) as a lens to analyze the experiences of trans men and women and sex- and gender-diverse peoples in different but connected geopolitical locations. The emphasis was on bringing into conversation what is underprioritized in much PE work and also transgender studies as a formation, and how, from their own academic and activist knowledge, methodological bases, and experiences, respondents might see the (re)configuration of trans* political economy toward liberatory, antiracist, decolonial, and economically transformative ends.
Keywords transgender studies, decolonial, coloniality, critical political economy, activism

Our objective for this issue is to demonstrate how questions of political economy can be taken up within trans studies. How do you define political economy (or economies) within your work?

Raewyn Connell: *Economy* originally meant "household management." That is the word's ancient Greek meaning, and its first meaning in English, too. *Political* originally meant the public affairs of the city. So political economy means, literally, public housekeeping. I like that idea, but I don't use the term much, because it is not widely understood. It's associated with an economistic Marxism, which is notoriously hard to combine with gender analysis. But gender analysis certainly needs a concept of the economic. In my work I have treated the economic as one of four basic dimensions of gender relations and gender practice

TSQ: Transgender Studies Quarterly ∗ Volume 4, Number 1 ∗ February 2017   **16**
DOI 10.1215/23289252-3711505   © 2017 Duke University Press

(Connell and Pearse 2015). Gender theorists and movements for gender justice need to speak about housework and factory work, corporations and markets, wages and incomes, finance and trade, money and unemployment. If we don't have a concept of the economic, we will see gender issues—and trans lives—in a very limited way. It's important not to get trapped in a systems model of capitalism. The predatory economic processes that create poverty for many women in the Global South, including transsexual women, and create dire situations for sex workers, including transsexual women, *travestis*, and *vestidas*, cannot be explained by a systems logic—whether it is the supposed declining-rate-of-profit or accumulation-by-dispossession. There are other predators besides our soulless corporations, and other forms of exploitation besides the extraction of surplus value. Colonial conquest was one! To understand the economic dimension of trans lives, we need to pay attention to the whole assembly of privilege and exploitation around them.

Nael Bhanji: I'm interested in how we can trace the trans body of color as a necessary yet disavowed presence within contemporary political and economic formations of violence and memorialization. In particular, I analyze the ways in which the Trans Day of Remembrance vigils and websites that memorialize the ghostly trans body of color can also metamorphose into calls for vigilance against the possible terrorist body of color. I suggest that we can trace the circulation of affects that structure homonational narratives of belonging in transsexual citizenship; these are narratives that emerge as history's ghostly residues within neoliberal narratives of government intervention in the face of terrorism. By analyzing narratives about trans-identified people of color who have been memorialized by the Trans Day of Remembrance—narratives that *explicitly* link post-9/11 nationalism to TDOR—my aim is to animate the seemingly disparate, violence-dependent trajectories of counterterrorism and transsexuality, the transsexual body and the terrorist body, and vigilant reactions and vigils that re-act. Political economies are affective as well as material (Hardt and Negri 2005), and the legitimation of the role of affect in political economy is a key component of my work, which follows a sense or feeling of identification within and through racialized scripts of neoliberal inclusion within the field of trans theory. I turn to affect theory because it provides a framework for conceptualizing the trans body as both a psychic and a material event. Paying attention to political economies means attending to the ways by which the trans body, enmeshed in systems of state surveillance and (in)security, emerges alongside, or in resistance to, the neoliberal, capitalist machinery that would render it (il)legible. By extension, this necessitates interrogating the biopolitical management of life (and death), the mechanisms of global capitalism, and how, and whose, (trans)sexual laboring bodies are ascribed with value, erased, or rendered invisible.

Viviane Namaste: Political economy refers to how resources are distributed and redistributed, and particularly the role of states in that process. Feminist theories of political economy have drawn attention to the gendered dimensions of thinking about political economy, arguing, for instance, that state-funded child care is an economic issue. In my earlier work, particularly *Invisible Lives: The Erasure of Transsexual and Transgendered People* (2000), I examined access to health care for transsexuals, a question fundamentally focused on the distribution of resources. In some of my more recent work, including *Oversight: Critical Reflections on Feminist Theories and Politics* (2015), I am interested in thinking about political economy globally by thinking through the movement of trans women across national borders as an effort to access the necessary economic resources, including medications for those who are HIV-positive, to live their bodies as they choose. These questions illustrate the importance of emphasizing the trans/gender politics of labor precarity, race, and migration as an integral component of the global political economic relations.

Qwo-Li Driskill: Settler colonialism(s), and other forms of colonialism, are inseparable from political economies. Within the academy, "studies" are also often a part of settler logics that, as Malea Powell (1999) has pointed out, lay claim and stake out territory in which bodies and thought can be disciplined. We might want to think about how trans studies can intervene in such a system, or if it can. Scholars in trans studies must think about how we can use trans studies to intervene in interlocking systems of power across, and outside, the academy. Dean Spade's *Normal Life: Administrative Violence, Critical Trans Politics, and the Limits of Law* (2015), as well as the work (both the writing and activism) in Eric Stanley and Nat Smith's *Captive Genders: Trans Embodiment and the Prison Industrial Complex* (2015), can inform trans political economies in ways that have us think critically about—and take action against—settler colonial institutions and systems that benefit socially and financially from the control and confinement of trans people, particularly trans people of color.

Some say trans studies has developed under the shadow of US queer theory and antinormative cultural studies, and hold that this theoretical hegemony has negative repercussions for many struggles to achieve economic justice on local, national, and global levels. Can you comment on this in relation to your own work?

Raewyn: I have serious problems with any form of politics focused on rejection of norms. For transsexual women, the most important political connection is with feminism, as I have argued in detail (Connell 2012). The next most important is with the labor movement. The experience of both movements is that social struggle must include attempts to *create* norms—norms like equality, nonviolence, recognition, respect. Social justice is a norm! A radical individual-ism, an insistence on personal expression as an overriding right, won't do it. If we hope specifically to link transsexual and transgender groups internationally, and build wider alliances in which these groups have a place, we need a language of common interests and we need to develop real capacities for mutual learning.

Nael: My work on queer theory endeavors to incorporate a transnational and diasporic framework. While I am aware that my focus on 9/11 and Euro-American queer theory can in fact reify the systems of oppression that I address in my writing, I am also indebted to the lessons I learn from grassroots activism at home in Kenya. In many ways, in order to address the *production* and circulation of the trans body within the public imaginaries, one must necessarily turn to those "shadows"—for it is precisely within those shadows that we may trace those scripts of "homing desires" and metaphors of borders and boundaries that are the "stuff" of racialized sexuality and (trans)national terror. The circulation of terror, and the disciplinary economies that support it, are no longer confined to the United States.

Viviane: I appreciate the concern with the ways in which dominant framings of an object of research have been determined by a specific theoretical framework that may, or may not, be actually connected to real people and their everyday lives. And I certainly share the concern that queer theory preempts many kinds of inquiry. While much of my earlier work critiqued such a framing, I think it is also necessary to think about how to proactively create different kinds of knowledge, and avoid getting stuck in a critique of queer theoretical projects that may or may not fundamentally change how a field organizes itself. My own historical work on the history of cabaret artists in Montreal, *C'était du spectacle! L'histoire des artistes transsexuelles à Montréal, 1955–1985* (2005), did not situate itself within any queer studies field. It simply provided a labor history of trans women in Montreal, including an examination of the ways in which laws and access to health care affected such work.

Qwo-Li: Trans studies is developing within settler colonial systems. Queer theory and antinormative cultural studies are no more or no less part of these than any other institution in settler nations. I would like to trouble the idea that "academic" and "nonacademic" work is really so separate. I don't know if I think there's "theoretical hegemony," because I don't think academic theory is any more or less significant than other kinds of theory. I do think that certain theories emerge in academe that folks find exciting and popular that then are disregarded when the next "cool" theory comes along, which I think is its own kind of problem—it's a particular kind of capital that is part of a very consumerist model. I do think that antinormative models (including in activist practices outside academe) are really important, even if some of those theories need to be questioned or complicated. I do see, however, how (particularly but not exclusively white) queer and trans movements have taken up antinormative politics in problematic ways that end up deciding who is "normative" and who is not, who is "gender binary" and who is not, even who is "trans" and who is "cis" in ways I find deeply troubling. This kind of behavior strips antinormative critiques of their larger critiques of oppressive systems, turns critiques of institutions and structures of power into critiques of individuals, makes new boxes and labels for people, and decides who is "in" and who is "out."

Trans- political economy opens spaces to think through the different ways that particular bodies are de/valued within society. Can you delve further into the coloniality of power/gender/race to demonstrate how some bodies are understood as being worth more while others are disposable? Furthermore, can you address the ways that many who are engaged in human rights advocacy work (e.g., asylum law and expert witness testimony) ascribe value to vulnerable bodies through discourses of suffering and victimization?

Raewyn: Gender is the way that human reproductive bodies are brought into the historical process that we call "society." Different gender orders manage this in different ways and have produced different forms of gender and different theorizing, too (Connell 2014). The creation of European empires and the global economy over the last five hundred years disrupted all existing gender orders (including in the imperial center) and produced the structures we live in today, including the entanglements of gender, class, race, migration, and sexuality. Different colonial regimes treated colonized bodies differently. The current upsurge of racism in rich countries, which we see in "border protection," Brexit, and the Trump campaign, has a lot to do with the economic insecurity among white men, especially working-class men, produced by forty years of neoliberalism. The upsurge is (at least in part) a symptom of *loss* of privilege and the failure of racial and international hierarchies, which right-wing populism offers to restore. In that case, refugee advocates who hope to change attitudes by stories of suffering and victimization are not likely to be successful. The people whom Donald Trump, Boris Johnson, the UK Independence Party, and John Howard have appealed to regard themselves as victims.

Viviane: Theoretically, some of the most productive work I know on the notion of value is that of the Italian social semiotician Ferruccio Rossi-Landi. He makes the important point that value, for Marx, is not simply about the economic. It is also fundamentally about meaning, and therefore deeply imbricated in language itself. To connect this to the question above, then, part of my scholarship seeks to begin with non-English-speaking contexts, as one way to speak back to an imposition of American frames of reference. The identification of which bodies count, and in which ways, within a global knowledge production apparatus speaks to how value is inscribed in and through Empire.

Nael: What does it mean when the gender liminal body of color can circulate only within public imaginaries of death and decay? How is racialized and queered bodily affect mined for both its literal and metaphorical value? How are trans bodies subsumed within rhetorics of authenticity and, therefore, consumption? A quick example of this necropolitical economy would be the cannibalistic "inheritance" and manipulation of the political, emotional, and aesthetic labor of trans women and transfeminine people of color—labor that is subsumed within narratives of trans and gay liberation while rendering invisible the trauma, pain, and violence that gave rise to these resistant art forms engineered as a means of survival and as a "fuck you" to the ongoing rhetorics of disposability.

Trans- theoretical and political analysis includes but exceeds trans∗ identity-based categorizations. What are some substantive issues that require immediate attention in the contemporary colonialist and capitalist economy?

Raewyn: There are four widespread issues that really matter. (1) *Housing*: under neoliberalism, secure housing is not regarded as a social right. There is a general housing affordability crisis, and young transsexual women and men live at the sharp end of it. (2) *Income security*: young people facing the very tough work of gender transition are also likely to be facing poverty, and often their education has been disrupted. If they go into sex work, the conditions are always insecure and sometimes downright dangerous. We need to build consensus for income-support systems. This may sound a long way from current trans politics, but a reliable income is required to make gender transition, or gender refusal, survivable in all social classes. (3) *Land rights*: imperialism meant seizing land from Indigenous communities. Colonial economies were built on the results, from the silver mines of Potosí to the sugar plantations of Queensland. It's unclear whether gender-changing groups had defined land rights within Indigenous societies; they certainly had none in colonial economies. In settler colonial societies such as Canada and Australia, claiming land rights has been a vital part of reasserting dignity and building a new economic position for Indigenous people. Land rights is perhaps the toughest issue for a social justice politics concerned with transition and transgender. Since land rights claims normally involve kinship, it seems important to find ways in which transition, or gender refusal, can be recognized in kinship structures. Those families who have made a place for transsexual sons and daughters (or even parents) provide positive starting points. (4) *The state*: in thinking about trans issues in a neoliberal world economy, it's important not to be confined by Global North understandings. Neoliberalism in the Global South, from the Pinochet dictatorship onward, was above all a new development strategy (Connell and Dados 2014) that tried to find some comparative advantage while integrating developing economies into global markets and smashing labor and socialist movements. A strong coercive state was helpful for such restructuring, so it is not surprising that masculinized military, paramilitary, and police forces remain powerful in the neoliberal world. If you ask where the death squads engaged in "social cleansing" of sex workers, homosexuals, and *travestis* come from, look no farther. The short-term goal is survival in the face of a militarized state, and the long-term goal is democratizing and demilitarizing the state. Unfortunately, a lot of trans activism in the Global North has adopted the rhetoric of individual rights, which limits its relevance to the rest of the world or, worse, means exporting around the world a political framework whose individualism is complicit with neoliberalism. It is only collective social power, an agenda of social justice, and a development strategy *not* built on social coercion that will change the way contemporary states work.

Nael: Several scholars have interrogated the distinct lack of an analysis of settler colonialism within contemporary queer and feminist theory. Scott Morgensen's (2010) exploration of the links between settler colonialism and modern sexuality illustrates how "settler sexuality" is intimately tied to the normative violence of settlement and disappearance, and also to the circulation of the figure of the "modern" non-Native queer as the subject of life. Of course, trans narratives, too, are complicit in the ongoing, and often appropriative, circulation of the "inherited" histories of Native peoples (Aizura 2006). If trans theory does not actively work toward both antiracism and decolonization, it is complicit with ongoing colonial violence.

Viviane: In many ways, the struggle to find decent, safe housing is of the utmost importance for trans people today. Yet this struggle is more than simply related to discrimination against trans people because of their gender. As my doctoral student Natalie Duchesne (2016) shows, access to stable housing is a broader political question in the absence of a state infrastructure to address the housing needs of the poor. Aside from housing, I would name the matter of migration—so many trans people move across the globe to access employment, and sometimes medication. But the process of immigration is daunting and challenging, and one of the most important issues faced by trans women when thinking about questions of colonialism and capitalism.

Qwo-Li: The most substantive issue Two-Spirit and Indigenous trans folks face is the ongoing settler colonialism that we have experienced for generations. Our lands and bodies are still under settler control. Indigenous children are still being taken away from their families and funneled into adoption and foster care. We are still struggling to awaken and/or continue our languages and lifeways after concerted efforts by settler states to destroy them. Indigenous activists in Canada have brought international attention to missing and murdered Indigenous women, and because of Two-Spirit activism there is increasing consciousness that many of those missing are Two-Spirit and/or trans. In the United States, Indigenous youth have the highest rates of suicide in the country (Jiang et al. 2015). Indigenous people in the United States experience vastly disproportionate rates of violence, poverty, homelessness, and incarceration and are more likely to be killed by police than any other race. While there is a gap in research when it comes to the ways transphobia and queerphobia intersect with—and are tools of—settler colonialism and racism in the lives of Two-Spirit and trans Indigenous people, clearly the ramifications of these interlocking systems on our lives are ever present.

What are some ongoing concrete struggles for economic justice that inspire you?

Raewyn: They all do! Not because they always triumph. Economic justice has actually been losing ground in the last generation, as neoliberalism has strengthened its grip and inequalities of income and wealth in most countries have widened. In our time, even keeping up the struggle is inspiring. I welcome news of union organizing, land rights campaigns, public housing programs, microcredit programs, community electric power generation, defense of public water supply, cooperative agriculture and forestry, defense of land against insane mining projects, and more. Often it is very small or very local campaigns that can bring new groups into action. What local struggles cannot do, separately, is shift state and corporate economic strategies. For that, connections between different social movements are essential. A coalition of movements does seem to have emerged recently in the USA, in the Sanders campaign for the Democratic presidential nomination. Something like that happened a little earlier in the Greek and Spanish mobilizations that produced Syriza and Podemos. It is doubtless a utopian idea, but I do think transsexual women have a certain expertise in living with contradiction and making unexpected connections. I'd like to think we can play a positive role in building coalitions on the scale needed for human society to survive.

Nael: I've spent the past few years attending trans pride parades, tracking TDOR websites, and observing TDOR vigils. In the past two years, there has been a concerted effort to integrate discourses about antitransgender violence with campaigns against antiblack violence. In particular, I have been deeply influenced by the work undertaken by the Audre Lorde Project (ALP) in New York, which centers the people who are most directly affected—black, transfeminine folk. Through ALP, TDOR and Black Lives Matter coalesce as a series of campaigns that run throughout the year and incorporate discourses of homelessness, antiblack violence, sex worker rights, and abolition activism into TDOR's public expressions of grief.

Viviane: I live in Quebec, so the 2012 student strike offered incredible inspiration for me. The matter was not simply about students striking to prevent a raise in tuition fees. It raised fundamental questions about what the political priorities of a nation should be. And Quebecois youth in particular raised the question of access to education. Grassroots struggles need to reframe how the state defines a particular issue if that framing does not reflect the values or worldviews of the people. I am inspired by many local forms of activism, struggles that privilege the local, in tremendous opposition to state power and large corporations.

Qwo-Li: #IdleNoMore is a movement that is about economic justice because it's a movement of Indigenous resistance to settler states, including economic colonialism and corporate and state violence against our lands and communities. Similarly, #BlackLivesMatter is not only a movement to end police violence and brutality; it's also a challenge to the entire prison-industrial complex and its white supremacist underpinnings. While both movements are part of a direct-action model, they're also both more than that—they critique the foundations of colonialism and racism and expose the deep relationship between capitalism, white supremacy, and settler colonialism.

Many activists and practitioners would argue that since the state and state-like formations themselves are part of the multiple forms of violence of which you speak, we must think outside the state. Where do you see the place of alternative forms of social action and coordination, even alternative forms of governance, as pertinent to transformative changes for communities?

Raewyn: The difficult fact is that the state is both a major form of repression and a key means of change and redistribution. States are the major terrorists in our world, in terms of the numbers of people killed. They also supply most of the schools, hospitals, and public transport. There's a gender politics in all this. I think that effective challenge to patriarchal power and toxic masculinities does require new ways of organizing a society's collective life. We need struggle "in and against" the state. We also need new models beyond what's imagined by contemporary states; we need "prefigurative politics," that is, positive examples of change. Such things as cooperative housing, cooperative farming and manufacturing, student-centered schools, free universities, and workers' learning centers have a long history. So there's a lot of experience for trans activism to build on. But there is also a lot of difficulty, because neoliberal institutions have moved in the other direction.

Viviane: I love this question. I wish that there were more spaces for thinking about what would bring about transformative change. I think that some of the collective organizing of sex workers could help point the way. I think, for instance, of research I did on the history of HIV in Paris. In that study, trans women told me how they would take up collections to transport a woman gravely ill with AIDS via ambulance from Italy to Paris. This example speaks to concrete realities of trans sex workers: gathering together the money to help a coworker and friend; choosing who would accompany her on the journey; negotiating with health services, the physical border, and immigration. This work happened in most ways without state support, although perhaps paradoxically different state institutions also needed to be negotiated. I think this example is useful for helping us identify what might need to occur entirely outside state structures, but also the very real needs sometimes filled by the state, such as access to health care.

Qwo-Li: I think here again of Malea Powell's (2002: 20) work, when she writes of Indigenous people in the academy, "We are already alternative." I think of this statement in relationship to alternative forms of governance and social action because Indigenous forms of governance and tactics for transformation are "already alternative" to dominant forms of governance as well as dominant forms of intervention. Settler colonization(s) deeply inform our ways of knowing to such an extent that thinking outside settler colonial frameworks becomes *unimaginable*. Craig Womack (1999: 230) writes, "The process of decolonizing one's mind, a first step before one can achieve a political consciousness and engage in activism, has to begin with imagining an alternative." The alternatives are also already present—both in cultural memories of other possibilities and in continuing practices of Indigenous peoples. While a rights-based model is a material legal reality that we have to contend with as marginalized peoples, it will always bring us up against settler structures that are infused with logics and practices that will always marginalize, oppress, and/or attempt to eradicate us. John Trudell connects Indigenous philosophies of responsibilities to movements for liberation. He argues, "It's not revolution we're after; it's liberation. We want to be free of a value system that's being imposed upon us. We do not want to participate in that value system. We don't want to change that value system. We want to remove it from our lives forever" (Trudell 1980).

Nael: A shift in the work that trans activists and trans studies are doing to focus on "responsibilities" instead of "rights" would change how we do our work. When I talk with students about Two-Spirit identities and communities, I talk about how Two-Spirit activism and identities focus on resuming and/or continuing our responsibilities in our communities. What if we talked about trans responsibilities instead of (or in addition to) trans rights? How might that change our movements and our understandings of ourselves "living in reciprocal relation with all of our seen and unseen relatives," as Melissa K. Nelson (2008) describes? A shift to "responsibilities" supports Dean Spade's (2015) concept of critical trans politics that "can inform strategies that take up law reform campaigns tactically: when doing so provides immediate relief to harmful conditions, helps mobilize and build political momentum for more transformative change, provides an incremental step in dismantling a harmful system, and makes sense when weighed against the dangers of legitimization and reification of violent systems."

Dan Irving is an associate professor at the Institute of Interdisciplinary Studies at Carleton University. He is coeditor of *Trans Activism in Canada: A Reader* (2014).

Vek Lewis is a senior lecturer in Latin American studies at the University of Sydney and the author of *Crossing Sex and Gender in Latin America* (2010).

Nael Bhanji is a PhD candidate in the women's studies program at York University. His research draws on psychoanalysis and affect theory to explore articulations of nationalism, racialization, and counterterrorism in an increasingly globalized trans movement. His work appears in *Transgender Migrations: The Bodies, Borders, and Politics of Transition* (2011), *The Transgender Studies Reader 2* (2013), and *Canadian Ethnic Studies*.

Raewyn Connell is one of Australia's leading social scientists. She is the coauthor of twenty-three books, including *Gender: In World Perspective* (2015). She has worked for the labor movement, peace movement, and women's movement, and for democratic change in education. Her website is www.raewynconnell.net, and she's on Twitter @raewynconnell.

Qwo-Li Driskill is a (noncitizen) Cherokee Two-Spirit and Queer writer, activist, and performer also of African, Irish, Lenape, Lumbee, and Osage *ascent*. S/he is the author of *Walking with Ghosts: Poems* (2005) and coeditor of *Sovereign Erotics: A Collection of Two-Spirit Literature* (2011) and *Queer Indigenous Studies: Critical Interventions in Theory, Politics, and Literature* (2011). Hir book *Asegi Stories: Cherokee Queer and Two-Spirit Memory* is forthcoming.

Viviane Namaste is a full professor and research chair in HIV/AIDS and sexual health in the Simone de Beauvoir Institute at Concordia University. She is the author of *Oversight: Critical Reflections on Feminist Research and Politics* (2016).

References

Aizura, Aren Z. 2006. "Of Borders and Homes: The Imaginary Community of (Trans)sexual Citizenship." *Inter-Asia Cultural Studies* 7, no. 2: 289–309.

Connell, Raewyn. 2012. "Transsexual Women and Feminist Thought: Toward New Understanding and New Politics." *Signs: Journal of Women in Culture and Society* 37, no. 4: 857–81.

———. 2014. "Rethinking Gender from the South." *Feminist Studies* 40, no. 3: 518–39.

Connell, Raewyn, and Nour Dados. 2014. "Where in the World Does Neoliberalism Come From? The Market Agenda in Southern Perspective." *Theory and Society* 43, no. 2: 117–38.

Connell, Raewyn, and Rebecca Pearse. 2015. *Gender: In World Perspective*. 3rd ed. Cambridge, MA: Polity.

Duchesne, Natalie. 2016. "The Politics of Trans: A Comparative Study of How Trans People Interact with Public Policies in Montréal and Toronto." PhD diss., Concordia University.

Hardt, Michael, and Antonio Negri. 2005. *Multitude: War and Democracy in the Age of Empire*. New York: Penguin.

Jiang, Caroline, Andreea Mitran, Arialdi Miniño, and Hanyu Ni. 2015. "Racial and Gender Disparities in Suicide among Young Adults Aged 18–24: United States, 2009–2013." www.cdc.gov/nchs/data/hestat/suicide/racial_and_gender_2009_2013.pdf.

Morgensen, Scott Lauria. 2010. "Settler Homonationalism: Theorizing Settler Colonialism within Queer Modernities." *GLQ* 16, nos. 1–2: 105–31.

Namaste, Viviane. 2000. *Invisible Lives: The Erasure of Transsexual and Transgendered People*. Chicago: University of Chicago Press.

———. 2005. *C'était du spectacle! L'histoire des artistes transsexuelles à Montréal, 1955–1985*. Montreal: McGill-Queen's University Press.

Nelson, Melissa K., ed. 2008. *Original Instructions: Indigenous Teachings for a Sustainable Future*. Rochester, VT: Inner Traditions/Bear.

Powell, Malea. 1999. "Blood and Scholarship: One Mixed-Blood's Story." In *Race, Rhetoric, and Composition*, edited by Keith Gilyard, 1–16. Portsmouth, NH: Boynton/Cook-Heinemann.

———. 2002. "Listening to Ghosts: An Alternative (Non)argument." In *ALT DIS: Alternative Discourses and the Academy*, edited by Christopher Schroeder, Helen Fox, and Patricia Bizzell, 11–22. Portsmouth, NH: Boyton/Cook-Heinemann.

Spade, Dean. 2015. *Normal Life: Administrative Violence, Critical Trans Politics, and the Limits of Law*. Durham, NC: Duke University Press.

Stanley, Eric A., and Nat Smith. 2015. *Captive Genders: Trans Embodiment and the Prison Industrial Complex*. Oakland, CA: AK.

Trudell, John. 1980. "We Are Power." Speech, July 18. History Is a Weapon. www.historyisaweapon.com/defcon1/trudellwearepower.html.

Womack, Craig S. 1999. *Red on Red: Native American Literary Separatism*. Minneapolis: University of Minnesota Press.

Capital T

Trans Visibility, Corporate Capitalism,
and Commodity Culture

EMMANUEL DAVID

Abstract This article examines the production of new regimes of transgender value and visibility. First, it explores the cultural commodification of transgender by exploring the rise of transgender-specific products and consumer markets. Second, it examines the counterpart of trans consumption — trans production — and investigates the emergence of trans-specific labor power and all-trans groups of workers. Third, it offers a critique of trans economic empowerment strategies that have drawn on freelance economies, independent contractors, trans class aspirations, and the global restructuring of work, in efforts to address issues of trans un/der/employment. The article argues that such strategies bolster precarious work conditions and economic insecurities and unwittingly contribute to economic imperialism. Taken together, this article examines links between transgender issues and flows of capital within neoliberal markets.
Keywords trans value, visibility, capitalism, work, neoliberalism

"Transgender Visibility: A Guide to Being You": these words appear on the cover of a thirty-page booklet produced in 2014 by the Human Rights Campaign (HRC), one of the most visible and well-funded mainstream gay rights organizations in the United States. Intended to guide readers through the process of self-discovery and disclosure, this resource offers practical advice to help trans people "meet the challenges and opportunities that living as authentically as possible can offer to each of us." The booklet includes with a message from HRC president Chad Griffin, who notes that "progress toward equality is made when we choose to share our lives with others" and considers this sharing to be the "greatest political action any of us can take." Griffin then suggests that the collective work of becoming visible has allowed issues like gender identity and expression to be incorporated into the law and has "inspired" corporations to expand employee protection and benefits programs to include gender identity and expression.

TSQ: Transgender Studies Quarterly ∗ Volume 4, Number 1 ∗ February 2017   **28**
DOI 10.1215/23289252-3711517   © 2017 Duke University Press

With its focus on transgender issues, this HRC pamphlet reflects a noticeable shift for mainstream, US-based gay equality organizations, described by some critics as the "gay establishment" (Sycamore 2016) or the "gay right wing" (Duggan 2003: 65) because of the focus on personal choices and privatized politics rather than structural inequalities, such as access to universal health care. More than just demonstrating how this mainstream gay and lesbian organization has expanded its focus to include trans issues, it appears to signal HRC's efforts to extend the proverbial olive branch to the trans community in an attempt to address the organization's past controversial support of a trans-exclusive version of the 2007 Employment Non-Discrimination Act (Vitulli 2010). Given recent successes of equality campaigns to help gays and lesbians gain full access to marriage, the market, and the military (Duggan 2011–12), trans struggles appear to be the logical next chapter of this progress story, and indeed many gay assimilationists and political lobbyists have lauded this new direction (Wolfson 2015).

The queer political and academic Left, however, has long been vocal in its opposition to the "equality" rhetoric advocated by mainstream gay and lesbian groups like HRC and the National LGBTQ Task Force, which some argue make up part of a broader conservative shift in LGBT politics since the early 1990s (Conrad 2014; Duggan 2003; Shepard 2001; Spade 2011; Sycamore 2016). Among these critical queer scholars is Yasmin Nair (2010: 4), who contends that mainstream causes like gay marriage have been central to the shrinking of LGBTQ movements' transformative potential. Similarly, Lisa Duggan (2003: 50) describes this neoliberal sexual politics as "the new homonormativity," a form of politics that "does not contest the dominant heteronormative assumptions and institutions, but upholds and sustains them, while promising the possibility of a demobilized gay constituency and a privatized, depoliticized gay culture anchored in domesticity and consumption." That is, mainstream gay organizations, with their corporate structures and "trickle-down" theories of equality (Duggan and Kim 2011–12), have relentlessly pushed for inclusion in society's dominant structures.

The HRC booklet's subtitle—"A Guide to Being You"—clearly reveals how HRC has extended its focus to include trans discourses in its identity-based equality campaigns. It makes appeals to a similarly depoliticized trans constituency that mobilizes notions of identity and self-actualization rather than transformative politics and collective resistance. It also exemplifies what critical queer and trans scholars have long warned about: that mainstream gay organizations might incorporate trans issues into their neoliberal discourses of individualism, privatization, and the retreat from the social. As Mattilda Bernstein Sycamore (2016) observes, "For decades, the gay establishment has been dominated by the agenda of the wealthy, one that views identity as an endpoint. *Gay* becomes simply another way to adorn every hideous hypocritical institution and camouflage its violence—gay marriage, gays in the military, gay cops, gay priests, what's next? Oh—let's get trans people into the mix." The HRC booklet's mention of trans inclusion in existing legal structures and corporations shows how these campaigns promote minority assimilation in sociolegal, political, and economic arenas. Even more, they rely on visibility strategies, or what David Getsy (2015: 39, 41) describes as the "evidence of existence" and the "protocols of identification." And as Nair (2010: 6) argues, "In a neoliberal economy, gay identity becomes a way to further capitalist exploitation." Could this also be true for trans identities?

All this points to how trans visibility has the potential to produce social, political, and economic value. Trans inclusion, it turns out, can be highly profitable, a source of yet untapped value that could be put to use to bolster the status quo. Here my thinking about the potentiality of trans value has been influenced by the anthropologist Michele Friedner (2014, 2015a, 2015b), whose work in critical disability studies demonstrates how deafness, rather than being devalued or a source of limitation, becomes a source of value—deaf value—under new labor regimes in postcolonial contexts. Friedner argues that deaf sociality has become an important site of recruitment and extraction, one in which the stigma of deafness is reinscribed and transformed into deaf capital. Taking a similar approach to issues of value and inclusion of queer and gender variant bodies, Aren Aizura (2014: 142) argues that "rather than excluding the disadvantaged . . . capital incorporates their needs, desires, into its fabric." As these scholars have observed, the socially marginalized—including queer and trans subjects— can become folded into global capitalism. Extending these lines of thought, we could ask about relationships between trans identities and historical formations of capital.

This article examines the uneasy relation between trans visibility politics and the production of trans value. While there is a growing body of literature on transgender experiences in the labor market, these writings usually focus on crucial dimensions of trans lived experiences such as employment discrimination and blocked access to full participation in existing institutions. There is far less scholarly attention given to how actors in the labor market, whether teams of investors, corporate sponsors, entrepreneurs, or venture capitalists, seek to cash in on the "cultural turn to transgender" (Hines 2010: 11). This requires a reorientation to thinking about trans as a valued condition.

This article is organized into four sections. The first explores the recent rise of transgender-specific products and consumer markets and shows how trans visibility is often tied to the courting of trans dollars. The second examines trans production by focusing on the emergence of trans-specific workforces, including those that promote trans employees as productive workers who offer the market a unique and sometimes brandable form of value. The third focuses on TransTech, a social enterprise company that seeks to cultivate trans entrepreneurs; this section discusses TransTech's reliance on freelance economies, independent contractors, trans class aspirations, and the global restructuring of work in its efforts to address trans un/der/employment. While the company's goal is to help trans workers in the United States overcome employment obstacles, I argue that the strategies it uses to do so potentially bolster precarious work conditions and economic insecurities in ways that might also unwittingly contribute to economic imperialism. The final section offers some concluding remarks about the links between transgender issues and capital in neoliberal markets.

Trans Markets and Consumer Economies

Transgender consumption activities, like global medical tourism, have existed for years (Aizura 2011; Gale 2015). Yet, as transgender issues gain visibility in popular culture, some companies have sought to stay ahead of the curve, taking advantage of segmented consumer markets that seem to be emerging from "America's transgender moment" (Griggs 2015). A recent *Washington Post* story outlines a number of players poised to profit from the developing market of services for trans people: therapists, plastic surgeons, endocrinologists, voice coaches, hair-removal specialists, and lawyers with subspecialties helping trans people transition (Contrera 2015). Articles in *Forbes* (Pearson 2015) and *Fortune* (McCue 2015) have remarked on new retailers sprouting up, offering consumer goods like shoes, lingerie, makeup, and tailored suits to transgender consumers. For example, NiK Kacy (www.nikkacy.com), a self-identified gender-fluid, queer, and trans person, created a luxury "gender-equal footwear" store where shoppers could purchase "masculine of center gender neutral shoes" that would provide solutions to the "limitations of shoe sizing set by the shoe industry based on gender." Demonstrating the proliferation of segmented markets, the site announced that it would soon expand with a "feminine of center collection" as part of Kacy's "desire for gender equality." The *Forbes* contributor noted that these niche markets are, at the moment, quite small, but predicted that the number of transgender individuals will likely increase as more people in the general population begin to accept trans people into their communities. The author added, "Included in that acceptance will be retailers, and the sooner they recognize the importance of their role serving this market group, the greater will be their long-term benefits." After discussing how merchants can increase sales and cultivate brand loyalty through "creative segmenting," the *Forbes* writer goes on to say that "[retailers] can identify select groups of shoppers, even within the transgender community, who should be catered to in different ways" (Pearson 2015).

Beyond promoting services and retail products for transgender shoppers, companies are also marketing getaway experiences to transgender travelers. In

September 2015 the *New York Times* (Daniel 2015) reported that Fort Lauderdale, Florida, had embarked on a new tourism campaign designed specifically to court transgender tourists. Discussing the city's TLGB campaign (the T was strategically placed first) called "Where Happy Meets Go Lucky," Richard Gray, managing director of the LGBT market for the Greater Fort Lauderdale Convention and Visitors Bureau, told reporters, "The one thing the trans market has in common with the L.G.B.T. market is we've all experienced discrimination, safety issues and a lack of acceptance. I want trans people to be like all travelers—free to be themselves, free to be accepted and, most of all, welcome and safe" (Daniel 2015). Concepts like freedom are refashioned into consumer strategies, reflecting what Duggan (2003: 65–66) describes as a "rhetorical recoding of key terms in the history of gay politics."

First-to-market claims abound when targeting aspirational, middle-class transgender consumers. Retail products, shopping, consumerism, first-mover discourses, and memorable headlines all converge in the example of the transgender marriage market. Consider this *US Weekly* headline in January 2016: "'Say Yes to the Dress' Is Featuring Its First Ever Transgender Bride: Meet Precious Davis" (Chan 2016). The article focused on an episode of TLC's reality show *Say Yes to the Dress: Atlanta* dedicated to the trans woman Precious Davis's search for the perfect wedding gown. "A wedding in a woman's life is a huge moment. It's almost healing for me that I will be honored as noble, I'm marrying my king, and we will start our family together. That is my activism," said Davis (Talusan 2016).

This spectacle of consumption shows how trans consumers get incorporated into what Chrys Ingraham (2008) has famously called the "wedding industrial complex." Ingraham argues that the wedding industry is virtually "recession proof," largely because of deeply ingrained ideologies of romance that encourage consumers to spend large amounts of money, some taking on considerable debt, to have the perfect wedding day (see also Whitehead 2011). Returning to radical critiques of inclusion (Conrad 2014), it reveals a great deal about the direction of the mainstream LGBT movement that participation in one of society's most conservative practices can be unselfconsciously described as "activism." When trans markets and movements converge, we are confronted with a historically specific consumer phenomenon that can be likened to what Nan Alamilla Boyd (1998) observed in the context of gay and lesbian visibility politics in the 1990s: "shopping for rights."

Putting Transgender to Work

Trans production, a counterpart to trans consumption, is the patterned location of trans people in the chains of material and cultural production. Much of the existing research on the productive activities of trans people has focused on trans labor in informal economies, such as entertainment, prostitution, and webcam work and Internet porn (Aizura 2014; Namaste 2004). Film and fashion are two important sites where trans labor markets begin to intersect with formal wage labor. In an essay on depictions of trans people in film, Julia Serano (2004) notes that nontransgender actors are often cast in transgender roles. The 2013 film *Dallas Buyers Club* is a recent case in point: the cisgender actor Jared Leto was cast as a trans woman living with HIV/AIDS, a role that earned him an Oscar for best supporting actor. Beyond criticisms that the film reproduced stereotypes of trans women as merely "men in drag," commentators pointed out that this casting further limited employment opportunities for transgender actors. "Why not cast a trans woman to play a trans woman?" asked Jos Truitt (2014) on Feministing .com. In 2015 another heated discussion unfolded with *The Danish Girl*, a film about transgender pioneer Lili Elbe, played by the cisgender actor Eddie Red- mayne (Pulver 2015).

To address limited employment opportunities for trans workers, some in the entertainment industry have begun creating roles for trans actors. For example, MTV's show *Faking It* launched an open casting call for transgender actors, both in speaking and supporting roles, to make the show more "inclusive" (Heffernan 2015). In addition to mainstream productions, subcultural efforts to employ trans subjects have also appeared. Take, for instance, the work of the trans recording artist Macy Rodman and her music video "Lazy Girl," which *Vice Magazine* described as a "trans anthem to millennial lethargy amidst the comforts and confines of capitalism" (Tourjee 2015), which features an all-transgender cast, as noted in *Original Plumbing* (Mac 2015). In an Indiegogo campaign to raise money for the follow-up video, "Violent Young Men," Rodman (2016) said: "It's hard for trans people to make an impact in the music industry, and it is my goal to make work . . . placing us at the center of pop imagery that influences so much of the world around us. . . . I want the visuals to match the work we've put into the music." Rodman's all-trans cast is noteworthy because it belongs to a larger trend of moving beyond mere inclusion or transgender "tokenism" (Schilt 2010: 116–19) and creating labor arrangements marketed as "all transgender." This dynamic is often framed as "another big stride in the acceptance and respect in the main- stream" for the trans community (Adleman 2015).

Like the first-to-market consumer campaigns mentioned earlier, there has been a surge in first "all transgender" enterprises. In 2015 Apple Model Man- agement billed itself as the first all-transgender modeling agency in Los Angeles (Adleman 2015). *Fortune* covered the story (Carlson 2015), and an MTV headline read "An All-Transgender Modeling Agency? Yup, That Is So Happening" (Davidson 2015). Soon thereafter, news stories, including one in *Forbes*'s "Entre- preneurs" section, drew attention to the opening of Trans Models, pitched as

New York City's first transgender modeling agency (Honigman 2015). While these agencies focus on trans people on the runway and in front of the camera, there have also been efforts to employ trans people behind the scenes. In an ad campaign for Other Stories, a clothing label owned by the H&M Group, not only were the models trans, but so was everyone involved in production—from makeup artists to stylists to photographers (Dockterman 2015).

One observer described the phenomenon of trans models as "tokenism at work" (Avila 2015). But much more is happening, for these assemblages extend beyond individual subjects and their inclusion. I would argue that these emergent organizational forms result from what David Valentine (2007) describes as the institutionalization of transgender as a category. With the uptake and institutionalization of trans in broader culture, organizational arrangements seem to be reconfiguring themselves. In this sense, the all-trans workforce resonates with what I describe elsewhere as "the purple collar" (David 2015) or the emergent patterns of trans people in occupations, from workplaces characterized by complete segregation to the dense clustering in particular jobs. The all-trans workforces reflect how the incorporation of trans workers—as trans—into specific parts of the labor market functions to produce new forms of value drawn specifically from the mobilization of trans labor power. While all-trans workforces can emerge as a self-organizing of trans subjects who aim to share economic resources in response to labor market anxieties, they might also result from companies, like those mentioned here, that use trans subjects to draw extra attention to their products and services.

Trans Entrepreneurs: The Case of TransTech Social Enterprises

"The smile I have today is because I know my value," said Angelica Ross, a self-identified trans woman of color and social entrepreneur, during a 2015 lecture.[1] In her talk, "Bridging Digital Divides: Reaching Liminal Spaces," Ross described founding TransTech Social Enterprises, a training academy that seeks to cultivate skills for transgender workers in the tech industry. Ross described workplace struggles that trans people face, especially when transitioning on the job. It was in the global restructuring of work that she saw the promise of telecommuting opportunities, which would allow trans people to become self-employed independent contractors able to work from home. Remote work environments were portrayed as a flexible, personal solution to the issue of trans discrimination at work, because they do not rely on how one looks or sounds. To strengthen her case, she said that remote jobs had been highly beneficial to people in other contexts, especially "stay-at-home moms."

In TransTech's training academy, "apprentices" work on commercial projects and learn skills, such as web coding, commercial web design, and data entry. As part of a "dual empowerment project," companies receive high-tech services at drastically cheaper prices, and apprentices develop portfolios to help gain future employment. This independent contract work, Ross said, could serve as a pathway to owning their own businesses.

In Ross's lecture, I learned that TransTech apprentices pay a participation fee, and if they do not have funds, the company buys into their careers and receives a percentage of future earnings. Looking to expand operations, Ross said that TransTech's telecommuting and remote employment opportunities could help employ trans people across the world, including the Hijra in India and trans and gender-nonconforming people in Thailand and Pakistan, who would be compensated at the living wage in their countries. In addition, her company could offer freelance working opportunities for trans communities around the world to "build their own bridges towards financial freedom while traditional forms of freedom are still unaccessible" (Ross 2015b).

TransTech was met with great enthusiasm in a number of venues, including the *Advocate, Chicago Tribune, Huffington Post*, and MSNBC (see Kellaway 2014; MacArthur 2015; Ross 2015b), and the company was even invited to participate in the White House's 2015 LGBTQ Tech and Innovation Summit (Wells 2015). It is tempting to buy into this fervor, given the positive coverage and the fact that TransTech has sought to improve the lives of its participants. But critical reflection is necessary to understand the underlying logics that guide these approaches to addressing trans employment struggles. One must consider how these neoliberal strategies might inadvertently bring about negative repercussions, bolstering new forms of exploitative employment practices in a globalized, service economy.

My observations are based on readings of cultural texts and materials in the public record, rather than on an in-depth, ethnographic study of this company, which would yield quite different results. Let me pause to note that this article is not intended as a critique of individuals who have dedicated their paid and unpaid time and energies to improving trans economic lives. Rather, I want to examine the global economic structures and new modes of governance that shape calls for market inclusion. Doing so helps better understand how trans people "have to build working lives in the face of gender inequalities and the insecurities of a globalizing economic order" (Connell 2012: 871). As such, I engage in what Duggan (2011–12) describes as a "friendly critique" of inclusion agendas with an end goal of "transforming these institutions in ways that meet the needs of more of us, rather than simply plead or settle for inclusion in the status quo."

I limit my discussion to three observations. One drawback of TransTech's approach is its reliance on flexible work. While telecommuting can offer some relief from on-the-job trans discrimination, the cultivation of self-employed independent contractors could leave many in precarious work positions. Some of this precarity arises from the restructuring of work in neoliberal contexts. In *Normal Life: Administrative Violence, Critical Trans Politics, and the Limits of Law,* Dean Spade (2011: 50–51) writes, "More workers have been forced into the contingent labor force, working as 'temps' of various kinds without job security or benefits. At the same time, these developments are lauded by proponents of neoliberalism as increased 'flexibility' and 'choice' in the job market, where workers are portrayed as having more of an entrepreneurial role in their own employment as independent contractors." These shifts are symptomatic of what the sociologist Allison Pugh (2015: 4) calls the "insecurity culture," a "culture of personal responsibility and risk, linked to the spread of precariousness at work, the neoliberal receding of the state, and the dominance of the market." Rather than strengthen worker solidarity and organized labor, TransTech redistributes responsibility to individuals in a contingent labor force. By focusing on the class aspirations and entrepreneurial spirit of transgender freelancers and contract workers, TransTech turns attention away from the economic context of work restructuring and its devastating effects on workers across the globe. Echoing discussions about "gig" and "sharing" economies that increasingly rely on contingent and temporary workers, many of whom are excluded from employer-provided benefits (King 2014; Scheiber 2015; Schor 2013), there is less attention in TransTech's model to workplace programs that reduce precarity, such as access to health insurance, pensions, or retirement benefits, or to union organizing and worker protection from ever-expanding work hours. While TransTech is portrayed as relief from employment discrimination, it potentially leaves some trans subjects in insecure economic positions because of their status as independent contractors and freelance workers who shoulder the weight of the global restructuring of work.

A second concern lies in the formation of new forms of worker surveillance. In her lecture, Ross mentioned regularly using software programs like Upwork to monitor telecommuting workers. These programs allow employers to log keystrokes, record mouse clicks, monitor time use, and take screenshots of workers' activities during a project. For Ross, collecting this information ensures efficiency for company projects, thereby reducing costs for consumers. So while remote work promises flexibility for trans employees, it does not necessarily offer less oversight or workplace surveillance. TransTech tracks worker productivity to maximize efficiency and control workers' time, and in doing so, the company's surveillance techniques follow the logic of profit. As Ross said of these programs: "Data is power and it drives dollars."

A third concern is related to how this freelance work can reinforce economic imperialism and a global "race to the bottom." When Ross mentioned that

TransTech could begin helping trans people across the world — in India, Thailand, and Pakistan — by offering them freelance work at their home country's living wage, she failed to mention that those wages would likely be just a fraction of those earned in the Global North. What emerges, then, are trans economic relations that rely on cheaper pay as work moves its way down the outsourcing supply chain. Comparisons could be made to Nancy Fraser's critique of mainstream feminism's recent push to have middle-class women "lean in" to corporate workplaces: "By definition, then, its beneficiaries can only be women of the professional-managerial class. And absent structural changes in capitalist society, those women can only benefit by leaning on others" (Gutting and Fraser 2015). One might ask if a similar "leaning in" by trans subjects in the Global North might entail "leaning on" trans subjects who perform outsourced work in the Global South.

The trans scholar Viviane Namaste (2005: 120) notes that "current articulations of transgender rights in North America are implicated in a broader project of imperialism," which she sees in the "specifically economic relations in which the interests of US corporations are imposed throughout the world" and in "the imposition of a particular (Anglophone) world view." My research (David 2015) on transgender workers employed as call center agents in the Philippines shows how their outsourced work lives are structured by unequal flows of affect and global capital; TransTech's global projects rely on this inequality. In doing so, TransTech's entrepreneurial model strengthens ruling relations rather than challenging them. What might emerge from this outsourcing is a dynamic not of solidarity but of trans-on-trans exploitation across North-South divides.

TransTech's economic empowerment projects routinely deploy discourses of value, visibility, and entrepreneurialism. This is apparent in one of its fundraising campaigns, which brought together fifteen trans leaders, advocates, and allies to raise $15,000 in fifteen days. A five-minute-long video, "15k 15 Days 15 People," began with Ross introducing the company: "I created TransTech because I believe there needs to be an employment and education structure that uses the wide variety of skills that trans people already possess." Then, to the upbeat tune of India Arie's song "Just Do You," the video showcased still photographs of TransTech participants holding placards with words like "Justice," "Resilience," "Sufficient," "Perseverance," and "Authenticity." The video highlighted endorsements from fifteen supporters, including musicians, trans activists, and an adult film star. Many speakers use the language of economic value. For example, Tiq Milan, a strategist at GLAAD, declares, "I support TransTech because trans folks need exclusive opportunities for empowerment and development." Another speaker, Myles Brady, described in the video as a "human rights activist, educator, and gentleman," says, "I support TransTech because I believe it will help empower trans individuals as economic agents and better their ability to access markets on competitive and fair terms." The activist Erik Roldan says, "I support TransTech because trans people are capable, talented, and hard working" and claims that the company offers apprentices spaces free of transphobia and microaggressions so that they "can focus on learning, thriving, and starting a career." Then there was the support offered by the trans activist Precious Davis, board president of TransTech Social Enterprises. She supports TransTech because she believes in the "investment of resources that empower and enable transgender people to be competitive players in today's increasingly technological world." At the video's end, Ross says:

> Trans people are twice as likely to be unemployed and we're determined to change that. . . . In our apprenticeship program, similar to a beauty school model, TransTech will offer creative tech services like web development, graphic design, media production, all that are worked on by the students and the educators at an affordable price for consumers. One hundred percent of the profits will go right back into the program.

She tells viewers that TransTech is based on a "social enterprise structure," which for her means aiming "to maximize economic improvement and well-being in the LGBT community rather than focusing on maximizing profits for external shareholders." Ross concludes the video by saying, "I know the devastating statistics and the pain that my community has endured. But I also know the incredible resilience and the possibilities that each one of us has to offer. We're not here to save anyone. We're here to empower, to educate, and to employ the trans community. That's our mission and we hope that you will help us make that happen."

The video is revealing of the neoliberal strategies used to address labor market anxieties. It portrays trans individuals as economic agents and competitive players, and it highlights desires to contribute to society through work. This focus resonated with corporate donors. In December 2014 TransTech announced a partnership with MillerCoors in a donor-matching campaign, noting that the company was recognized by HRC as one of the "Best Places to Work for LGBT Equality" (TransTech 2014; MacArthur 2015).

These discourses raise concerns about movement co-optation and corporatization. Rickke Mananzala and Dean Spade (2008: 58) note, "The emergence of the nonprofit sector has created a cultural shift in social justice activism, including professionalization, corporatization, and competition between groups for scarce resources." Much of what is described as trans activism is increasingly linked to incorporation into existing markets and corporate economic structures, complete with the adoption of "labor practices that reflect business values more than social justice values" (58). These business values are evident in how Ross imagines the company's future. Ross told the *Advocate* (Kellaway 2014), "It is my mission to make TransTech the Apple of the nonprofit industry!" But as INCITE! Women of Color Against Violence (2009) has famously pointed out, politics and private interests threaten to co-opt social movements, forming what they call the "non-profit industrial complex."

Ray Filar (2015), in "Trans™: How the Trans Movement Got Sold Out," outlines numerous ways that corporations in the United States profit from transgender visibility. After noting a rise of mainstream trans visibility in film and consumer culture, Filar writes: "This partial acceptability stems from the trans movement's push for inclusion. It's a respectability drive, supported by a bevy of companies who are jumping at the chance to use trans or non-normative gender expression to sell their products. Trans-ness is sexy." Filar's observations recall debates about co-optation, commercialization, and commodification in the gay and lesbian community in the 1990s (Chasin 2000; Gluckman and Reeds 1997; Hennessy 1994–95; Sender 2004). Filar then turned attention to lessons for the trans liberation movement: "Movements are taken out of the hands of the radical, angry, non-respectable, non-conforming people who did the years of unrewarded hard graft to make it all happen. Then gradually they are overrun by . . . career activists out to make a name for themselves." These shifts resonate with Dan Irving's (2012: 157) observations about the entanglements of economic logics, cultural spheres, and technologies of the self: "As CEOs of 'Me, Inc.,' we are responsible for managing our own advancement. We develop our worth through education, self-branding, and promotion."

Circling back to links between trans visibility and the mainstreaming of activism in probusiness and nonprofit settings, we could examine how TransTech has struck a chord with corporate audiences and mainstream LGBT organizations, including HRC, which offered office space to Ross in its Washington headquarters. In 2015 Ross delivered the keynote at the 2015 HRC Corporate Equality Index awards. During her speech, she spoke about blocked employment opportunities as well as discrimination on the job. She then elaborated on the promise of trans value for the business sector: "But we are not the problem. We are the solution. The problem really comes down to business and economics. It is time that corporate America starts to recognize the value in the trans community" (Ross 2015a). Ross's speech makes clear how TransTech is inextricably tied to market forces and business values. At the same time, one can also recognize the potential benefits offered to trans employees. For those who cannot claim membership in an emerging "trans elite" (Sycamore 2016), opportunities like those promoted by TransTech are important livelihood options in a world where wealth and life chances are unevenly distributed. Paraphrasing Karl Marx, it would be advantageous to remind ourselves that it is people who make history, including Ross and other trans entrepreneurs, but not under material circumstances of their own making.

Conclusions

Examining trans markets, labor, aspirations, and entrepreneurship, this article highlights some of the paradoxes of our neoliberal times. As the anthropologist Carla Freeman (2014: 47–48) writes in *Entrepreneurial Selves*, "Entrepreneurialism today represents simultaneously greater pressure placed upon the individual to create her or his own livelihood in the absence or changing face of formal sector employment and opportunities to break out of traditional confines of gender, race, and class." Freeman notes that entrepreneurial practices "suggest radical transformations" in institutions and cultural life: "These are at once creative and onerous, spaces of aspiration and precarity, engaging and reconstituting both reputation and respectability" (48). In its focus on the production, circulation, and extraction of transgender value, this article takes seriously trans-political economy approaches that encourage moving beyond the language of self-determination and self-actualization (Irving 2014; see also Irving 2008, 2009), which all too easily become mere strategies of market inclusion without questioning capital's insidious and adaptive force. It may seem counterintuitive, but inclusion and visibility could deepen social divides and strengthen oppressive global relations.

Rather than simply celebrate shifts from exclusion to inclusion, from devaluation to valuation, trans studies should pay attention to the political-economic conditions of work, labor, and economic insecurities. Future research is needed to better understand the conditions that give rise to production and consumption practices as well as all trans workplaces and the organizational and institutional dynamics that unfold within them. Such critical approaches would also help focus attention on how trans labor and value intersect with the neoliberal restructuring of work across the globe and the upward redistribution of wealth.

Concerns about institutional inclusion are also political. Focusing on how new inclusivity practices can undercut social justice movements, Morgan Bassichis, Alexander Lee, and Dean Spade (2014: 662) write: "Be careful of all those welcome mats! . . . Other movements and other moments have been drained of their original power and purpose and appropriated for purposes opposing their principles, either in governments working to dilute and derail transformation or by corporations looking to turn civil unrest into a fashion statement (or both)." In sum, the current moment of increased queer and trans visibility offers the powerful prospects of social transformation and political change, but there is also a seductive pull toward marketplace activism and commodity cultures that view trans as a source of value. If trans visibility is indeed becoming valuable, one must ask the perennial question, "for whom and in whose interests"?

Emmanuel David is assistant professor of women and gender studies and codirector of the LGBTQ Certificate Program at the University of Colorado Boulder. His recent work has appeared in *Gender and Society, GLQ,* and *Radical History Review.*

Notes

This article's subtitle refers to Rosemary Hennessy's 1994–95 essay "Queer Visibility in Commodity Culture."

1. Unless otherwise credited, all quotes from Ross come from my written notes of her lecture, "Bridging Digital Divides: Reaching Liminal Spaces," at the University of Colorado Boulder on September 21, 2015.

References

Adleman, Nicole. 2015. "First All Transgender Modeling Agency Opens in Los Angeles—Get the Scoop!" *E! Online,* July 27. www.eonline.com/news/680548/first-all-transgender-modeling -agency-opens-in-los-angeles-get-the-scoop.

Aizura, Aren. 2011. "The Romance of the Amazing Scalpel: 'Race,' Labour, and Affect in Thai Gender Reassignment Clinics." In *Queer Bangkok*, edited by Peter A. Jackson, 142–62. Hong Kong: Hong Kong University Press.

———. 2014. "Trans Feminine Value, Racialized Others, and the Limits of Necropolitics." In *Queer Necropolitics*, edited by Jin Haritaworn, Adi Kuntsman, and Silvia Posocco, 129–47. New York: Routledge.

Avila, Theresa. 2015. "This Is the Conversation We Need to Be Having about Trans Models in Fashion." *Mic*, September 8. mic.com/articles/124950/this-is-the-conversation-we-need -to-be-having-about-trans-models-in-fashion.

Bassichis, Morgan, Alexander Lee, and Dean Spade. 2014. "Building an Abolitionist Trans and Queer Movement with Everything We've Got." In *The Transgender Studies Reader 2*, edited by Susan Stryker and Aren Z. Aizura, 653–67. New York: Routledge.

Boyd, Nan Alamilla. 1998. "Shopping for Rights: Gays, Lesbians, and Visibility Politics." *Denver University Law Review* 75, no. 4: 1361–73.

Carlson, Erin. 2015. "Meet the World's First Transgender Modeling Agency." *Fortune*, July 28. fortune.com/2015/07/28/first-transgender-modeling-agency/.

Chan, Anna. 2016. "'Say Yes to the Dress' Is Featuring Its First Ever Transgender Bride: Meet Precious Davis." *US Weekly*, January 16. www.usmagazine.com/entertainment/news/say -yes-to-the-dress-is-featuring-its-first-trans-bride-w161801.

Chasin, Alexandra. 2000. *Selling Out: The Gay and Lesbian Movement Goes to Market*. New York: Palgrave.

Connell, Raewyn. 2012. "Transsexual Women and Feminist Thought: Toward New Understanding and New Politics." *Signs* 37, no. 4: 857–81.

Conrad, Ryan, ed. 2014. *Against Equality: Queer Revolution Not Mere Inclusion*. Baltimore: AK.

Contrera, Jessica. 2015. "Learning How to Be a Lady? For the Transgender Market, Coaches Help." *Washington Post*, June 5. www.washingtonpost.com/lifestyle/style/learning-to-act-like-a -lady-for-the-transgender-market-coaches-help/2015/06/05/17bad4c8-03ba-11e5-a428 -c984eb077d4e_story.html.

Daniel, Diane. 2015. "Courting Transgender Tourists." *New York Times*, September 16. www .nytimes.com/2015/09/20/travel/lgbt-gay-travel.html.

David, Emmanuel. 2015. "Purple-Collar Labor: Transgender Workers and Queer Value at Global Call Centers in the Philippines." *Gender and Society* 29, no. 2: 169–94.

Davidson, Danica. 2015. "An All-Transgender Modeling Agency? Yup, That Is So Happening." MTV, July 22. www.mtv.com/news/2221213/transgender-modeling-agency/.

Dockterman, Eliana. 2015. "H&M Sister Store Features Transgender Models in Ad Campaign." *Time*, August 15. time.com/3999546/other-stories-transgender-models/.

Duggan, Lisa. 2003. *The Twilight of Equality? Neoliberalism, Cultural Politics, and the Attack on Democracy*. Boston: Beacon.

———. 2011–12. "After Neoliberalism? From Crisis to Organizing for Queer Economic Justice." *Scholar and Feminist Online* 10, nos. 1–2. sfonline.barnard.edu/a-new-queer-agenda /after-neoliberalism-from-crisis-to-organizing-for-queer-economic-justice/.

Duggan, Lisa, and Richard Kim. 2011–12. "Preface." *Scholar and Feminist Online* 10, nos. 1–2. sfonline.barnard.edu/a-new-queer-agenda/preface/.

Filar, Ray. 2015. "Trans™: How the Trans Movement Got Sold Out." *openDemocracy*, November 25. www.opendemocracy.net/transformation/ray-filar/how-trans-movement-sold-out.

Freeman, Carla. 2014. *Entrepreneurial Selves: Neoliberal Respectability and the Making of a Caribbean Middle Class*. Durham, NC: Duke University Press.

Friedner, Michele. 2014. "Deaf Capital: An Exploration of the Relationship between Stigma and Value in Deaf Multilevel Marketing Participation in Urban India." *Medical Anthropology Quarterly* 28, no. 4: 502–18.

———. 2015a. "Deaf Bodies and Corporate Bodies: New Regimes of Value in Bangalore's Business Process Outsourcing Sector." *JRAI: Journal of the Royal Anthropological Institute*, n.s., 21: 313–29.

———. 2015b. *Valuing Deaf Worlds in Urban India*. New Brunswick, NJ: Rutgers University Press.

Gale, Jason. 2015. "Transgender Tourism: For $2,000 a New Life Begins." *Bloomberg*, October 26. www.bloomberg.com/news/articles/2015-10-26/transgender-tourism-for-2-000-a-new-life -begins.

Getsy, David. 2015. "Appearing Differently: Abstraction's Transgender and Queer Capacities. David J. Getsy in Conversation with William J. Simmons." In *Pink Labour on Golden Streets: Queer Art Practices*, edited by Christiane Erharter, Dietmar Schwärzler, Ruby Sircar, and Hans Scheirl, 38–55. Berlin: Sternberg.

Gluckman, Amy, and Betsy Reeds, eds. 1997. *Homo Economics: Capitalism, Community, and Lesbian and Gay Life*. New York: Routledge.

Griggs, Brandon. 2015. "America's Transgender Moment." CNN, June 1. www.cnn.com/2015/04 /23/living/transgender-moment-jenner-feat/.

Gutting, Gary, and Nancy Fraser. 2015. "A Feminism Where 'Lean In' Means Leaning on Others." *New York Times*, October 15. opinionator.blogs.nytimes.com/2015/10/15/a-feminism -where-lean-in-means-leaning-on-others.

Heffernan, Dani. 2015. "MTV's 'Faking It' Launches Casting Call for Transgender Actors." GLAAD, November 4. www.glaad.org/blog/mtvs-faking-it-launches-casting-call-trans gender-actors.

Hennessy, Rosemary. 1994–95. "Queer Visibility in Commodity Culture." *Cultural Critique*, no. 29: 31–76.

Hines, Sally. 2010. Introduction to *Transgender Identities: Towards a Social Analysis of Gender Diversity*, edited by Sally Hines and Tam Sanger, 1–24. New York: Routledge.

Honigman, Brian. 2015. "Peche Di: How She Started New York's First Transgender Modeling Agency." *Forbes*, October 10. www.forbes.com/sites/brianhonigman/2015/10/25/peche-di -transgender-modeling-agency/.

Human Rights Campaign. 2014. "Transgender Visibility: A Guide to Being You." www.hrc.org
/resources/transgender-visibility-guide.

INCITE! Women of Color Against Violence. 2009. *The Revolution Will Not Be Funded: Beyond the
Non-Profit Industrial Complex.* New York: South End.

Ingraham, Chrys. 2008. *White Weddings: Romancing Heterosexuality in Popular Culture.* 2nd ed.
New York: Routledge.

Irving, Dan. 2008. "Normalized Transgressions: Legitimizing the Transsexual Body as Productive."
Radical History Review 100: 38–59.

———. 2009. "The Self-Made Trans Man as Risky Business: A Critical Examination of Gaining
Recognition for Trans Rights through Economic Discourse." *Temple Law Review* 18, no. 2:
375–95.

———. 2012. "Elusive Subjects: Notes on the Relationship between Critical Political Economy and
Trans Studies." In *Transfeminist Perspectives: In and beyond Transgender and Gender
Studies*, edited by Anne Enke, 153–69. Philadelphia: Temple University Press.

———. 2014. "Capital." *TSQ* 1, nos. 1–2: 50–52.

Kellaway, Mitch. 2014. "WATCH: TransTech Offers Employment Solutions for Aspiring Transgender Coders." *Advocate*, September 11. www.advocate.com/politics/transgender/2014
/09/11/watch-transtech-offers-employment-solutions-aspiring-transgender.

King, Martha. 2014. "Protecting and Representing Workers in the New Gig Economy: The Case of
the Freelancers Union." In *New Labor in New York: Precarious Workers and the Future of
the Labor Movement*, edited by Ruth Milkman and Ed Ott, 150–70. Ithaca, NY: Cornell
University Press.

Mac, Amos. 2015. "Premier: Macy Rodman's 'Lazy Girl' with All Trans Cast." *Original Plumbing*,
September 20. originalplumbing.com/index.php/the-basics/video/item/897-premier-macy
-rodman-s-lazy-girl-with-all-trans-girl-cast.

MacArthur, Kate. 2015. "Angelica Ross, TransTech, and Voice and Value for Transgender People."
Chicago Tribune, June 4. chicagotribune.com/bluesky/originals/ct-angelica-ross-transtech
-social-enterprise-bsi-20150604-story.html.

Mananzala, Rickke, and Dean Spade. 2008. "The Nonprofit Industrial Complex and Trans
Resistance." *Sexuality Research and Social Policy* 5, no. 1: 55–71.

McCue, Matt. 2015. "These Retailers Are Betting on Transgender Customers." *Fortune*, May 21.
fortune.com/2015/05/21/transgender-retail-growing/.

Nair, Yasmin. 2010. "Against Equality, against Marriage: An Introduction." In *Against Equality:
Queer Critiques of Marriage*, edited by Ryan Conrad, 1–9. Lewiston, ME: Against Equality
Publishing Collective.

Namaste, Viviane. 2004. "Beyond Leisure Studies: A Labour History of Male to Female Transsexual and Transvestite Artists in Montreal, 1955–1985." *Atlantis* 29, no. 1: 4–11.

———. 2005. "Against Transgender Rights: Understanding the Imperialism of Contemporary
Transgender Politics." In *Sex Change, Social Change: Reflections on Identity, Institutions,
and Imperialism*, 103–26. Toronto: Women's Press.

Pearson, Bryan. 2015. "Curating for Transgender Customers: How Five Retailers Size Up." *Forbes*,
July 30. www.forbes.com/sites/bryanpearson/2015/07/30/curating-for-transgender
-customers-how-5-retailers-size-up/.

Pugh, Allison. 2015. *The Tumbleweed Society: Working and Caring in an Age of Insecurity.*
New York: Oxford University Press.

Pulver, Andrew. 2015. "Danish Girl Director Tom Hooper: Film Industry Has 'Problem' with
Transgender Actors." *Guardian*, September 15. www.theguardian.com/film/2015/sep/05
/danish-girl-eddie-redmayne-tom-hooper-transgender-actors-venice.

Rodman, Macy. 2016. "Macy Rodman's New Music Video: Violent Young Men." Indiegogo.com. www.indiegogo.com/projects/macy-rodman-s-new-music-video-violent-young-men#/.

Ross, Angelica. 2015a. "Keynote Angelica Ross / HRC Corporate Equality Index Awards 2015." www.youtube.com/watch?v=Y2Q8oWWqZ3M.

———. 2015b. "One Lucky Black Trans Girl." *Huffington Post*, June 10. www.huffingtonpost .com/angelica-ross/one-lucky-black-trans-gir_b_7553524.html.

Scheiber, Noam. 2015. "Growth in the 'Gig Economy' Fuels Work Force Anxieties." *New York Times*, July 13.

Schilt, Kristen. 2010. *Just One of the Guys? Transgender Men and the Persistence of Gender Inequality*. Chicago: University of Chicago Press.

Schor, Juliet. 2013. "After the Jobs Disappear." *New York Times*, October 15

Sender, Katherine. 2004. *Business, Not Politics: The Making of the Gay Market*. New York: Columbia University Press.

Serano, Julia. 2004. "Skirt Chasers: Why the Media Depicts the Trans Revolution in Lipstick and Heels." *Bitch*, no. 26: 41–47.

Shepard, Benjamin H. 2001. "The Queer/Gay Assimilationist Split: The Suits vs. the Sluts." *Monthly Review* 53, no. 1: 49–62.

Spade, Dean. 2011. *Normal Life: Administrative Violence, Critical Trans Politics, and the Limits of Law*. Brooklyn: South End.

Sycamore, Mattilda Berstein. 2016. "'Transgender Troops' Should Be an Oxymoron." *Truthout*, June 29. www.truth-out.org/opinion/item/36622-transgender-troops-should-be-an-oxymoron.

Talusan, Meredith. 2016. "Meet the Very First Transgender Bride on 'Say Yes to the Dress.'" *BuzzFeed*, January 14. www.buzzfeed.com/meredithtalusan/meet-the-very-first-trans -woman-on-say-yes-to-the-dress.

Tourjee, Diana. 2015. "'Lazy Girl' by Artist Macy Rodman Is an Anthem for Transgender Mil-lennials." *Vice*, October 25. broadly.vice.com/en_us/article/lazy-girl-by-artist-macy -rodman-is-an-anthem-for-transgender-millennials.

TransTech. 2014. "TransTech Announces Donor Matching Program with MillerCoors." Press release. *Windy City Times*, December 18. www.windycitymediagroup.com/lgbt/-Trans Tech-announces-donor-matching-program-with-MillerCoors-/50044.html.

Truitt, Jos. 2014. "The Golden Globes Gave Jared Leto an Award for Playing a Trans Woman Because Hollywood Is Terrible." *Feministing*, January 13. feministing.com/2014/01/13/the -golden-globes-give-jared-leto-an-award-for-playing-a-trans-woman-because-hollywood -is-terrible/.

Valentine, David. 2007. *Imagining Transgender: An Ethnography of a Category*. Durham, NC: Duke University Press.

Vitulli, Elias. 2010. "A Defining Moment in Civil Rights History? The Employment Non-Discrimination Act, Trans-Inclusion, and Homonormativity." *Sexuality Research and Social Policy* 7, no. 3: 155–67.

Wells, Georgia. 2015. "White House Takes a Stand to Support LGBTQ Techies." *Wall Street Journal*, August 10. blogs.wsj.com/digits/2015/08/10/white-house-takes-a-stand-to-support-lgbtq -techies/.

Whitehead, Jaye Cee. 2011. *The Nuptial Deal: Same-Sex Marriage and Neo-Liberal Governance*. Chicago: University of Chicago Press.

Wolfson, Evan. 2015. "Gay Rights: What Comes Next." *New York Times*, June 27.

The Afterlife of Data

Identity, Surveillance, and Capitalism
in Trans Credit Reporting

LARS Z. MACKENZIE

Abstract Credit reports, once solely used to determine individual creditworthiness, have in the past several decades become a tool for authentication processes not directly related to one's capacity to take on debt, namely, in rental housing and employment applications. When trans people change their first names to better align with their gender identities, they often become illegible to credit reporting systems. In this article, the author examines online discussion board posts about trans people's experiences with their credit reports, arguing that the issues trans people encounter illuminate the complex logics of neoliberal capitalism, predatory lending, and the "afterlife" of identification data enabled by big data surveillance.
Keywords data, credit reporting, legal transition, housing, debt

Posting to a discussion board on a website for transgender people,[1] Caitlin[2] expresses frustration that the three major US credit reporting agencies (CRAs),[3] Equifax, Experian, and TransUnion, will not acknowledge her legal name change. She writes:

> I have had no luck getting the three credit bureaus to stop reporting my old name under my S[ocial] S[ecurity] N[umber], they just tell me to change my name with my creditors. I was told by an Experian rep to file a request online and upload proof of my identity. I did all that and just got a letter saying they couldn't find credit history for my new name.

Caitlin describes a common experience among trans people attempting to navigate administrative systems that presume identity is stable, consistent, and coherent. After making legal name changes, reporting the changes, and documenting the provenance of their identification data, people like Caitlin cannot tie their new legal identities to their credit histories: why? Although she obtained a

TSQ: Transgender Studies Quarterly ★ Volume 4, Number 1 ★ February 2017   **45**
DOI 10.1215/23289252-3711529   © 2017 Duke University Press

court-ordered name change, Caitlin's outdated identification data sticks to her because of the massive collection and coordination of data by financial institutions. These data are intended to protect individuals from identity theft and to protect lenders, employers, and landlords from making risky investments. Unlike a cisgender woman who changes her surname after marriage, Caitlin's first name change is illegible and suspect to credit reporting systems, even when it is legally sanctioned and documented. She remains marked as her previous (male) name on her credit report, which is used to determine her trustworthiness as a consumer, employee, and tenant. Outdated data stick, maintaining a connection between a past and a present identity and drawing a trans history into focus.

In this article, I examine what the "afterlife of data" reveals about the relationship between identification systems and neoliberal capitalism for trans people who obtain legal name changes. I focus on name changes because, as the opening example demonstrates, a mismatch between legal and other names in a credit file separates people from their credit history or raises suspicion of a fraudulent or trans identity. While scholarship in trans studies has documented how the public sector administers official trans name and sex-designator changes (Spade 2008, 2011), I argue that official identity production is not limited to the public sector. In the United States, the private sector plays an increasingly important role in creating and verifying identities through the use of financial data. In credit reporting systems, trans peoples' identities can be produced or expunged by financial institutions, even when no legal basis for this action exists. Indeed, turning to the private sector reveals how debt, credit, and capital produce legible identities and how consumer data sharing reproduces housing and employment insecurity for trans people through their credit reports.

Centering trans identities in credit reporting practices reveals everyday strategies for manipulation and resistance against capitalism, identification, and surveillance. This article engages in critical trans politics, which Dean Spade (2011: 19) articulates as "a trans politics that demands more than legal recognition and inclusion, seeking instead to transform current logics of state, civil society security, and social equality." Writing against an inclusionary impulse for integration into the credit reporting system, I argue for a transformation of systems in which trans people, people with "bad" credit, no credit, and those with unstable or inconsistent identities are subject to administrative and state violence because of their financial, criminal, or trans histories.

Haunted by Data

The software developer Maciej Ceglowski compares big data to nuclear waste. In a keynote address at Strata + Hadoop World 2015, an international big data conference, Ceglowski (2015) remarked, "The data we are all collecting around people has the same really odd property [as nuclear waste]: it has a lifespan that is longer than any institution that manages it." In this conception, big data is nuclear, toxic. It is dangerous long after it has been created and forgotten because the massive amounts of data collected about people are not disposable: they could be useful at some point, particularly when consumer data are used in national security intelligence (Lyon 2014).

Ceglowski's metaphor is instructive for thinking about trans identity management. The identification data created about trans people do not disappear when individuals change their name. Although describing an identity that may no longer exist (legally or otherwise), it lives on, tied to their other identifying characteristics: their Social Security number (SSN), last known addresses, debts. Outdated data may be sold by third-party data brokers, surrendered to the police and the federal government by search engines and social media sites, or stored indefinitely in data warehouses. Data stick to individuals, matching them to moments when their past selves made contact with the Internet, the state, retailers, and banks. After a legal name change, a trans person's previous name sticks to credit reports, background checks, and other privately owned and operated authentication technologies that reference a past. Its value may decay over time, but it is still capable of causing harm.

Trans identity management has a queer temporality.[4] As most trans people cannot change all their data in a legal transition, at some or most points in time, they will legally exist as (at least) two identities. Kadji Amin (2014: 219) remarks, "Transgender experiences are constituted by yet exceed normative temporalities." The very trouble that trans identities pose to administrative systems is this capacity for multiplicity that makes it possible for trans people (at least through their data) to exist in multiple forms in the past, present, and future. Trans people are indeed haunted by identification data in their credit reports; their previous names have an afterlife that extends indeterminately, sometimes long after a legal name change. Avery Gordon ([1997] 2008: xvi) describes haunting as "one way in which abusive systems of power make themselves known and their impacts felt in everyday life, especially . . . when their oppressive nature is denied (as in free labor or national security)." The "abusive systems" of identification haunt trans people, as the state and financial sectors' investment in data collection as a risk-aversion and capital accumulation measure ensures that a trans person's former name might stick to that person indefinitely, emerging in unforeseen moments. While the state may allow some trans people to update all their IDs, big data surveillance and credit reporting practices tie traces of a trans person's former identity to the present or, as in the opening example, make a trans person's legal identity effectively invalid.

Credit Reporting Agencies

Credit reporting is a form of financial monitoring that produces identity out of economic activity. Structured by federal legislation and the needs of financial institutions, contemporary CRAs track and report consumer credit history, enabling financial data to stand in for a person's identity as a potential debtor, consumer, employee, and tenant. Kelly Gates (2010: 419) explains that prior to the 2008 financial crisis, US financial institutions constructed "an expansive network infrastructure" that was capable of systematically identifying and monitoring individuals. She attests, "Thanks significantly to this process, 'identity' itself came to be understood as a disembodied aggregate of transaction-generated data, a digital representation of the person constructed over time and space based on the perpetual collection of more data" (419). Contemporary CRAs are at the center of this network, collecting data and representing individuals in the form of credit reports and credit scores.

Credit reports disclose information about consumer credit history and current accounts, including medical debt, mortgages, education loans, open and closed credit cards, and any accounts sent to debt collection. They include seven to ten years of credit history, though demographic information, such as name(s) and addresses, may be reported indefinitely.[5] Credit reports were once solely used to determine individual creditworthiness, but in the past several decades they have become a tool for other authentication processes: applications for employment, property rentals, and home, health, and automobile insurance. In other words, credit reports now authorize activities not directly related to one's capacity to take on debt. In this way, credit reports are a tool of neoliberal capitalism, which privatizes access to basic goods and services, rewarding individuals capable of self-management in an increasingly precarious financial landscape.

The notion that an individual's credit history could and should be used in this manner is perhaps unsurprising within the US political economy. Credit reports and credit scores are racialized and classed calculi. A "good" credit score enables a proliferating number of life chances, while a "bad" credit score or no credit history is a sign of riskiness and a failure to adhere to proper self-management. Bad credit or no credit history further exploits low-income people, people of color, and those working in informal economies. Credit reports codify bankruptcies, defaulted payments, and closed accounts as the failings of risky persons, stripping away any consideration of the structures that enforce poverty and encourage debt: centuries of economic disenfranchisement, state policies, and the financial institutions themselves.

Currently, the types of positive accounts reported in a credit file are those associated with the middle class: prime mortgages, automobile and education loans, and credit cards. Making consistent payments on these accounts generates a positive credit report. Alternatively, histories of predatory lending make it more likely for low-income, Black, and Latino/a people to have negative credit histories, as high interest rates cause many to default on payments and file for bankruptcy (Rugh and Massey 2010; Wyly et al. 2009). For people of color sold subprime mortgages prior to the US housing market crash, a low credit score not only raises interest rates on their debts but also decreases their ability to obtain employment and rental housing. A low credit score and history of bankruptcy enable landlords and employers to rescind offers and lenders to raise interest rates, generating capital for financial corporations.

Credit reporting practices are an instructive example of what Spade (2011: 29) calls "administrative violence," defined as "administrative norms or regularities [that] create structured insecurity and (mal)distributive life chances across populations." When creditworthiness is tied to the necessities of daily life, such as employment and housing, credit history and credit scores come to stand in for a person's potential trustworthiness as an employee or tenant. Further, being outed by a credit report in a job or rental property application process increases the housing and employment insecurity trans people already face. Trans people of color face unemployment rates at four times the US national average and homelessness at twice the national average, and trans people own their homes at less than half the rate of the general public. Just over 40 percent of trans people rely on rental properties for shelter, and 44 percent of trans people report being denied a job because of their gender identity, making this issue of being outed by a credit check increasingly pressing (Grant et al. 2011).

Anyone with an SSN or an Individual Tax Identification Number is eligible for a credit report. However, credit files are generated only when individuals take out credit and creditors report debt or make an inquiry on a person's account (e.g., when an individual applies for a credit card). Equifax, Experian, and TransUnion each produce credit files with reported credit data. While credit files generated by each CRA should be identical, they sometimes differ, particularly because smaller financial institutions might report to just one or two of the CRAs to avoid the fees required to set up an account with each agency (Equifax 2014). Further, the three CRAs are private corporations, each with proprietary products for sale in consumer, business, and government markets.

Selective reporting and widespread errors cause inconsistencies among reports generated by different CRAs. In 2013 the Federal Trade Commission reported that 40 million people in the United States have errors on their credit reports and 26 million have lower credit scores because of errors. During a congressional hearing on this issue, several US representatives remarked that they had errors in their credit files they had trouble correcting. Representative Ed Perlmutter (D-CO) expressed his concern, stating, "This is the kind of situation where you are guilty until proven innocent, and given that situation, you have to get the reporting right the first time." When getting data "right the first time" is a prerequisite for accurate credit reports, trans people and others whose identification data change over time in unexpected or suspect ways can expect little recourse. Representative Mimi Walters (R-CA) echoes this sentiment:

> Sadly, the burden is too often placed on the consumers to prove information on their reports as false rather than on the consumer reporting agencies and furnishers. Errors on credit reports are very difficult for consumers to dispute, and it is even harder to have these inaccuracies actually removed from reports, causing heartache and pain for millions across the country. It is time to change that paradigm and ensure that a bad credit score will no longer haunt a consumer for years on end.[6]

A credit report full of difficult-to-remove inaccuracies resonates with other documents that record a history of state-imposed identification on trans people: birth certificates that cannot be changed and IDs that do not match one's gender identity or preferred name. Credit reporting systems can and do accommodate name changes, for instance, for people who change their last names after marriage. However, trans first-name changes require different considerations. When a name change is acknowledged by a CRA, all known previous legal names are listed in the demographic section of the credit report, either as "Formerly Known As . . . " or "Also Known As . . . " Across credit reports, a trans person may be formerly *and* also known as their previous name, suggesting that the past slips readily into the present, confounding the logics of normative time. This practice, which is much less likely to cause issues for a cisgender married person's name change, outs trans people to those accessing the report, leaving trans people unable to choose if, when, how, and to whom they disclose their trans history or identity. The difficulty of removing errors from a credit report forces trans people to either persistently reveal their trans history to employers and landlords or establish new credit identities by taking on risky, high-interest debt. When the impetus rests on individuals to verify their identities and prove their trustworthiness through their credit histories, the credit report can indeed "haunt a consumer for years on end," particularly for trans people whose bodies and identities are already illegible to these systems.

Fraud Alert: Trans Credit Reporting

Trans people's experiences with credit reporting demonstrate the insidious ways that consumer credit reports can plot lives through data points. In this section, I examine discussions on three separate online forums, written by trans people who experienced issues with their credit reports because of a legal name change, and those who gave advice to their peers about credit reporting and debt. All three forums cater specifically to trans participants. Two of the three are hosted on websites dedicated to trans people, and the third is a subsection of a larger, general, popular discussion forum website. On the two trans-specific sites, commentators were likely to reply multiple times in a thread; on the other site, participation was more ephemeral. Trans people use discussion boards as spaces to strategize how they might manipulate and resist oppressive policies, procedures, and systems across different experiences. Because the impacts of the afterlife of data are long-lasting and unpredictable, it is difficult to ascertain the long-term effects of the strategies trans people employ to manipulate credit reporting data. Further research into this question is necessary, though the question may be elusive precisely because identification data reemerges unexpectedly. However, discussion board posts demonstrate the range and complexity of the problems trans people encounter with their credit reports. While nearly all commentators say that their name change interferes with their credit in some way, they report a spectrum of different experiences about if and when a former name appears on a credit report. While none of the commentators mention the impact that their subject positions (beyond identifying as trans) have on their access to their credit history, this range of experiences is undoubtedly influenced by the commentators' race, gender, class, and citizenship statuses.

Posting to a thread about credit report inconsistencies, Kim expresses frustration at the impossible bind she finds herself in. She cannot access her credit report because of a name change that occurred seven months earlier. Kim is attempting to rent an apartment, but the landlord cannot validate her credit history as part of the application because her name change has not been reported to the CRAs. Her previous name is associated with her credit history, leaving her current name creditless. She explains:

> In other words, they won't [update my credit report] until I have credit in my new name and I can't get credit in my new name because there is no official file in that name. I currently do not have any credit cards or debt. . . . I am applying for a rental and will have to include a letter stating that I am a transsexual and give my prior name so they can run a credit check.

Kim voices her complaint to inquire if this has happened to anyone else. In response, a forum participant posts a template letter that Kim can use to request a name change in the credit agency's systems. A few weeks later, Kim posts again in this thread. She writes that she submitted a letter with proof of her court-ordered name change to all three CRAs. TransUnion sent her a credit report with her previous legal name listed as her primary name and her current legal name underneath as "Also Known As." Equifax did not change her records at all and sent her a report with only her previous name listed, stating that her name did not match any records in their system. Amid this frustration, Kim writes that what is most troublesome is that her credit report will reveal her trans status when she applies for housing. Indeed, landlords running the credit check will continue to have a relationship with Kim if she becomes their tenant. Being outed as trans in this situation has potentially longer-lasting consequences and larger risks than credit checks conducted for other types of applications, such as for a loan or credit card.

Kim states that even though she lives in Oregon, where it is illegal to discriminate based on gender identity, "we all know" that such discrimination is hard to prove and frequently occurs. A résumé-testing study conducted in Washington, DC, demonstrated significant bias against applicants presumed to be trans on paper. DC's antidiscrimination laws protect gender identity, but researchers found that 48 percent of tested employers preferred less-qualified cisgender applicants to more-qualified trans applicants in the first stages of the job application process (Rainey and Imse 2015). Kim's fears about revealing her gender history are well founded, even in a state where gender identity is a protected status.

In the scheme of things, Kim appears to have significant economic privilege. The Federal Reserve (2015) reports that as of October 2015, US consumers owe $3.48 trillion in debt. Kim's conundrum of carrying no debt puts her in an atypical position. At the same time, her case is important for examining why commonplace reliance on credit reporting in employment and housing decisions is particularly harmful for trans people, beyond what we already know about a credit report's ability to reify racialized and classed discrimination. Her credit history, used to evaluate her trustworthiness as a tenant, is associated with her previous name, and thus Kim cannot connect her credit history to her current name without coming out as trans. Further, her credit history reflects what she *owes* or has *owed*, not how much she *earns*. To obtain an apartment without coming out to the landlord, Kim is required to have debt, or a recent history of indebtedness, under her new name. A record of debt, rather than earning power, determines her capacity as a tenant. This is not a question of whether Kim makes enough money per month to pay rent. Her future landlord could verify this information with her employer. Rather, the credit check brings about another set of questions: Does Kim carry too much debt? Does she pay her bills on time? Who has trusted her before? Donncha Marron (2009: 108) explains that the credit report "provides a central resource for future credit consumption, presenting itself as a report card of the individual's capacity to self-govern." A "good" credit report contains a long history of open accounts, no missed payments, and a low proportion of debts to total available credit. In other words, though having no debt may functionally make Kim more likely to pay her rent on time, using a credit report for a rental application actually requires that she have *some* well-managed debt under her current name rather than none at all. Importantly, debt would validate Kim's name change in ways that her court order cannot.

Kim encountered a particular problem based on how credit reports manage data. Unlike "credit invisibles," the 26 million, predominantly young, low-income, Black, and Latino/a people in the United States who lack formal credit histories, Kim has been in debt, but it has been repaid in full (Holland 2015). CRAs collect and report what creditors disclose about their account holders. For Kim's credit file to list her name as the primary account holder, her creditors must affirm that she owns her accounts and report this information to the CRAs. When Kim requested that the CRAs update her name, she was unsuccessful because she has no open lines of credit and thus has no creditors to report her updated name. Though Kim has paid off her debt, there is no way for her potential landlord to access this information because the CRAs will not change her credit file until her creditors verify the change. Though Kim is legally "Kim" with the state, her data cannot change until she becomes a debtor again; "Kim" is made legible through recurring debt. Maurizio Lazzarato ([2013] 2015: 89) explains, "Credit has not been given in order to be reimbursed but rather to be in continual flux." The particular way that data about Kim's identity as a financial subject circulate, or, in this case, do not, shapes where and how she is able to live.

Forum participants suggest that Kim can force an update on her credit report by taking out debt. One commentator suggests that Kim should open an account at a different bank and apply for a credit card to force her previous credit history to merge with her new name. She will have to disclose her trans identity to bank tellers there, but the embarrassment will not last long, and she could close the account after a few months. Another commentator agrees, stating that a bank practically begged this person to apply for a credit card after opening an account, and suggests that Kim take out a small personal loan and pay it back immediately to establish a credit history. These suggestions emerge across multiple discussion threads: open a new credit card, take out a loan, and borrow money to establish financial subjectivity through debt. Kim's insistence on remaining debtless may be her largest obstacle: credit, especially in the form of a credit card, is easy to come by. Since the 1978 deregulation on consumer interest rates, credit card companies have drastically raised rates and extended credit to riskier borrowers, capitalizing on revolving debt remaining in their accounts each month. By the early 2000s "consumer credit became the most profitable sector of banking" (Gates 2010: 420).

While Kim stresses that she wishes to avoid taking on debt, even if she wanted to, she may have trouble opening a new account. Her previous name is still attached to her SSN in her credit file, which would produce a fraud alert if she attempted to apply for credit under the name Kim. Another forum poster remarked:

> [It] makes no sense how you can go through so much trouble . . . to change name [*sic*] because they are like "We want to make sure you aren't avoiding taxes, or debts, or changing your name for a bad reason" and then your name is changed, the S[ocial] S[ecurity] A[dministration] has the changed name, and even with your SSN being the same these credit companies are like "fraud alert."

A fraud alert triggered by a trans person using a new name demonstrates key logics of the surveillance of trans subjects. Toby Beauchamp (2009: 361) writes, "Concealing and revealing trans identity actually depend on one another, demonstrating the impossibility of thinking these actions as binary opposites. To conceal one's trans status under the law requires full disclosure to the medico-legal system, which keeps on public record all steps taken toward transition." To push Beauchamp's point farther, trans identification data exceed public records; it is also managed in the private financial sector. Many trans people are required to fully and persistently disclose their trans history, not just "under the law," but also to the countless private institutions that collect, manage, and report their consumer data. Trans people may not only medically and legally transition but also (attempt to) transition the innumerable remnants of the consumer data connecting their former name to their current name.

Indeed, Experian (2015) explains that previous names are reported on credit reports to protect consumers against fraud: "Name variations and unknown names can be an indicator that an identity thief is using your identity to apply for new credit. If that happens, the list of names on your report can enable you to take rapid action to prevent ongoing credit fraud." Trans name changes are flagged as potentially fraudulent because they change in unexpected ways. Removing a former or incorrect name from a credit report is nearly impossible for this reason: all names associated with an individual continue to be reported to prevent fraud. However, retaining an incorrect or former name on a credit report also legitimizes the connection between those names and the credit file, thus enabling fraudulent activity (any person listed on the credit report can claim ownership of the credit history) and outing trans people.

In another thread, Derek presents a way to build a "stealth" credit profile. Derek created a new financial identity by applying for an introductory-rate credit card in his new legal name. He explains, "You can start with store cards, an . . . introductory card, a phone contract. . . . That's how I did it and there is literally no record of my previous existence in the system." Rather than link his previous credit history to his present, Derek elects to start over by obtaining high-interest credit. For Derek, an empty credit file is more desirable than having his previous name listed on his credit report, especially if his concerns are finding a job or an apartment. A landlord or employer may not care how long Derek's credit history is, just that he has one. However, the cost of obtaining high-interest credit to avoid revealing a trans history is high if Derek needs a loan: potential lenders will likely see Derek's lack of history as a liability.

In what seems the opposite of Kim's concerns, another participant, Chris, begins a discussion thread inquiring about the *absence* of his previous name on his credit report. He wonders: has his credit been erased because he changed his name? Chris checked with all three CRAs and found no trace of his previous name, unlike many other participants whose names appeared on one or more reports as "Formerly . . . " or "Also Known As." When Kim spoke to the CRAs, she was told that if they changed her primary name in her credit file, her previous name would always be listed as well. She remarks that her former name *might* be removed only if she contacts every creditor she has ever had and asks them to report her name change. Chris experiences his name change with the same CRAs differently. He is not even sure that his previous credit history is connected to his identity any longer. This difference in experiences recurred throughout discussion threads: the most common experience trans people relayed about their credit report was confusion and inconsistency. Actions taken by any one person frequently yielded vastly different results when done by another. While Kim is an exception for having no creditors, other trans participants who do have open credit lines report seeing former names on their reports, unlike Chris.

Although Chris's previous name does not show up in his file, his prior identity is not fully subsumed in his name change. Chris notes that he receives credit card offers in the mail for his birth name but not his legal name. While Chris's previous name is not listed on his credit report, he is extended credit in that name — a name that for all intents and purposes should not identify him any longer. The practice of receiving "preapproved" credit card offers in the mail began in the 1990s, when consumers previously deemed too risky to be extended credit were seen as highly profitable markets for high-interest-rate credit cards. Gates (2010: 37) explains, "Such consumers were inundated with aggressive direct-market campaigns: rather than requiring consumers to apply for a credit line directly, creditors sent offers, even the cards themselves, to consumers who had not requested them." The haphazard extension of high-interest, predatory credit cards to two identities with the same SSN is evidence of the infrastructure of credit card company databases that do not erase past demographic (or third-party) data, the fractured nature of identities, and the aggressive and expansive extension of credit for profit.

Extending credit to individuals who may no longer legally exist illuminates the structuring logics underlying the use of credit reports in employment and housing decisions. Credit reports aim to protect the transference of property to "proper" financial subjects; a credit report generated for a nonexistent person with good credit and consistent gender identification might be more likely to result in a successful application than one of a person with a visible trans history. Further, depending on which name(s) are present on a credit report, a trans person may apply for credit cards under two different names, be approved for one, both, or neither. This proliferation of identities is profitable for credit card companies so long as account holders remain responsible for paying back their debts.

Major credit card companies' aggressive extension of credit also presents an opportunity for trans people. Some trans forum participants comment that before a legal transition, they are able to add authorized users to their credit card accounts in their preferred names. People who have not changed their name but have a credit card in their birth name could request a card for an authorized user in a name that better aligns with their gender identity. Some credit card companies allow primary account holders to add authorized users by simply providing the user's name and address. These users' identities need not be further authenticated as long as the primary account holder is liable for their purchases. While this is a practice that might benefit trans people who cannot or do not want to legally transition, it also points to the fractured, inconsistent practices of financial institutions' management of consumer data, which put private information at risk. Identities can be easily created through debt, but how are they accounted for later? As another poster remarks, "It's funny, apparently it's easy enough for our identities to be stolen . . . but so hard for us to prove who we are." A high-interest credit card forces a new credit file after a name change *and* puts trans people at higher risks of debt accumulation. The afterlife of trans identity data enables Chris and his previous name to exist simultaneously in different spaces of the financial sector, tucked deep in database fields that customer service representatives do not know how to, or perhaps do not want to, change. Current and previous names circulate as commodities and indictments.

The Promise of Data Errors?

Financial and legal identities are made up of keystrokes, faxed pages, photocopies, data fields, and phone calls. While for many, errors on their credit reports cause serious issues, data errors also present an opportunity to manipulate identification systems. Especially prior to the contemporary moment of increased trans visibility in dominant media, trans people who are able to "pass" as cisgender have successfully convinced data entry clerks that the "M" or "F" on their IDs were erroneously entered. Banking on clerks' limited knowledge about trans people and passing privileges, trans people have been able to obtain legal sex changes at the Department of Motor Vehicles without authorizing letters from medical professionals. One such person shared her story on a popular trans-oriented website:

> I just told the clerks that my license said I was 5′8″ and that I was male (!!). I told them that, well, I'm female and 5′6″ and they graciously changed it without requesting the letter from my doctor I had with me. The clerk that finally entered the data correction said that the person who entered the data . . . "must have had their fingers on the wrong keys." The moral of the story is, approach the sex change on the license as a mistake in data entry and you might have a very easy time. (James 2015)

While discussion board participants report that databases' inabilities to accommodate gender transitions cause issues for credit reports, this contributor's comments pervade stories about legal transition. Just like sex, data are socially constructed. In this case, the data about one's sex can be changed with a keystroke. This point is crucial: "Approach the sex change . . . as a mistake in data entry and you might have a very easy time." The notion that a mistake in data entry would benefit someone flies in the face of the cases above, where data inconsistencies cause denials. Identification information is supposed to be an accurate, reliable, and unique technology to identify individuals, yet such data are constructed by multiple offices and produced, edited, and maintained by humans who interpret information differently and make errors. The person requesting that her driver's license read "F" instead of "M" appeared female to the clerk, and the clerk read her identification card as having an error. While other trans people who want to change their sex on their licenses may have to have expensive or unwanted medical interventions to obtain this change, for this woman, this proof was unnecessary. Data about sex could be changed on the spot.

Errors on credit reports are far more common than errors on driver's licenses, often with long-lasting negative effects. One discussion board commentator suggests that the high prevalence of credit reporting errors might work to the advantage of trans people who cannot remove a former name from their report. She explains that the large number of errors in credit reports can help trans people, "If someone asks me, 'why is this other name on your credit report?' I can just say, 'haha, guess some guy named Michael has a similar SSN as me and someone at a bank screwed up somewhere.'" Another poster commented that if her employer ever asked her why there was a male name on her credit report, she would say that the male name is her brother, and when they were children, her mother mixed up her SSN with her brother's when setting up a bank account, thus leaving his name permanently attached to her credit report. While the discon-nected yet interrelated processes that go into producing a credit report are a bureaucratic nightmare for some, these examples demonstrate that the materiality of the bureaucracy may work in the favor of illegible subjects at certain moments, disrupting the presumed omnipotent power of data systems to tell the truth of a person's identity. Trans people take advantage of the confusing and chaotic processes of data identity production and push back against neoliberal capitalism, surveillance over their bodies, and the assertion that institutions must have the final word on which data are produced about them.

Conclusion

Trans peoples' experiences with their credit reports draw our attention to how bodies are governed not only by legal administrative systems but also increasingly through their consumer data. Trans people's identities challenge the assumptions of credit reporting systems that equate multiple names with fraudulent activity and push us to think beyond the reliance on error-laden credit checks for broad verification and the increased securitization of identities.

Both the predatory logics of neoliberal capitalism and opportunities for subversion are revealed when looking to the credit report as a site where trans identities are produced and managed. Debt propels the afterlife of trans identity into the future and halts illegible, improper subjects in the past. Those who encounter trouble accessing debt or verifying their identities—undocumented immigrants, sex workers, trans people with inconsistent IDs—live in shared housing, work in informal economies, pay with cash, use payday loans and high-fee check-cashing services, and, overall, pay more for services than those with established credit histories.

The status of credit shifted drastically in the United States over the twentieth century. In the early 1910s paying for goods with credit signaled a lack of personal responsibility, but by the 1960s, credit was a marker of high social status (Hyman 2011). In the beginning of the twenty-first century, with consumer debt at an all-time high and millions struggling to repay their debts, another relationship with credit, debt, and data is possible. The issues trans people face with credit reporting demonstrate that it is imperative that we no longer rely on perpetual indebtedness, or extensive data sharing and identity verification, to access the means to livable lives.

Lars Z. Mackenzie is a doctoral candidate in feminist studies at the University of Minnesota. His dissertation examines how trans people navigate administrative systems, with a focus on their changing identification data.

Notes

1. Hereafter *trans*. While *transgender* and *trans* can signify differently, I use *trans* to capture a broad range of people who identify as transgender, transsexual, and/or gender nonconforming.
2. All names have been changed to protect the privacy of discussion board participants.
3. Credit reporting agencies are commonly referred to as credit bureaus.
4. For a discussion of trans bodies and queer temporality, see Halberstam 2005.
5. Closed accounts will remain in a person's credit file for seven years. Bankruptcy will remain in a credit file for ten years. See Fair Credit Reporting Act, 15 U.S.C. § 1681.
6. US Congress, House Committee on Financial Services, *Overview of the Credit Reporting System: Hearings, September 10, 2014*, 113th Cong., 2nd sess. (Washington, DC: GPO, 2015), financialservices.house.gov/uploadedfiles/113-97.pdf.

References

Amin, Kadji. 2014. "Temporality." *TSQ* 1, nos. 1–2: 219–22.

Beauchamp, Toby. 2009. "Artful Concealment and Strategic Visibility: Transgender Bodies and U.S. State Surveillance after 9/11." *Surveillance and Society* 6, no. 4: 1–11.

Ceglowski, Maciej. 2015. "Haunted by Data." idlewords.com/talks/haunted_by_data.htm (accessed October 5, 2015).

Equifax. 2014. "Eight Things You Don't Know about Your Credit Score." Equifax Finance Blog. January 9. blog.equifax.com/credit/eight-things-you-dont-know-about-your-credit -score/.

Experian. 2013. "Why Previous Names Appear on Your Credit Report." September 10. www .experian.com/blogs/ask-experian/why-previous-names-appear-on-your-credit-report/.

Federal Reserve. 2015. "Consumer Credit—G.19 Release." December 7. www.federalreserve.gov /releases/g19/20151207/.

Federal Trade Commission. 2013. "In FTC Study, Five Percent of Consumers Had Errors on Their Credit Reports That Could Result in Less Favorable Terms for Loans." Press release, February 11. www.ftc.gov/news-events/press-releases/2013/02/ftc-study-five -percent-consumers-had-errors-their-credit-reports/.

Gates, Kelly. 2010. "The Securitization of Financial Identity and the Expansion of the Consumer Credit Industry." *Journal of Communication Inquiry* 34, no. 4: 417–31.

Gordon, Avery. (1997) 2008. *Ghostly Matters: Haunting and the Sociological Imagination.* Minneapolis: University of Minnesota Press.

Grant, Jaime M., et al. 2011. *Injustice at Every Turn: A Report of the National Transgender Discrimination Survey.* Washington, DC: National Center for Transgender Equality and National Gay and Lesbian Task Force. www.thetaskforce.org/static_html/downloads /reports/reports/ntds_full.pdf.

Halberstam, Judith. 2005. *In a Queer Time and Place: Transgender Bodies and Subcultural Lives.* New York: New York University Press.

Holland, Kelley. 2015. "45 Million Americans Are Living without a Credit Score." CNBC. May 5. www.cnbc.com/2015/05/05/credit-invisible-26-million-have-no-credit-score.html/.

Hyman, Louis. 2011. "Ending Discrimination, Legitimating Debt: The Political Economy of Race, Gender, and Credit Access in the 1960s and 1970s." *Enterprise & Society* 12, no. 1: 200–232.

James, Andrea. 2015. "Legal Name Change Tips." Trans Road Map. www.tsroadmap.com/reality /name-change-tips.html (accessed October 1).

Lazzarato, Maurizio. (2013) 2015. *Governing by Debt.* South Pasadena, CA: Semiotext(e).

Lyon, David. 2014. "Surveillance, Snowden, and Big Data: Capacities, Consequences, Critique." *Big Data & Society* 1, no. 2: 1–13. doi:10.1177/2053951714541861.

Marron, Donncha. 2009. *Consumer Credit in the United States: A Sociological Perspective from the Nineteenth Century to the Present.* New York: Palgrave Macmillan.

Rainey, Teresa, and Elliot Imse. 2015. *Qualified and Transgender: A Report on Results of Resume Testing for Employment Discrimination Based on Gender Identity.* Washington, DC: Office of Human Resources. ohr.dc.gov/sites/default/files/dc/sites/ohr/publication/attachments /QualifiedandTransgender_FullReport_1.pdf.

Rugh, Jacob, and Douglas Massey. 2010. "Racial Segregation and the American Foreclosure Crisis." *American Sociological Review* 75, no. 5: 629–51.

Spade, Dean. 2008. "Documenting Gender." *Hastings Law Journal* 59, no. 1: 731–842.

———. 2011. *Normal Life: Administrative Violence, Critical Trans Politics, and the Limits of Law.* Brooklyn, NY: South End.

Wyly, Elvin, et al. 2009. "Cartographies of Race and Class: Mapping the Class-Monopoly Rents of American Subprime Mortgage Capital." *International Journal of Urban and Regional Research* 33, no. 2: 332–54.

Categories and Queues

The Structural Realities of Gender
and the South African Asylum System

B CAMMINGA

Abstract South Africa is the only country on the African continent that not only recognizes but also constitutionally protects and offers asylum to transgender-identified individuals. On entering the country, an individual has fourteen days to report to a Refugee Reception Office and apply for asylum. To access a center, asylum seekers are required to queue. Faced with two separate lines, one for men and one for women—much like the issues surrounding transgender access to public bathrooms— gender refugees approaching the South African state for asylum are immediately forced to make a choice. This queue also creates the conditions for surveillance, particularly as different regions are serviced on different days, which brings together the same asylum seekers from similar regions on the continent. This can make life for those who transition in South Africa doubly exposing, as they possibly move between queues witnessed by local communities. This article questions the necessity of an ever-ubiquitous system of sex/gender identification in the lives of asylum seekers, noting current developments internationally, regionally, and locally in relation to the development of third-gender categories, "X" category passports, the suppression of gender markers, and wider debates about the removal and necessity of sex/gender identifiers on documents and their impact.
Keywords refugees, migration, state administration, transgender realities

A seemingly banal administrative system the world over, gender manifests most often, for transgender people, even those with some access and privilege, as nodes of confrontation, but its presence, as a site of discipline and exclusion—often violently so—is felt most strongly by those who are poor or rely on the state most acutely for support (Spade 2011: 11). South Africa is the only country on the African continent that recognizes sexual orientation[1] and gender[2]—including gender identity/expression—as human rights, enshrined in its Constitution.[3] In recent years, partly because of these far-reaching constitutional protections, the country has seen the emergence of a relatively new class of refugee[4]—those who identify as transgender, or "gender refugees."[5] In essence, these are *people who can make claims to refugee status, fleeing their countries of*

TSQ: Transgender Studies Quarterly ★ Volume 4, Number 1 ★ February 2017   **61**
DOI 10.1215/23289252-3711541   © 2017 Duke University Press

origin based on the persecution of their gender identity—turning to a state that is not their own for refuge and assistance. Drawing on interviews conducted between 2012 and 2015 with transgender-identified asylum seekers from Africa living in South Africa, this article argues that there are two interconnected sites of discipline in relation to asylum at work in the country.[6] The first can be considered universal—paperwork/documentation. The second, a focus of this article, and possibly a peculiarity of the South African asylum system, functions as an initial site of surveillance at the very entrance to any Refugee Reception Office— the queue.

Harald Bauder (2008: 316) notes that citizenship is a "strategically produced form of capital, which manifests itself in formal (legal and institutional) as well as informal (practiced and cultural) forms." Viviane K. Namaste has been critical of how institutions, for instance, asylum, manage the lives of transgender people. She also argues that one of the most severe limitations of what she terms "Anglo-American scholarship" on trans people is that it lacks "any sustained analysis of how . . . [transsexual/transgender] . . . people are situated (and/or situate themselves) outside institutions" (Namaste 2000: 269). Although probably not intended as literally by Namaste, I use the queue as a fruitful way to analyze the deployment of gender "outside institutions." This article argues that South Africa presents, in some ways, a unique opportunity to understand how gender refugees are situated in relation to the institution of asylum and how this affects their ability to access citizenship, experience social integration, and actualize "embodied cultural capital" (Bauder 2008: 318). This discussion of institutions and management—in particular, the notion of queuing—allows transgender to function as an analytic posing wider questions about the necessity of sex/gender as a category of classification for notions of citizenship, human rights, and viability of transgender lives in asylum systems more broadly.

The Refugee Process in South Africa

Once entering South Africa, an asylum seeker has fourteen days to report to a Refugee Reception Office (RRO), run by the aptly named Department of Home Affairs (DHA), and apply for asylum. There are several RROs throughout South Africa, but the most prominent are in the larger cities of Cape Town and Johannesburg. At the RRO asylum seekers are required to furnish a Section 23 permit and any proof of identification stipulating country of origin and a travel document, should they be in possession of one. A Refugee Reception Officer will conduct an initial eligibility interview, with the assistance of a translator if necessary, to establish identity and reasons for asylum application. An Eligibility Determination Form is completed, applicants are fingerprinted, and their data and image are captured in the refugee system. These are then printed, signed, dated, stamped, and issued as a Section 22 Asylum Seekers Permit, which gives applicants the right to work and study in South Africa and protects them from deportation. Given that the country practices local integration, rather than encampment as found elsewhere in Africa, asylum seekers experience freedom of movement within the country. Moreover, for those who identify as transgender, the permit is crucial to gaining access to state-subsidized gender-affirming health care, although this in itself is limited.[7] I touch on some of the broader implications of health care access, but exploring these linkages in greater detail is beyond the scope of this article. The initial permit is valid for six months while asylum seekers await their second interview — a status determination hearing — with a Refugee Status Determination Officer (RSDO) and the outcome of their asylum application. The document is not allowed to expire and must be renewed by applicants pending a decision on their status. The RSDO must, on conclusion of the status determination hearing, either grant asylum; reject the application as manifestly unfounded, abusive, or fraudulent; reject the claim as unfounded; or refer any question pertaining to the law to the Standing Committee for Refugee Affairs. If granted asylum, refugees are issued a Section 24 permit, allowing them to remain in South Africa for four years. If not granted asylum, refugees have the right to appeal the decision to the Refugee Appeals Board (DHA 2014).

The *Home* of Home Affairs

Jay Prosser (1998: 204), on trans bodies and existence, asks quite productively: "What are the politics of home?" Aren Aizura (2006: 295) notes that for Prosser, "'home' is doubly inflected as the task of finding a home in the body, and being able to call the state home." For first-time arrivals, or "newcomers," wanting to apply for an asylum seeker permit in South Africa, the first step is *not* entering an RRO but finding one. Arguably, the *home* intended by the DHA for asylum seekers is seemingly a constantly perplexing, vexed, and elusive edifice. Over the past several years it has become increasingly difficult to both find and access RROs, as they themselves are constantly moving, closing, or restructuring. For example, between 2003 and 2004 the Johannesburg RRO moved three times in six months. According to Human Rights Watch, during this time there were no notices providing information on where the offices had relocated. This created "confusion and, potentially, the risk of arrest, detention, and deportation for those who were due to renew their permits but found the former offices shut" (Human Rights Watch 2005: 13).

It is well documented that asylum seekers in general in South Africa struggle to gain access to RROs. Queuing daily, the amount of time they queue often exceeds that of their fourteen-day visa. Daniel, a transgender-identified asylum seeker from East Africa, explains that you can wait in the queue all day and night, only to be told: "No, we are not working on newcomers today." Over the years the number of people waiting outside the ever-migratory RROs has steadily increased, but the capacity to assist those queuing has not been able to keep pace (Cornelius and Jordan 2014). Many have been forced to wait outside the offices for days; some sleep there overnight. The documentation—the "paper"—asylum seekers receive is critical to their survival. Not only does it establish that they have made their presence in the country known through the correct legal channels, but it allows access to rights conferred on asylum seekers, such as access to health care, including gender-affirming health care, education, and social services. Though the general condition of the queues has been described as "completely inhumane" (South African National AIDS Council 2008), fear of arrest has meant that asylum seekers, including gender refugees, would rather remain in the queue and near the RRO, for an indefinite period of time, no matter the conditions, than risk being caught without documentation (Theron 2011). These experiences are concerns for everyone who attempts to access an RRO in South Africa—what sets the experience of gender refugees apart from those of other asylum seekers is the very nature of this system outside an RRO.

"There Is No Queue for Gender Change"

State actors produce and police gender in myriad ways.[8] These are often influenced by perceptions of culture, historical legislative approaches, international norms and treaties, transnational organizations, and individual perceptions of what can be read as stable from the site of the body. State systems require standardized classifications and metrics for measuring, in essence taking "exceptionally complex, illegible, and local social practices" such as gender and forcing them into "a legible and administratively convenient format" (Scott 1999: 3). So intimately intertwined are perceptions of citizenship and gender that Benedict Anderson (2006: 5) suggests, "Everyone can, should, will 'have' a nationality, as he or she 'has' a gender." In essence, citizenship—acknowledgment, protection, rights, and personhood—pivots on any given state's perceptions and categorical understandings of gender. Moreover, being perceived as "correctly" gendered or fitting into the state's available framework functions as a "symbolically legitimate form of cultural capital" (Skeggs 2004: 24). This capital, for Bauder (2008: 316), is interchangeable in its social, economic, and cultural forms and is intimately linked to the reproduction of the social order. Citizenship, then, as a form of capital, in this view, is tied to constructions of identity and belonging along with struggles related to recognition.

Much like the issues surrounding transgender access to public bathrooms in both the United States[9] and South Africa,[10] gender refugees approaching the South African state for asylum are immediately forced to make a choice between two separate lines, one for men and one for women. Arguably, the queue makes clear that not only are there two distinct categories of people that Home Affairs expects to interact with but these categories are based on unchanging, visibly readable anatomical difference. Moreover, these "anatomical distinctions are a legitimate way of organising and sorting people" and, by extension, are the legitimate categories to be sorted as a human being (Cohen 2012: 168). Alex, a trans-identified person from Central Africa, illustrates the difficulty in making the right choice on the first day of approaching an RRO:

> There was a lot of people and there was confusion. . . . You know there was two queues and you have [to] choose. Am I gonna be to the girl's queue or the men's queue? I was like in the middle. I was just in the middle. . . . There were people fighting there. Everyone wanted to go inside to get the permit.

Akraam, a trans woman from the Horn of Africa, explains the trauma of gendered surveillance and being the object of discussion in the queue:

> I can hear people talking, "why is he like this?" and in [a] loud voice too to make me feel bad. "This man is supposed to be a man. He is a disgrace." Discussing about me when I'm in the queue. I ignore it. . . . Even though I'm hurting inside, I just show just pretend that I'm confident.

Simply having to queue with many others and choosing to identify as either male or female is compounded by the fact that specific countries or regions queue on certain days. For participants, then, some of whom are either living in stealth in South Africa—living outside their country-of-origin communities in South Africa—or are living in country-of-origin communities in South Africa because they provide support but are not out to them, there is very real concern about being seen. Moreover, regional days can change, often with little information or notice, which means an applicant can end up queuing with the wrong group for quite some time without ever being informed otherwise. The assumption would be that other members of the queue would provide clarity or information, but for gender refugees the aim is to remain as inconspicuous as possible, often not talking to another soul. Kelly from East Africa goes to Home Affairs in a disguise—baggy stereotypical male attire, no makeup or handbag:

> I dress differently because I don't want to be called those names. I don't want trouble with people. . . . I put on big jeans, big shirt . . . no one bothers me . . . I stand in the men's queue. There is nothing you can do, my dear. I have to balance it.

Kelly notes that disguise is not uncommon—"those transgender things like dresses are for at night"—and that this is the approach of most transgender-identified people in order to avoid detection. This may seem counterintuitive in a system, like asylum, that hinges on self-exposure for access: "A sphere of immigration law that focuses on taking in the vulnerable, not only can asylum law cope with dissident expressions—be they political, sexual or gender related—it requires them" (Solomon 2005: 20). The queue evidently takes on the function of surveillance, particularly as different regions report on different days, meaning that during the process to renew asylum documentation, the same asylum seekers from similar regions on the continent often gather together.

Ava, from East Africa, was one of the first asylum seekers to access gender-affirming health care and transition in South Africa. Her story shows how gender and nationhood are mutually constitutive; at least this is the case in South Africa currently. In Ava's case the ability to claim rights and protection from the South African state, possibly any state, has become more elusive the farther she has moved from the gender/sex she was assigned at birth. As it currently stands in South Africa, for gender refugees who embrace a particular iteration of transgender—something that signifies transition to the "opposite sex"—there is very little room for recognition in the South African asylum system. The Alteration of Sex Description and Sex Status Act No. 49 of 2003, which facilitates the ability of South African citizens to alter sex/gender markers on identity documents, does not apply to asylum seekers or foreign nationals.[11] Asylum seekers do have the right to access state health care, meaning that, as with Ava, access to state-provided gender-affirming health care such as hormones is entirely possible and fairly easily attained, at least for hormones. Access and availability of surgical interventions is far more limited, as the waiting list in the public health care system is prohibitively long. Ava, as an asylum seeker, also pays a reduced fee. She initially applied for asylum from the men's queue and like Kelly attempted to disguise herself.

> It's a problem when you stand in the queue, people look at me and I was like, "Oh my God, I don't know what to do!" . . . I try when I go to "boy it up." I'm going to be a boy and everything but the figure it shows you, so I remove my earrings and everything, but people still notice it, you know?

This option became untenable once she began to take hormones. She became concerned about returning to Home Affairs to renew her asylum application, which would mean being faced with asylum seekers from the same region on the same day, some of whom already knew her.

> I was thinking how are these people going to treat me? Now should I go to the women's queue? The problem is the security; they come and check if you [are] in the right queue. . . . they read all the details (from her papers). So what if they read you are male and you [are] in the queue of females?

The closer it came to the time for Ava to return to Home Affairs, the more anxious she became and the more documents she accrued—from her doctor, her counselor, and her endocrinologist—to provide proof should anyone confront her. Alex astutely describes the experience of the queue, the tension from hiding and being visible to people from one's country of origin and to asylum seekers from the same region, as well as the role of security officials in surveying correct sex/gender, which combine to create a "double oppression" faced by asylum seekers who are transgender. One way to mitigate this would be to have asylum seeker papers adjusted to reflect self-identification. Ava was one of the first to request this; to her mind this would at least present the possibility, should she be in the women's queue, of having security ostensibly checking her paper and leaving her in place, thereby tacitly supporting her claim to her queue of choice. Though this may seem a relatively simple solution, the response of Home Affairs officials to her request suggests a far more intricate relationship between the administrative uses of sex/gender, asylum, statehood, and citizenship.

> She [the Home Affairs official] saw my paper . . . then she looked at me. . . . Look at the paper and look at me. . . . She asked me is this your paper? . . . I was like "yes," but she can't deny it because she had to check my fingerprints. . . . It was positive, it was me. Then she looked at me again and then she said, "So what happened?" I told her actually I am in a process, I am transgender. . . . I always go to Home Affairs with my papers for doctors, I took them out and showed them. She read them and she was like, "OK I think you are the first person I have seen, so why don't you change?" . . . Then she went to the manager and told her the story in front of a whole lot of other people. . . . She was asking permission to actually change the picture and change the gender to female. The manager refused . . . then she said "*I feel sorry for you because if the police or something happens, then you will be in trouble. This person here, this paper, and you there is two different people. . . . This is a legal paper. It is you and everywhere you go in South Africa they will see it's your fingerprint but . . . there is no way they can confirm. The only way is here at Home Affairs. It says it's male but when I see you, you [are a] complete female and your face, when I see this face of yours and I see this face on the paper, it's not same person. So if you go to the police or somewhere else, they may even detain you for weeks to try and find out if this paper is you.*"

The manager suggested that in order to have her documents rectified, Ava would need to make a request to the Appeals Board. Yet, as noted, access to the Appeals Board only becomes available to asylum seekers once a negative decision is made on a claim to refugee status and not before. The question of "two different people" is critical here. As Ava explains:

> They were saying, "if we change her gender, we are naturalizing her to South Africa because she is not going to be recognized [by her country of origin]." . . . I am not allowed to change that paper because I am not a South African citizen and South Africa has no right to change other nationalities'—other people from other countries'—genders. If they do so it means I will become definitely a South African because that country [her country of origin] does not recognize me as a woman and there is no legal binding paper in that constitution that says they must give me that. . . . I am no longer the same person who left that country.

Arguably the situation comes down to an issue of citizenship and naturalization. Ava is not a South African citizen. If the South African state were to adjust her gender on her asylum paper, to their mind, they would effectively be naturalizing her. To be clear, the country she has left does not recognize her as a woman, while the South African state argues that were it to do so, she would then no longer legally be the same person who left her country of origin. The physical experiences of the queue—the uncertainty, the surveillance, the anxiety, and the fear of reprisal—have for Ava become self-perpetuating beyond it because of the nature of her documentation.

The impact of this nonrecognition is monumental for the survival of gender refugees—a direct block to accessing what Bauder (208: 319) might call "embodied cultural capital." As Ava explains, this is not exceptional in the South African asylum system but part and parcel of how a system that can only see dichotomy functions.

> It's not a life. I am actually living like someone who is illegal in a country where I am using legal papers because everywhere you go they will tell you "no this is not you." . . . It's like life stops because that is the only thing you use for identification. This is the thing that you use to the banks, this is the thing you use for employment for jobs, this is the thing that you [are] going to use at school and this is the thing that everybody, everywhere you go, everybody looks at . . . [the paper] . . . and looks at you again and questions . . . "This is not your paper?" . . . What if you go to apply for a job and they bring you in and you put female [on the form] and you go to an interview. They [are] going to bring that stuff that says male and they don't see a male in front of them. . . . What are you going to do?

The constant inability to function on a day-to-day basis has driven her to the point of corruption. Note here that it is an amalgamation of the repetitive nature of her life as an asylum seeker, in combination with incongruent documents as a transgender person, and the almost routineness of this experience:

> I am tired of every time having to explain, I am tired of having to go . . . [to the RRO] . . . all the time. So I have two papers: I [have] a fake that says it is me — female and I have a legal one [which says male]. . . . I paid R250 I use the same names . . . the new picture of me and the gender female not male. . . . I just have to walk with it or to apply for jobs maybe . . . if they ask me [for] my ID then I will bring them that paper . . . [the fake one] so I don't have to show them the real one because if I show them the real one telling the whole fucking story I don't want that. I am tired.

Eithne Luibhéid (2002: 44) notes in the closing chapter of *Entry Denied* that fraud and the subversion made possible through forged documents may be dismissed as lawless by the state but can also be usefully read "as a competing system of knowledge that is brought against the state." It is arguable that Ava, in this instance, has responded to her exclusion by reading the possible form of capital that "false" (though correct for her image, name, and gender marker) documentation might open up to her. As Bauder (2008: 318) notes, "Individuals and social groups do not simply respond to market forces but, rather, strategically create, valorize, and endorse different forms of capital."

Sex/Gender: What Are the Options?

There is within South Africa a clear lack of institutional coordination and cohesion between asylum and state-sponsored health care. Documents, as proof of a gendered identity, come to play a critical role in this discordance and function as a barrier to accessing particular kinds of capital for gender refugees. As Namaste (2006: 164) has noted, this is not uncommon with regard to the daily working of state administrative practices. The *complexity* of situations in the administration of gender is in fact a "function of its administration" (164). There is a connection here between the performance of gender, its use as an administrative tool, nationhood, and citizenship. In terms of the constitutional rights provided by the South African state and the theoretical possibilities of this in relation to asylum, South Africa represents a space in which transgender-identified asylum seekers might find themselves, or imagine themselves, to be included in the "we" of the nation. That transgender would perform a particular type of labor for citizenship in South Africa. However, in the South African asylum system, parts of which can be extrapolated to asylum systems (and state systems) globally for transgender-identified asylum seekers like Ava, the nature of the wider regulatory framework based on a bifurcated system of sex/gender is a direct impediment to the actualization of this imaginary/citizenship. For South Africa, as I have argued, this issue is acutely visible for both the queue and the nature of documentation, where one can be read as the physical manifestation of the other — both key sites of discipline and surveillance. V. Spike Peterson argues that the state system at its heart is based historically on the differentiation of gender. She adds that the codification of binary sex difference is an outcome of the historical heterosexism that has underpinned much of the creation of the world's legal systems, in large part influenced by Western scripts and understandings of governance. The "either/or thinking that this imposes fuels hierarchical constructions of difference and social relations of domination" (Peterson 2010: 54). Since 2000, discussions about sex/gender markers, their meaning, and their utility have been in flux, presenting several options for addressing these issues in South Africa. While some states, namely, Bangladesh, India, Pakistan, and Nepal, countries with historically acknowledged "third gender populations,"[12] have added third-gender categories, others such as Australia and New Zealand have attempted to expand the possibilities for self-definition, introducing an "X" category on passports, and still others, such as the Netherlands, have opened the debate over the necessity of sex/gender markers and registration more generally.

Although perhaps more equitable for countries with historically acknowledged third-gender populations who may envision themselves as neither male nor female, the third-gender stance in general has been critiqued for limiting the possibilities for self-definition and reinstating rigid biological determinism (Cauterucci 2015). As Mauro Cabral notes:

> People tend to identify a third sex with freedom from the gender binary, but that is not necessarily the case. If only trans and/or intersex people can access that third category, or if they are compulsively assigned to a third sex, then the gender binary gets stronger, not weaker. (Quoted in Byrne 2014: 22)

In essence, adding a third category would be much like adding a third queue: this may well work for Alex, who acknowledges "standing in the middle," but for Ava, who identifies as a woman, this would be highly problematic. As she points out,

> If there was a separate queue . . . I would not support it. . . . Even if there were many transgender there would be . . . bullying. . . . For me, if you are trans it means you are transitioning. You [are] becoming something. . . . I have this belief. . . . I know I am a female.

Activists have noted that a more inclusive approach, something Ava certainly desires, would be to increase the options for people to self-identify or define their sex/gender (Byrne 2014). In the case of the queue this would arguably translate into a single, combined queue rather than several queues.

In 2005 Australia began a wider discussion about the place and necessity of the recording of sex/gender and concomitant visibility in documents. Since then, both New Zealand and Australia have implemented the possibility of replacing M or F on passports with X (unspecified or indeterminate). This shift has affected the use of sex/gender on international travel documents such as passports and may eventually have a direct impact on refugee documents. Assigned by the United Nations, the International Civil Aviation Organization (ICAO) controls the standards and stipulations for passports internationally. Under ICAO rules there are in fact three designations for sex on passports—M, F, or X. Initially X was introduced in 1945 as a result of the sheer volume of refugees who needed to be processed after World War II. Notably at the time of its creation nowhere was it stipulated that X would eventually need to be resolved into an M or F designation (OII Australia 2011). Currently the ICAO allows X as a marker on passports to signify "sex unspecified." Thus far ICAO has argued that it would be too costly to enact universally (New Zealand 2012: 3).

The Netherlands has perhaps been the most far-reaching in discussions on the necessity of gender markers. In 2012 the Dutch organization Feministisch Netwerk GroenLinks began a campaign for the "abolishing of gender as a legal distinction" (FEMNET 2011: 4). The group has argued that sex/gender is a private matter much like ethnic origin, sexual orientation, and political opinion and that if states are determined to treat people equally, with no distinction or difference, then there is no need for sex/gender to be registered. Moreover, given the continuing issues worldwide with doing so, they have argued that it has become increasingly evident that sex/gender is too complex to register. As they point out, the most common argument for maintaining sex/gender is the need for positive discrimination, but society is able to practice this in relation to ethnic minorities and disabilities without registration or visible information on documents (10). For FEMNET, the registration of sex/gender continues to affirm for society, regardless of what might be argued about social construction, that there are two kinds of people and that the difference between them is so essential that it must be registered (van den Brink 2009: 167).

There have certainly been legal challenges by transgender people over rights and identity issues on the African continent. Victor Mukasa won a court battle against Uganda's attorney general in 2008, which established that the articles of Uganda's Constitution, in particular the right to privacy and freedom from torture or inhumane and degrading treatment, apply to all people regardless of sexual orientation and gender identity (Hivos 2008). This certainly may create some room to challenge sex/gender and identity categories in the future.[13] Audrey Mbugua, a trans activist from Kenya, won a court battle in 2014 to have her name amended on her official school-leaving certificate (Chigorimbo 2015). Along with this, Mbugua has also been involved in a case, led by LGBT rights activist Solomon Gichira, in the Kenyan High Court to establish a third-gender category for people who do not identify as male or female in Kenya (Matata 2015).

Anne Fausto-Sterling has argued, perhaps as a kind of middle ground, that to ensure legal protection for all but particularly those who are "gender-diverse," the suppression of the category of gender from official documents would be most prudent. As she notes, "Surely attributes both more visible (such as height, build and eye colour) and less visible (fingerprints and genetic profiles) would be more expedient" (Fausto-Sterling 2000: 23). To suggest that South Africa consider either suppressing the registration of sex/gender is not outlandish, particularly as the country has been moving since at least 2004 toward a Smart Card biometric-based identity system that would include refugees (Rulashe 2004). In fact, this point was raised by the South African intersex activist Sally Gross in discussions with Home Affairs in 2012 on the poor implementation of Act 49. Those present seemed quite amenable to her suggestion. As Gross notes:

> If ID was shifted to a biometric system it would actually remove the problem (regarding sex/gender) because fingerprints or retinal patterns do not change. The issue of gender would become irrelevant. So that would be rather an elegant solution. (Quoted in Portfolio Committee on Home Affairs 2012)

In essence, the DHA may need to collect information on the sex/gender of asylum claimants, but this does not necessarily mean that this information needs to be reflected on documentation in general. Notably, Gross, in her conversations with the Portfolio Committee, was suggesting this as an option for South African society in general, but it would most certainly have an impact on refugee documents and asylum papers.[14] In essence, it would not be about abolishing categories but mooting them, disinvesting from them while allowing people the room to self-identify. This would theoretically mean creating a combined queue in which those lined up may have specific sex/gender designations across a spectrum of possibility, but security would be unable to ascertain these from documents; more than this, ascertaining them would have no point. Moreover, for those stuck in a legal limbo like Ava, the grounds on which the state denies the possibility of personhood would no longer be a factor.

Conclusion

The asylum process in South Africa, as reported by myriad organizations and international bodies, is by no means easy for anyone (Amit 2015). It is widely acknowledged that the system is overburdened, generally corrupt, and poorly managed, but there are specific issues that make this process that much more difficult for those who identify as transgender. Some issues, like the queue, are perhaps peculiar to the South African system. It signals the perception of Home Affairs that there are two and only two sex/genders—discernible, definable, and easily differentiated. Moreover, these genders are often determined by what the security guards see when they move up and down the queues checking that people are in the "right" place. As Luibhéid (2002: 53) argues, though, it is not about individual officials, although they do carry prejudice, but about the makeup and underlying assumptions of the system itself—the "techniques and systems of knowledge on which its daily operations depend." Sex/gender diversity the world over, in its many geopolitical iterations, questions the need for sex/gender to be visible on identity documents. For Bauder (2008: 327), the imagining and reimagining of citizenship and the possibilities of accessing capital related to it is not simply the realm of legal bodies; people, in this case gender refugees, articulate the realities of "ever changing systems of distinction and exclusion." As categories expand, collapse, solidify, and possibly disappear, legal systems will need to adjust in order to address the wider structural concerns about the facilitation of the movement of people, not only in South Africa. Scholars have certainly grappled with this issue in the recent past, but notably it has been only in relation to the relatively privileged position of international air travel, licensing documents, or adequate documentation for citizens of states (Currah and Mulqueen 2011).

This article has mapped the experiences of gender refugees who have attempted to access the South African asylum system and has noted the barriers to their gaining access and adequate documentation. It has also suggested that issues of access and documentation directly inhibit gender refugees' abilities to draw on any form of "embodied capital"—nonrecognition being a key stumbling block to not only social integration but everyday survival. This article, drawing on the work of South African activists such as Gross and international and regional developments, has suggested some possible solutions for addressing these issues. The erasure of sex/gender markers may seem unreal or prove difficult to implement; indeed, this is why this article suggests suppression. Certainly in South Africa's transition to a biometric-based smart card system, this is a possibility. Such cards may not directly address wider structural concerns, which are global issues over the administrative uses of sex/gender, but it may offer the beginnings of relief and greater social integration. Certainly more research and thinking is needed, not just on South Africa but internationally, on the meanings of human rights, citizenship, personhood, documentation, and the right to self-definition of sex/gender as it pertains to people who may not be citizens of a given state but have turned to that state for refuge and asylum.

B Camminga is a doctoral fellow at the Institute for Humanities in Africa (HUMA), at the University of Cape Town, South Africa, whose research interests include transgender rights, the bureaucratization of gender in relation to transgender bodies and asylum regimes, and the history of trans phenomena in South Africa.

Notes

1. In *The National Coalition for Gay and Lesbian Equality v. Minister of Justice and Others* (1998) at paragraph 21, the Constitutional Court stated that sexual orientation, as in Section 9(3) of the South African Constitution, "be given a generous interpretation" and thus was extended to include the prohibition of discrimination against transsexual people. The judgment did more than just recognize transsexuality; it provided a space for the varying ways that individuals come to identify themselves using a mixture of signifiers and language, while acknowledging that the *language* is contingent but not the experience the language attempts to name or describe. By extension this also opens the possibility for transgender. See de Vos 2009.

2. A 2010 decision in the South African labor court on the unfair dismissal of a trans person further suggests a possible reading of gender to include gender identity/expression. See *Ehlers v. Bohler Uddeholm Africa* (Pty) Ltd (JS296/09) [2010] ZALC 117; (2010) 31 ILJ 2383 (LC) (13 August 2010); and Theron 2011.

3. Section 9(3) of the Bill of Rights of the South African Constitution is referred to as the "Equality Clause." The clause affirms the rights to nondiscrimination and equality on the basis of sexual orientation and gender among other grounds.

4. In 1951 the UN passed the Geneva Convention relating to the Status of Refugees. The convention defines a refugee as "any person who is outside their country of origin and unable or unwilling to return there or to avail themselves of its protection, on account of a well-founded fear of persecution for reasons of race, religion, nationality, membership of a particular group, or political opinion." Prior to 1990, claims to refugee status based on sexual or gender-based persecution were not recognized within the convention. International LGBT organizations rallied around notions of sexual orientation and gender identity as human rights, building an increasingly influential lobby (Kollman and Waites 2009).

5. For recent work also addressing issues of transgender asylum, see Shakhsari 2013.

6. Pseudonyms along with only regional, instead of national, origins have been used to protect the identities of the participants who took part in this project.

7. It is far easier to access hormonal care than surgical interventions. Asylum seekers pay a reduced fee at public hospitals for hormonal care. The access points are limited to a handful of public hospitals across the country. These spaces are often overburdened and struggle to manage demand (Theron 2014).

8. Ava, interviewed April 9, 2014.

9. See Kogan 2009.

10. In South Africa this debate has been largely prevalent at institutions of higher learning (Chang 2016).

11. In the parliamentary discussions leading up to the act, South African activists argued that any bill, considering that it was being written for South Africa, would need to draw on international standards while remaining cognizant of the country's unique social and economic position, including the provision "for legal recognition of a change in sex identity . . . [for] . . . foreign-born people." The chair of the committee clarified that the legislation was intended for South African citizens only, as the National Population Register did not contain the details of foreigners and thus it would not apply to them (Parliamentary Monitoring Group 2003).

12. Constructed slightly differently in each of the Asian nations but usually as Transgender, Hijra, "Khawaja Sarra," or "Other."

13.　The United Nations Commission against Torture recently released findings about the Convention against Torture, "explicitly recommending the repeal of 'abusive' preconditions to legal gender recognition and called for respect for transgender people's 'autonomy and physical and psychological integrity'" (Yeung 2016). These arguably could be extended to wider legal litigation with regard to legal gender recognition through necessary documentation.

14.　The Smart Cards were meant to phase out the maroon refugee identification documents as early as 2005, although this has yet to take place (Human Rights Watch 2005: 35).

References

Aizura, Aren Z. 2006. "Of Borders and Homes: The Imaginary Community of (Trans) Sexual." *Inter-Asia Cultural Studies* 7, no. 2: 289–309.

Amit, Ron. 2015. *Queue Here for Corruption: Measuring Irregularities in South Africa's Asylum System*. Johannesburg: Lawyers for Human Rights African Centre for Migration and Society.

Anderson, Benedict. 2006. *Imagined Communities*. London: Verso.

Bauder, Harald. 2008. "Citizenship as Capital: The Distinction of Migrant Labor." *Alternatives* 33: 315–33.

Byrne, Jack. 2014. *License to Be Yourself*. New York: Open Society Foundations.

Cauterucci, Christina. 2015. "France Now Recognizes a 'Neutral Gender'—but It's Just as Narrow as the First Two." *Slate*, October 15. www.slate.com/blogs/outward/2015/10/15/france_s_new_third_gender_is_just_as_narrow_as_the_first_two.html.

Chang, Dion. 2016. "On My Radar: Toilet Wars, Transgender Rights." *City Press*, June 5. city-press.news24.com/Voices/on-my-radar-toilet-wars-transgender-rights-20160605.

Chigorimbo, Shamiso. 2015. "Africa: International—Where Are Diverse Gender Identities in the Sixteen Day Campaign?" *All Africa*, November 27. allafrica.com/stories/201511271282.html.

Cohen, David S. 2012. "Sex Segregation, Masculinities, and Gender-Variant Individuals." In *Masculinities and the Law: A Multidimensional Approach*, edited by Anne C. McGinley and Frank Rudy Cooper, 167–86. New York: New York University Press.

Cornelius, Jerome, and Bobby Jordan. 2014. "Asylum Seekers Get Cold Shoulder." *Timeslive*, December 8. www.timeslive.co.za/thetimes/2014/12/08/asylum-seekers-get-cold-shoulder.

Currah, Paisley, and Tara Mulqueen. 2011. "Securitizing Gender: Identity, Biometrics, and Transgender Bodies at the Airport." *Social Research* 78, no. 2: 557–82.

de Vos, Pierre. 2009. "From Heteronormativity to Full Sexual Citizenship? Equality and Sexual Freedom in Laurie Ackermann's Constitutional Jurisprudence." In *Dignity, Freedom, and the Post-Apartheid Legal Order: The Critical Jurisprudence of Laurie Ackerman*, edited by Jaco Barnard, Drucilla Cornell, and François Du Bois, 254–72. Cape Town: Juta.

DHA (Department of Home Affairs of the Republic of South Africa). 2014. "Department of Home Affairs—Refugee Status and Asylum." www.home-affairs.gov.za/index.php/refugee-status-asylum.

Fausto-Sterling, Anne. 2000. "The Five Sexes, Revisited." *Sciences*, July–August, 18–23.

FEMNET (Feministisch Netwerk GroenLinks). 2011. "* Verplicht veld? Pleidooi voor verkennen van mogelijkheden voor afschaffen van geslacht als juridisch onderscheid" ("* Required Field? Suggestion to Investigate the Removal of Sex as a Legal Distinction"). femnet.groenlinks.nl/sites/default/files/downloads/page/verplicht_veld.pdf.

Hivos. 2008. "Human Rights Victory: Ugandan Transgender, Lesbian, and Gay Human Rights Upheld in the High Court of Uganda." December 23. www.tigweb.org/action-tools /projects/download/28239/law.pdf.

Human Rights Watch. 2005. "Living on the Margins: Inadequate Protection for Refugees and Asylum Seekers in Johannesburg." www.hrw.org/report/2005/11/16/living-margins /inadequate-protection-refugees-and-asylum-seekers-johannesburg.

Kogan, Terry. S. 2009. "Transsexuals in Public Restrooms: Law, Cultural Geography, and Etsitty v. Utah Transit Authority." *Temple Political and Civil Rights Law Review* 18, no. 2: 673–99.

Kollman, Kelly, and Matthew Waites. 2009. "The Global Politics of Lesbian, Gay, Bisexual, and Transgender Human Rights: An Introduction." *Contemporary Politics* 15, no. 1: 1–17.

Luibhéid, Eithne. 2002. *Entry Denied: Controlling Sexuality at the Border.* Minneapolis: University of Minnesota Press.

Matata, Lydia. 2015. "Identifying as Neither Male nor Female, Some Kenyans Seek a Third Option on Official Documents." *Global Press Journal*, December 2. globalpressjournal.com/africa /kenya/identifying-neither-male-nor-female-some-kenyans-seek-third-option-official -documents.

Namaste, Viviane K. 2000. *Invisible Lives: The Erasure of Transsexual and Transgendered People.* Chicago: University of Chicago Press.

———. 2006. "Changes of Name and Sex for Transsexuals in Quebec: Understanding the Arbitrary Nature of Institutions." In *Sociology for Changing the World*, edited by Caelie Frampton, Gary Kinsman, A. K. Thompson, and Kate Tilleczek, 160–74. Halifax, NS: Fernwood.

New Zealand. 2012. "A Review of the Requirement to Display the Holder's Gender on Travel Documents." International Civil Aviation Organization Information Paper (TAG/ MRTD/21-IP/4). Montreal: International Civil Aviation Organization.

OII Australia. 2011. "On Australian Passports and 'X' for Sex — OII Australia — Intersex Australia." October 9. oii.org.au/14763/on-x-passports/.

Parliamentary Monitoring Group. 2003. *Alteration of Sex Description and Sex Status Bill: Hearings. (Portfolio Committee on Home Affairs).* Cape Town: Parliamentary Monitoring Group.

Peterson, V. Spike. 2010. "Political Identities / Nationalism as Heterosexism." *International Feminist Journal of Politics* 1, no. 1: 34–65.

Portfolio Committee on Home Affairs. 2012. *Gender Dynamix on Alteration of Sex Description and Sex Status Act Implementation; Lawyers for Human Rights on Statelessness; CoRMSA on Closure of Refugee Reception Offices in Metro Areas, Department of Home Affairs.* Cape Town: Parliamentary Monitoring Group.

Prosser, Jay. 1998. *Second Skins: The Body Narratives of Transsexuality.* New York: Columbia University Press.

Rulashe, Pumla. 2004. "Refugees Lobby for Identity in South Africa." *UNHCR*, May 1. www .unhcr.org/406c1c3c4.html.

Scott, James. C. 1999. *Seeing Like a State: How Certain Schemes to Improve the Human Condition Have Failed.* New Haven, CT: Yale University Press.

Shakhsari, Sima. 2013. "Transnational Governmentality and the Politics of Life and Death." *International Journal of Middle East Studies* 45, no. 2: 340–42.

Skeggs, Beverly. 2004. "Context and Background: Pierre Bourdieu's Analysis of Class, Gender, and Sexuality." In *Feminism after Bourdieu*, edited by Lisa Adkins and Beverly Skeggs, 19–35. London: Blackwell.

Solomon, Alisa. 2005. "Trans/Migrant: Christian Madrazo's All-American Story." In *Queer Migrations: Sexuality, US Citizenship, and Border Crossings*, edited by Eithne Luibhéid and Lionel Cantu Jr., 3–29. Minneapolis: University of Minnesota Press.

South African National AIDS Council. 2008. *Vulnerable Groups: Refugees, Asylum Seekers, and Undocumented Persons: "The Health Situation of Vulnerable Groups in SA."* Report to the Portfolio Committee on Home Affairs, Cape Town.

Spade, Dean. 2011. *Normal Life: Administrative Violence, Critical Trans Politics, and the Limits of the Law*. Brooklyn, NY: South End.

Theron, Liesl. 2011. "When a Progressive Constitution Is Not Enough, and Other Challenges." Paper presented at the International Association for the Study of Forced Migration, Kampala, July.

———. 2014. "Rooted in the Past, Reaching for the Future: Report of the 2nd Trans* Health, Advocacy, and Research Conference." Cape Town: Gender DynamiX, Transgender and Intersex Africa (TIA), Social, Health and Empowerment Feminist Collective of Transgender and Intersex Women of Africa (SHE).

van den Brink, Marjolein. 2009. "Onpraktisch, oninteressat en ongepast." In *Vrouw & Recht: De beweging, de mensen, de issues*, edited by Margeet de Boer and Marjan Wijers, 165–70. Amsterdam: Pallas Publications.

Yeung, Geoffrey. 2016. "Using the Convention against Torture to Advance Transgender and Intersex Rights." Oxford Human Rights Hub, May 16. ohrh.law.ox.ac.uk/using-the-convention-against-torture-to-advance-transgender-and-intersex-rights/.

The Value of Transgender

Waria *Affective Labor for Transnational Media Markets in Indonesia*

BENJAMIN HEGARTY

Abstract The globalization of transgender and its relationship to human rights has been accompanied by increased media interest in those so identified around the world. In Indonesia, this mostly involves the representation of male-to-female transgender-identified *waria*. While most mass media representations do portray them in narrow terms as the victims of violence, this does not undermine the value of transgender for *waria*. Seeing interaction with mass media in economic terms, many *waria* charge money for interviews and other media appearances. This article describes how *waria* understand affective labor for transnational mass media markets. They do so in terms of the historically understood association between work and visible claims for national belonging and recognition in Indonesia. Although such possibilities are situated in a context characterized by inequality, *waria* do consider the global scope of transgender to be of value as a way to expand their claims. A perspective that analyzes the circulation of transgender as it relates to global political economy helps clarify how the category produces uneven forms of value as it encounters diverse national and local contexts.
Keywords *waria*, Indonesia, affective labor, mass media, political economy

I n the current climate of popular interest in transgender, journalists and others have traveled around the world to make documentaries, photographs, and films about those whom they identify as belonging to the category.[1] An increasing number of productions are made in Indonesia, both because of its history of visible vernacular forms of gender and sexual diversity and greater ease of access in recent years. Mass media representations of transgender in Indonesia focus almost exclusively on *waria*.[2] While representations draw on a range of categories to articulate *waria* to their audiences — earlier films, for example, use "transvestite" or "third gender" — more recently "transgender" is used frequently with reference to the subjects of these accounts.

The term *transgender* has come to be understood by most *waria* and used by some, partly because of its use by journalists and researchers. Recent interest

TSQ: Transgender Studies Quarterly * Volume 4, Number 1 * February 2017
DOI 10.1215/23289252-3711553 © 2017 Duke University Press

from the media is also related to the emergence of transgender as a political movement related to LGBT rights (Valentine 2007). My own role as a researcher working among *waria* in the smaller city of Yogyakarta in the central part of the island of Java and the large capital city Jakarta in 2014 and 2015 placed me in an ambiguous position in the context of these media representations. This was particularly pronounced because these two cities are the most commonly visited by journalists and filmmakers. In the context of my research I was legible as a foreign researcher, albeit one who was somewhat unusual. Unlike most journalists and researchers, who came only once, asked a set list of questions, and then left, I was a more regular presence over the almost eighteen months that I spent there.

As such, this article draws on ethnographic data to define the importance of affective labor to *waria*, rather than providing a detailed textual analysis of the documentaries produced about them. This was made possible because I participated in *waria* social life as much as possible and rarely carried out formal interviews (known in Indonesian as *wawancara*), which carried with them connotations of payment. This enabled me to observe everyday interactions between *waria* and journalists during this period. This was fairly easy in Yogyakarta and Jakarta, given that on average about four foreign journalists and countless Indonesian journalists visited each month. Each visit by a journalist was anticipated eagerly by my *waria* friends, who enthusiastically invited me to observe, participate, and document the productions made. It was during these interactions that I observed how *waria* see the value of transgender in its ability to provide work. I do not suggest that all the *waria* whom I interacted with, let alone all *waria* in Indonesia, appear in such representations only out of a desire for payment. While its ability to provide an income is certainly welcomed by some *waria*, the value of transgender also relates to historical understandings of the relationship between national belonging, labor, and material success in Indonesia (see Boellstorff 2005).

I have been following the production of professional and amateur films and documentaries in Indonesia since the early 2010s, when *waria* started to appear frequently in the mainstream mass media. I have also followed public discourse about *waria* in both the Indonesian and international media. I observed in detail the filming of eight professional productions in Indonesia, informally interviewed two Western journalists, and spoke with the *waria* subjects of these films while filmmaking was under way and after the fact. I witnessed the production of about twenty professional and amateur films, documentaries, and photography features over hundreds of hours. I am not suggesting that *waria* participate uniformly in such representations or that they are a homogeneous group that universally shares the sentiments I describe. Rather, for the most part, the *waria* whom I observed taking part in mass media productions about transgender in Yogyakarta and Jakarta are poor, and for the most part older. They rely on diverse forms of precarious labor, including being research and documentary subjects, to make ends meet.

The reductionist and commercial nature of most representations of *waria*, while often unpleasant, was not a surprise; a mercenary attitude is expected of the mass media. What interested me was the ways in which *waria* stressed the importance of the paid affective labor they provided for transnational mass media markets. Academic discussions about the political and economic aspects of transnational transgender representation tend to dismiss such participation as a money-making exercise or the unwitting reproduction of a Western exoticizing impulse (see Morris 1994; Towle and Morgan 2002). A more recent body of literature in transgender studies critiques the selective emphasis on violence and suffering as a form of "trans necropolitics" in which transgender figures are reduced to function in the role of victim or potential victim (Haritaworn and Snorton 2013). Haritaworn and Snorton describe how the lives of trans people of color are considered disposable in the accrual of political and social value for white LGBT and queer activists in the Global North. The documentaries I describe resemble a logic that may also relate to a long history of exoticizing Western representations made about Southeast Asia (see Lim 2014: chap. 1). Yet, while this may be the case, my observations suggest that *waria* understand them according to other criteria.

The question that I pose in this article is, why do *waria* participate enthusiastically in popular mass media representations about transgender? In doing so, I reflect on how the global category transgender is transforming the meanings of the Indonesian category *waria*. What I have found is that the growth of mass media interest in transgender globally has provided one source of income to *waria*. Furthermore, while such economic exchanges and representations might be exploitative and objectionable, they do provide a site for *waria* to engage with the category transgender. In emphasizing their ability and desire to provide affective labor for media representations, *waria* relate transgender to historical understandings which associate national belonging with productivity and consumption. I describe *waria* mass media performances as affective labor to emphasize the relationship between political economy and gender performativity (see Hochschild 2004; and Judy, Negri, and Hardt 1999). While affective labor is performed for an imagined audience, it is crucially linked to projects of self-cultivation and improvement, heightened under the conditions of neoliberal capitalism and body-centered transnational media markets. For example, Dredge Byung'chu Käng (2014a) describes feminine Thai gay men's cover performances of female Korean popular music idols as affective labor. These gender transformations in Thailand are emerging in the context of greater popular culture flows within Asia (567). These reflect a reshaping of relationships with what are considered to be more developed parts of Asia, such as Korea and Japan, with the affective labor involved in cover dance emerging as one site for participating in a cosmopolitan regional imaginary shaped by middle-class consumerism (568). Similarly, *waria* performances for transnational mass media markets can be understood as a form of affective labor, albeit one that must be understood as related to class aspiration, national belonging, and gender performativity in Indonesia.

For *waria* who link affective labor to claims for social acceptance, the motivations for interacting with the mass media extend beyond economic benefits alone. *Waria* understand labor for mass media representations as a form of *prestasi*, an Indonesian concept that can be translated as "good deeds" (Boellstorff 2007: 105–12). Tom Boellstorff defines *prestasi* for *waria* as a "performative theory of recognition" driven by "a desire joining everyday belonging to national belonging through the performance of good deeds or accomplishments" (105). As visible everyday claims for recognition, *prestasi* often takes place through recognized forms of work. For example, since at least the 1970s, many *waria* have transformed Indonesian men and women into ideal heteronormative gender roles through their work in salons (111). The historical relationship between *prestasi* and labor is important in shaping *waria* attitudes toward new mass media markets related to the category transgender. I suggest that forms of work frequently double as *prestasi* in Indonesia because of an increasing emphasis on productivity in discourses about citizenship (see Rudnyckyj 2010). *Prestasi* reveals how the category *waria* is implicated in national experiences of class and economy now understood on global terms, reflected here in its relationship to transgender.

Despite offering avenues for *prestasi*, the emergent relationship between *waria* and transgender also risks reproducing global hierarchies of value in the neoliberal political economy. This is particularly so because although an emergent understanding of transgender in Indonesia makes certain experiences visible, it may also elide those of the most socially vulnerable. In this regard, my observations in Indonesia echo those of scholars working in other parts of the world. For example, in research about *transformistas* in Venezuela, Marcia Ochoa (2008: 158) describes how local activists drew on globalized transgender politics to distance themselves from practices widely considered deviant. Vek Lewis has described this as a form of "recuperative politics" (quoted in Namaste 2011: 195) through which the global economic and political framework of LGBT and transgender politics produces some categories and practices—and those who identify with them—as abject. Such a relationship may have the unexpected consequence of transforming *waria* into a category capable only of naming marginality and exclusion.

In this article I describe contemporary understandings of affective labor that *waria* undertake for Western mass media productions framed by the category transgender. I first describe the category *waria*, situating it in the context of histories of gender and sexuality in Indonesia. I show how the production of representations of *waria* as victims in mass media accounts emerges through globalized understandings of the category transgender. I then describe *waria* understandings of transnational mass media productions in detail, showing how engagement with transgender is defined by its relationship to affective labor. This marks it not only as a way to make money but crucially as an extension of the relationship between work and claims for belonging in Indonesia. *Waria* have their own understandings of the value of affective labor, which challenges the superficiality of media representations and offers an understanding of the emergent global effects of the category transgender.

Indonesian Transgender, Mass Media, and Affective Labor

Indonesia has a diverse vocabulary for understanding expressions and practices related to gender and sexuality. Anthropologists in particular have discussed transgender in the context of various practices and subjectivities, described in studies of female-bodied masculinities such as *tomboi* (Blackwood 2010), male-bodied femininity usually described as *banci* or *béncong*[3] (Oetomo 2000), and *waria*[4] (Boellstorff 2007). These descriptions are often placed in the context of research about sexuality, particularly *gay* men (Boellstorff 2005) and *lesbi* women (Wieringa 2007).

From 1967 to 1998 the Indonesian government was led by an authoritarian president, Suharto, whose military-backed developmentalist agenda was supported by the United States.[5] While earlier research on gender and sexuality thus focused necessarily on its relationship to state power (Oetomo 1996; Suryakusuma 1996), more recent scholarship describes how new subjectivities are entangled with experiences that link national modernity, local patterns of gender and kinship, and globalized ideas that travel via the mass media (Blackwood 2005, 2010; Wieringa 2007). Elsewhere in Southeast Asia, scholars have noted the impact of global capitalism, identifying a transnational male-to-female transgender imaginary linked to femininity, consumption, and race (Aizura 2010; Jackson 2009). This has important implications for the phenomena I describe, given that media representations depict *waria* as part of a transnational transgender imaginary, in which they are most often compared to Thai *ladyboys*.[6] However, here I describe *waria* in the context of Indonesian history, given that the category is embedded within a particular experience of national modernity.

Most accounts (Boellstorff 2007; Oetomo 2000) describe *waria* subjectivity as associated with the desire for romantic and sexual relations with cisgendered, heterosexual men, the adoption of feminine dress, makeup, and comportment (*déndong* or *dandan*) at least some of the time, and participation in visible forms of employment such as salons and fashion design. However, much like *kathoey* in Thailand (Käng 2014b) and *bakla* in the Philippines (Benedicto 2014), *waria* experiences in Indonesia intersect with concerns other than gender performativity, such as class and sexuality. Recent political and social reform (*reformasi*) in Indonesia since the end of the Suharto presidency in 1998 has led to the rapid expansion of the media and its influence in everyday life (Strassler 2009). In the context of access to information and increased ability to shape media content, *waria* have at times distinguished themselves from the activism of gay men, articulating themselves as belonging to the more recent global category transgender (Boellstorff 2011). Similar distinctions have emerged in the context of lesbian activist groups in Jakarta, who use *transgender* to describe some *tombois* who identify as men, thus delineating lesbian identity as associated only with women and women's bodies (Blackwood 2010: 198–202). Less explored, however, is how *waria* experiences of the category transgender are shaped by their interaction with the production of media representations. While I stress the importance of affective labor for transnational mass media, I situate *waria* understandings of the value of transgender in relation to national histories of gender, class, and the economy in particular.

While mass media appearances by *waria* have increased since the 1980s, there is a long and well-documented history of male-bodied individuals who either appear in female attire or are categorized as feminine, throughout Indonesia. However, such categorizations depend on problematic concepts of the feminine and female that may not have been relevant in the historical period or cultural context in which such figures appeared. The terms *banci* and *béncong*, both of which are now considered derogatory, were historically used with reference to those whom Western scholars referred to as "transvestites," mostly described as performers and prostitutes (see also van der Kroef 1992; and Bleys 1996). The key historical event leading to the creation and popularization of the contemporary term *waria* in the late 1970s was the growth of Indonesian nationalism and the emergence of a unified identity in a geographically and culturally vast nation (Boellstorff 2005). Accounts of "transvestite" *ludruk* drama on the island of Java underscore this link to a modern, national subjectivity and audience (Peacock 1968; Hatley 1971). At the same time, similar figures appear to have a history that extends both prior to the Indonesian nation and beyond its borders (Peletz 2006). For example, Benedict Anderson (1972) suggests that the prominence of figures who combine masculine and feminine elements in a single body is one aspect of general mythological understandings of power in Java. It has been claimed that this is a common feature of understandings of gender and sexuality throughout the Indonesian archipelago (see also Atkinson 1992; Davies 2010).

There are, however, problems associated with linking such historical representations too closely with the lives of contemporary Indonesians, which may "assume an essentialized, cross-cultural and transhistorical transgender identity" (Blackwood 2005: 850) as well as potentially collapse the meanings of transgender and homosexuality (see Davies 2010: 61). Indeed, the literature on female-bodied masculinity in Indonesia either avoids using the category transgender (Wieringa 2007) or else engages with it cautiously (Blackwood 2010). I thus follow David Valentine's (2007) concern for tracing the problematic and productive tension through which categories relate theoretical understandings of personhood to everyday practices and subjectivities. I do so by acknowledging that more recent forms of *waria* affective labor are shaped by long histories of scholarly and popular representations of gender and sexuality in Indonesia and Southeast Asia.

Transnational Media Markets and Transgender in Indonesia

The following section charts how an emergent popular understanding of transgender, focused on narratives of victimhood and violence, has shaped understandings of the category for *waria*.[7] At the same time, *waria* themselves do not necessarily see this framing as problematic.

The representations made by journalists, researchers, and filmmakers I describe are usually not intended for audiences in Indonesia, but most often those in the United States, Europe, and Australia.[8] *Waria* rarely hear back from producers or are invited to watch the final production, and thus they are rarely able to provide input prior to the release of the films. Documentaries have titles that range from bland, such as *The Warias* (2011), produced by *Vice* magazine, to exoticizing, for example, *High Heels and Hijabs* (2015), produced by SBS Television in Australia. Both of these documentaries focus on a limited range of experiences, linking *waria* to specific experiences of violence, discrimination, and suffering.

Waria share an understanding that such appearances are a form of paid work. While the best-known *waria* command a large individual fee for appearances, most receive a small amount paid to them directly of about 50,000 to 100,000 Indonesian rupiah (between US$4 and US$7) for short interviews. A separate and larger fee is often paid to local *waria* organizations. Occasionally the leaders of various organizations encourage the growth of such a market by capitalizing on the presence of journalists and researchers. These leaders are central to assembling *waria* labor and making it accessible to global mass media markets. While journalists do wield a certain degree of power over the form and content of the representation, their ability to evoke desired performances is of course complicated by the perspectives of *waria* themselves.

Having been asked similar questions repeatedly by journalists and researchers, *waria* have an understanding of the kinds of questions to be asked, and thus a rehearsed set of answers. Observing many such interactions over time, it became apparent that their answers were part of a shared narrative, made up of particular tropes. The focus on *waria* as victims of violence, for instance, addressed two aspects of victimhood. The first presents *waria* as a stigmatized identity category in Indonesia, and the second is the related problem of their visible participation in sex work.

I observed the filming of one documentary intended for foreign audiences at the beginning of 2015. It was made by a German journalist for a European television station. It was filmed entirely in Yogyakarta, and shooting was completed in three days. The brevity of the production process and interest in only a limited set of questions was representative of the twenty-odd films I had seen made during my fieldwork. When I asked the journalist what drew him to make a documentary about *waria*, he responded, "I thought it would be a good story for a film about disadvantage. My television station producers asked for something about inclusion for a weeklong series of programs about tolerance in Germany." An interest in marginality thus preceded any knowledge of *waria* lives, shaping the focus of the representation from the outset.

On the first day of the film shoot, one *waria*'s house was transformed into a small television studio. I sat on the floor behind the camera, taking on an uneasy role as the interpreter. Bright lights illuminated the space, and several *waria* gathered there. Three additional *waria* arrived wearing glamorous clothing and makeup. As was common, interviews supplemented staged versions of everyday activities to present a perspective on *waria* for audiences unfamiliar with Indonesia.

After spending some time arranging the setting, which included getting mirrors, makeup, and wigs in frame, the journalist asked several questions. They were mostly based on familiar and problematic tropes about transgender lives in Western contexts. He also asked about the relationship between *waria* and sex work.

> "When did you become transgender?"
>> "Do you want to have a sex change?"
>> "Do you see yourself as a real woman, or a woman trapped in a man's body? For instance, how do you see yourself in the mirror as you do yourself up?"
>> "Why do you wear makeup?"
>> "What employment opportunities are available, if you do not do sex work?"

Each *waria* took a turn answering these questions directly to the camera. Each spoke as an experienced interview subject who had been asked similar questions many times before. Their responses were strikingly uniform.

"I knew I was a *waria* from when I was a small child. Since I was little I have liked men and worn dresses."

"I wanted to have a sex change but my family didn't want me to. I wanted it at the time [when I was young] but now I am too old for it. Even if I were to have a sex change, I would not be a perfect woman. If there is a way to have an operation and have a child I want to do it."

"I am a woman, because when I am with women and *waria* I feel that it is right."

"Actually during the day I do not [wear makeup] but when I want to go out I put makeup on so I am seen as more beautiful and interesting. I want to change myself so that people see me as beautiful."

"There has been no chance for me to stop. I would like to have a business if I could."

After this brief interview, the journalist asked the *waria* to hand out condoms as a staged version of HIV/AIDS prevention activities. His interest moved toward a more concerted focus on sex work and was supposed to include a scene of *waria* at a nearby red-light district. On this occasion heavy rain disrupted the plan. Just before the journalist left for the evening, I realized that he had not said when or where it would be screened. When I asked, he told me the name of the television channel and program, but avoided my offer to take his contact details and follow up with him.

Waria occasionally criticized the presence of journalists. For instance, one *waria* was angry after witnessing a particularly insensitive exchange. "Who do they think they are? They just come and look at her, they just report on her and give us no benefits, and they just see her as an object," she seethed. During filming for the same documentary, another *waria* expressed irritation at a journalist getting too close during her attempts to pray. "They should know that there are times when you cannot be sticking a camera in our faces. It is not ethical [*kurang etis*]," she asserted. Yet both of these were young people, who had other sources of income, and tended to see participation in such productions as passé. I did not once hear one of the fifty-odd poorer and older *waria* who more frequently participated criticize journalists or researchers in this way. For example, when I asked the *waria* subjects of this documentary how they considered their roles in such representations, they were fairly ambivalent. For example, after the journalist had left, discussion quickly turned to how to distribute the 200,000 Indonesian rupiah (US$15) he had paid them equitably.

Representations of *waria* as transgender emphasize a narrative of victimhood. However, *waria*'s own understandings of the value of their affective labor, shaped by Indonesian's national history, challenge these limiting representations. I suggest that *waria* do not locate the value of transgender solely in the financial benefit that they derive from mass media appearances. Rather, *waria* affective labor is related to a historical understanding of such work as "good deeds" (Boellstorff 2007: 105–12), which link everyday practices to possibilities for national belonging. However, while forms of *prestasi* for *waria* have been historically defined in national economic and class terms, they now take place increasingly with reference to the global imaginary of the category transgender.

Histories of Affective Labor and the Value of Transgender

In this section I expand on the relationship between historical experiences of affective labor for the mass media in Indonesia and its relationship to the value of transgender for *waria*. I do so by focusing on my conversations with one *waria* in her late sixties, whom I call Mira. Her perspective underscores how *waria* see the value of transgender not only in the financial benefits that it offers but in the hope that it presents expanded possibility for opportunities *prestasi*. Appearing in documentaries is *prestasi* because it is both work and a form of visible recognition. These national histories shape *waria* understandings of more recent transnational markets for, and understandings of, the category transgender.

I met with Mira the day after the film shoot described in the previous section. I mentioned to her some of my concerns about the large numbers of journalists making films about *waria* in Yogyakarta. In response, she spontaneously described her own experiences of affective labor for the national mass media over the past twenty years. Initially I was surprised by Mira's lack of interest in what I saw as the problematic framing of *waria* as victims and what some *waria* and I perceived as the unethical behavior of some journalists. Instead, she focused on voicing disapproval of those *waria* whom she described as either too "commercial" (*komersil*) or "inauthentic" (*palsu*). Moreover, she stated that while charging money was absolutely necessary, it was important not to be excessively greedy. When I again directed her attention to my concerns about the relevance of the finished film or documentary, she replied that it did not matter as much as the labor that *waria* had put into it. She ignored my concerns about journalists representing *waria* as victims, instead describing her concerns about whether the labor was commensurate with the amount paid, on the one hand, and the quality of the work performed, on the other.

To explain this point, Mira described her own experiences of affective labor. She explained how a well-known Indonesian soap opera invited *waria* to appear on the show in the late 1990s. She described how one group of *waria* had asked for 2 million Indonesian rupiah (US$150) per person as the fee. According to Mira, this was widely condemned at the time for being too expensive. Most of all, she expressed alarm at the potential harm that such a request might have on *waria*'s ability to continue this kind of labor in future. She explained, "We are just extras, right? In the background we only speak a small amount of dialogue." She continued to stress that the amount charged should be commensurate with the work: "If you want, then for one person you can charge 250,000 [Indonesian rupiah; US$19] per person. Not more, though!"

When I followed up with Mira on what was wrong with taking so much money, she stressed a connection between affective labor and commanding a certain amount of "self-worth" (*harga diri*). This suggests the centrality of economy and class to understandings of the self for *waria*. She expressed that taking excessive amounts of money devalued not only an individual's worth but the overall "value" (*nilai*) of that labor for *waria* collectively. Drawing out a comparison with sex work in detail, she explained, "If you put up a tariff that large, right, that's commercial. As for me, no. For instance, in [the] past when I was doing sex work [*nyebong*], I wasn't only looking for money. I'm not one of those greedy people. If he isn't handsome, well, I just say no." her metaphor reflected the ideal that economic transactions should not place too much emphasis on only making money. This is not to say that all *waria* believed this to be so; indeed, rumors circulated about those who had benefited from recent media interest in transgender and charged excessively, growing rich from the results. Similarly, Mira criticized others for their willingness to do anything for a fee.

Mira stressed that the visibility made possible by such labor marked it out as especially important to *waria*. As such, she stated that those who undertake it should consider its value beyond only monetary gain. "There are people, as long as they get something, they think it is better than nothing. As for me, I'm not like that. I don't look for money," she explained. Turning to *waria* participation in foreign documentaries, Mira expressed her disapproval of those who provide answers simply to satisfy only their own desires. Mira laughed as she explained to me how one *waria* had inflated her own standing in an interview with a journalist. "They asked her like this, 'How is the environment around where you live, with your neighbors?' she answered, 'They think I'm a woman.' 'What is your work?' and she answered, 'I'm a bridal wear designer.' Like that! And to think that she's just a busker [*pengamen*]!" In voicing her disapproval for *waria* who did not prioritize the collective value of affective labor, Mira affirmed its importance as *prestasi*.

Such claims for recognition have a long history for *waria* in Indonesia. The very first *waria* organizations in the 1970s emerged out of claims for protection and a desire for national belonging. This belonging is most often articulated through an emphasis on work that amounts to *prestasi*, as indicated by Mira. Indeed, her comments echo Boellstorff's (2007: 105) observation that *waria* link a sense of self to notions of quality and value: "Warias must become high quality [*jadi waria yang berkualitas*] with 'high quality' referring both to beauty and good deeds." Yet, even though *waria* participation in cabaret, dance, film, television, commercial advertising, salon, fashion design, and weddings (Murtagh 2013; Davies 2010: 46; Boellstorff 2007: 88; 2005: 143; Blackwood 2005: 849) are well described, it is rarely explained in terms of affective labor and its relationship to class and economy.

A perspective linking *prestasi* and affective labor helps to understand *waria* experiences of mass media interest in transgender. Most *waria* I spoke with described the emphasis on victimhood as unimportant, given that either way the work is *prestasi*. Further, by asserting that their affective labor amounts to *prestasi*, some *waria* emphasized that financial rewards should not overshadow the possibilities offered by the category transgender. However, affective labor for transnational mass media markets has also altered how *waria* understand *prestasi*. This is particularly important because, as Mira explained, *prestasi* is not only about making money. It is also a form of self-cultivation made possible through a performance for an imagined audience. It is through affective labor for the mass media that *waria* have increasingly come to see victimization—in particular, the evocation of pity—as an important part of a performative repertoire through which they articulate claims for class mobility. For *waria*, therefore, the value produced through a relationship to transgender hinges on this ironic connection between victimization and *prestasi*.

Political Economy and Transgender Labor in Indonesia

The transformations I describe in Indonesia are related to an emergent understanding of global transgender rights. For example, the subtitle of the Australian television documentary *High Heels and Hijabs* is *Transgender Rights in Indonesia*. This documentary focuses almost entirely on *waria*, who, as I have described, are ideally suited to mass media appearances for a range of reasons. The *waria* who appear in it might be understood as motivated solely by economic interests. However, such practices must be analyzed with reference to broader national histories. In particular, I have stressed the important relationship between historically important claims for belonging and forms of affective labor for *waria*. These observations suggest that focusing on political economy yields insights into the practices that animate globalization of the category transgender. The recent experiences of the mass media I have described produce a relationship between the national category *waria* and the global scope of transgender. This may reflect the historical fascination with the "transgender native" as an object of curiosity (Towle and Morgan 2002). However, as *waria*'s own enthusiasm for this fascination shows, the affective labor of the "transgender native" is crucial in making these representations possible. And these representations, in turn, play a role in what Valentine (2007) calls "imagining transgender."

What, then, does an emergent relationship with the global category transgender mean for *waria*? How does it relate to the national and local histories that I have described? The value of transgender for *waria* is oriented toward the understanding that it provides a market for affective labor and, through it, opportunities for *prestasi*. This benefit of transgender to *waria* suggests one example of how the category offers "networks of resistance and transformation" (Stryker 2013: 552). Furthermore, it reveals that the global effects of the category transgender are related to national and transnational experiences of political economy. I have argued that *waria*'s willingness to participate in productions about transgender emerged in the context of an association with the national mass media, which may also be reflected in their participation in other forms of stage performance in Indonesia. Given this association, *waria* see it as entirely reasonable that people would want to make films about them and that they would be willing to pay money to do so.

However, while such labor offers a source of income, *waria* say that greed and self-interest should not overshadow its value as *prestasi*. The emergence of a stress on affective labor for media representations among *waria* is related to broader economic and social transformations in Indonesia. Since the 1980s, *prestasi* has been mobilized as a way to recuperate the meaning of the category *waria* into a more respectable set of practices related to productivity and a desire to work. This has consistently emphasized the importance of middle-class forms of labor, most commonly salon work, while excluding and criticizing sex work in particular. This is where *prestasi* consistently comes up against its limits; respectable formal employment and conformity with middle-class family values has never been a realistic or desirable option for many *waria*. And indeed, despite economic insecurity many *waria* that I know enjoy life on the streets, which they say is as much about having fun as it is about making money.

The reality is that, for many *waria* and other Indonesians, making money is a precarious affair. I stress here that the income generated from mass media representations is important in the context of dwindling economic opportunities among the urban poor more generally.[9] In such a context there is little room for *waria* to proactively engage with media producers or to shift the perspective of such productions beyond narrowly prescribed concerns.

Waria labor for transnational mass media markets is one way that the cultural value of transgender is produced globally. My findings are in some ways consistent with other critiques (Haritaworn and Snorton 2013); *waria* are mostly represented as abject figures framed as victims from the outset. The association between *waria* and transgender is also representative of broader transformations in which the market economy is central to Indonesian social life. At this stage it appears that the association between *waria* and transgender has, if anything, strengthened the relationship between ideal forms of productivity, normative middle-class aspirations and *prestasi* as a "performative theory of recognition" (Boellstorff 2007: 105). That the category transgender is producing new forms of cultural value—and its other—in locations as diverse as Southeast Asia and Latin America suggests a relationship with neoliberal economic transformations globally. In Indonesia, this has resulted in a diminished ability for *waria* to articulate broader concerns including access to health care, adequate housing, and safe employment. That a considerable component of the affective labor invested in *prestasi* is now devoted to evoking experiences of victimization suggests the limits of this discourse.

I have been concerned with tracing the emergent category transgender as a set of practices understood by *waria* who participate in mass media representations in Indonesia. Describing how transgender is animated globally helps clarify the ways in which it produces new forms of inequality and exclusion alongside possibilities for political mobilization. *Waria* see the value of transgender in its ability to offer new, global claims for recognition. This focus expands a politics of respectability that privileges normative productivity. Yet, even while redemptive, middle-class forms of activism have a long history in Indonesia, an emergent relationship to transgender appears to offer *waria* even narrower ways to imagine their future. The relationship between *waria* and transgender thus appears defined increasingly by the marginality that it produces, even as their affective labor remains essential to new forms of cultural value required by expanding global markets.

Benjamin Hegarty is a PhD candidate in the School of Archaeology and Anthropology at the Australian National University. His dissertation research combines historical and anthropological methods to explore how mass media markets and global political economy have shaped experiences of the gendered body and possibilities for queer intimacy in Indonesia since the 1960s.

Acknowledgments

All translations from Indonesian to English are my own. Ethnographic research was conducted in Yogyakarta and Jakarta, Indonesia. The research was conducted with funds from the Prime Minister's Endeavour Scholarship for PhD research and the Australian National University. An enormous thanks to the generous comments offered by two anonymous reviewers and to special issue editors Vek Lewis and Dan Irving. I also offer gratitude to Ferdiansyah Thajib and Sandeep Nanwani, who kindly offered their thoughts on this article and the broader questions that it raises.

Notes

1.   I use *transgender* with reference to its hegemonic Western or global meaning throughout this article. What I refer to as the value of transgender is the value of using or adopting the category as understood by *waria*.

2.   The category *waria* was established in the late 1970s by the Indonesian government, replacing the earlier category *wadam*, which was in widespread use by the early 1970s (for summaries of this history, see Boellstorff 2007: 85–87; and Oetomo 2000: 58). *Waria* is a combination of the words for woman (*wanita*) and man (*pria*) and is considered polite. It is often used in official contexts.

3.   *Banci* and *béncong* can refer to a diverse range of people and practices in Indonesia, for example, *waria*, gay men, cross-gender play, or behavior at odds with one's sex (Oetomo 2000). It is sometimes used as an offensive slur but is also used by *waria* and *gay* men to refer to one another and themselves.

4.   See note 2 for a definition and brief history of the term *waria*.

5.   The complex events of the October 1965 coup, its suppression, and Suharto's subsequent thirty-two-year rule has been analyzed in detail (see Anderson 2008 for an overview). Suharto resigned in May 1998 after a period of social and economic instability (Strassler 2009).

6.   For an overview of this category in the Thai context, see Jackson and Sullivan 1999. The processes of producing the global category transgender as a form of cultural and economic value takes place in locations beyond Southeast Asia, most notably in Latin America. This indicates the importance of comparative perspectives in future scholarship that addresses the relationship between transnational genders/sexualities and political economy.

7.   It is also of note that recently LGBT NGOs in Indonesia also emphasize a generalized experience of violence. See, for example, Hidayat 2016.

8.   I list a number of illustrative media representations here, rather than a complete survey. These include online articles, film and television documentaries, and photographic features. Articles include Brooks 2011; and O'Shea 2015. Photographs include Rayman 2015; and Soukup 2016. Independent and educational documentaries include Kiwa and Toomistu 2011; and Huang 2011. Mainstream media articles often refer to television programs or documentaries. See, for example, Huang 2012; Killalea 2015; and Engebreston 2014.

9.   *Waria*'s ability to make money has been diminished by the recent introduction of regional and local bylaws that criminalize street-based work. In Yogyakarta a law which effectively punishes various street-based economic activities was introduced in 2014. Aimed at eradicating begging and homelessness, this and similar legal instruments are framed as methods for social protection, poverty reduction, and gentrification by local and regional governments around Indonesia. In this context, affective labor for mass media markets has become even more important economically to many *waria*.

References

Aizura, Aren Z. 2010. "Feminine Transformations: Gender Reassignment Surgical Tourism in Thailand." *Medical Anthropology* 29, no. 4: 424–43.

Anderson, Benedict. 1972. "The Idea of Power in Javanese Culture." In *Culture and Politics in Indonesia*, edited by Claire Holt, 1–69. Ithaca, NY: Cornell University Press.

———. 2008. "Exit Suharto: Obituary for a Mediocre Tyrant." *New Left Review*, n.s., no. 50: 27–59.

Atkinson, Jane Monnig. 1990. "How Gender Makes a Difference in Wana Society." In *Power and Difference: Gender in Island Southeast Asia*, edited by Jane Monnig Atkinson and Shelly Errington, 59–93. Stanford, CA: Stanford University Press.

Benedicto, Bobby. 2014. *Under Bright Lights: Gay Manila and the Global Scene*. Minneapolis: University of Minnesota Press.

Blackwood, Evelyn. 2005. "Gender Transgression in Colonial and Postcolonial Indonesia." *Journal of Asian Studies* 64, no. 4: 849–79.

———. 2010. *Falling into the Lesbi World: Desire and Difference in Indonesia*. Honolulu: University of Hawai'i Press.

Bleys, Rudi C. 1996. *The Geography of Perversion: Male-to-Male Sexual Behaviour outside the West and the Ethnographic Imagination, 1750–1918*. New York: New York University Press.

Boellstorff, Tom. 2005. *The Gay Archipelago: Sexuality and Nation in Indonesia*. Princeton, NJ: Princeton University Press.

———. 2007. "Warias, National Transvestites." In *A Coincidence of Desires: Anthropology, Queer Studies, Indonesia*, 78–113. Durham, NC: Duke University Press.

———. 2011. "But Do Not Identify as Gay: A Proleptic Genealogy of the MSM Category." *Cultural Anthropology* 26, no. 2: 287–312.

Brooks, Hannah. 2011. "Warias, Come Out and Plaaayayay." *Vice*, October 13. www.vice.com /read/warias-come-out-and-plaaayayay-0000007-v18n10.

Davies, Sharyn Graham. 2010. *Gender Diversity in Indonesia: Sexuality, Islam, and Queer Selves*. London: Routledge.

Engebreston, Jess. 2014. "Transgender Women Find a Safe Place to Practice Their Faith in Indonesia." *The World*, July 3. www.pri.org/stories/2014-07-03/transgender-women-find-safe -place-practice-their-faith-indonesia.

Haritaworn, Jin, and C. Riley Snorton. 2013. "Trans Necropolitics: A Transnational Reflection on Violence, Death, and the Trans of Color Afterlife." In *The Transgender Studies Reader 2*, edited by Susan Stryker and Aren Aizura, 66–76. New York: Routledge.

Hatley, Barbara. 1971. "Wayang and Ludruk: Polarities in Java." *The Drama Review: TDR* 15, no. 2: 88–101.

Hidayat, Arief. 2016. "89,3 Persen LGBT di Indonesia Pernah Alami Kekerasan" ("89.3 Percent of LGBT in Indonesia Have Experienced Violence"). *Tempo*, January 27. nasional.tempo.co /read/news/2016/01/27/063739961/89-3-persen-lgbt-di-indonesia-pernah-alami-kekerasan.

Hochschild, Arlie. 2004. "Love and Gold." In *Global Woman: Nannies, Maids, and Sex Workers in the New Economy*, edited by Arlie Hochschild and Barbara Ehrenreich, 34–46. New York: Metropolitan Books.

Huang, Kathy. 2011. *Tales of the Waria*. Independent Television Service (ITVS) in association with the Center for Asian American Media (CAAM). www.thewaria.com.

———. 2012. "Tales of the Waria: Inside Indonesia's Third-Gender Community." *Huffington Post*. May 26. www.huffingtonpost.com/kathy-huang/tales-of-the-waria-indonesia_b_1546629 .html.

Jackson, Peter A. 2009. "Capitalism and Global Queering: National Markets, Parallels among Sexual Cultures, and Multiple Queer Modernities." *GLQ* 15, no. 3: 357–95.

Jackson, Peter A., and Gerard Sullivan. 1999. *Lady Boys, Tom Boys, Rent Boys: Male and Female Homosexualities in Contemporary Thailand*. New York: Harrington Park.

Judy, Ronald A. T., Antonio Negri, and Michael Hardt. 1999. "Dossier: Scattered Speculations on Value." *boundary 2* 26, no. 2: 73–100.

Käng, Dredge Byung'chu. 2014a. "Idols of Development: Transnational Transgender Performance in Thai K-Pop Cover Dance." *TSQ* 1, no. 4: 559–71.

———. 2014b. "Conceptualizing Thai Genderscapes: Transformation and Continuity in the Thai Sex/Gender System." In *Contemporary Socio-Cultural and Political Perspectives in Thailand*, edited by Pranee Liamputtong, 427–47. Dordrecht, the Netherlands: Springer.

Killalea, Debra. 2015. "Dateline Explores Transgender Culture in Indonesia." *News.com.au*, March 31. www.news.com.au/lifestyle/real-life/true-stories/dateline-explores-transgender-culture-in-indonesia/news-story/feede7f2051811412788e1a1e9b831b9.

Lim, Eng-Beng. 2014. *Brown Boys and Rice Queens: Spellbinding Performance in the Asias*. New York: New York University Press.

Morris, Rosalind C. 1994. "Three Sexes and Four Sexualities: Redressing the Discourses on Gender and Sexuality in Contemporary Thailand." *positions* 2, no. 1: 15–43.

Murtagh, Ben. 2013. *Genders and Sexualities in Indonesian Cinema: Constructing Gay, Lesbi and Waria Identities on Screen*. London: Routledge.

Namaste, Viviane. 2011. "Critical Research and Activisms on Trans Issues in Latin America: An Interview with Vek Lewis." In *Sex Change, Social Change: Reflections on Identity, Institutions, and Imperialism*, 181–203. Toronto: Women's Press.

Ochoa, Marcia. 2008. "Perverse Citizenship: Divas, Marginality, and Participation in 'Loca-Lization.'" *WSQ* 36, nos. 3–4: 146–69.

Oetomo, Dédé. 1996. "Gender and Sexual Orientation in Indonesia." In *Fantasizing the Feminine in Indonesia*, edited by Laurie J. Sears, 259–69. Durham, NC: Duke University Press.

———. 2000. "Masculinity in Indonesia." In *Framing the Sexual Subject: The Politics of Gender, Sexuality, and Power*, edited by Richard Parker, Regina Barbosa, and Peter Aggleton, 46–59. Berkeley: University of California Press.

O'Shea, David. 2015. "High Heels and Hijabs: Transgender Rights in Indonesia." SBS, March 31. www.sbs.com.au/news/dateline/story/high-heels-and-hijabs-transgender-rights-indonesia.

Peacock, James L. 1968. *Rites of Modernization: Symbolic and Social Aspects of Indonesian Proletarian Drama*. Chicago: University of Chicago Press.

Peletz, Michael G. 2006. "Transgenderism and Gender Pluralism in Southeast Asia since Early Modern Times." *Current Anthropology* 47, no. 2: 309–40.

Rayman, Noah. 2015. "Inside Indonesia's Islamic Boarding School for Transgender People." *Time*, April 20. time.com/3753080/indonesia-transgender-muslim-islam/.

Rudnyckyj, Daromir. 2010. *Spiritual Economies: Islam, Globalization, and the Afterlife of Development*. Ithaca, NY: Cornell University Press.

Soukup, Brianna. 2016. "Warias of Indonesia." www.briannasoukup.com/warias-of-indonesia/ (accessed January 15, 2016).

Strassler, Karen. 2009. "The Face of Money: Currency, Crisis, and Remediation in Post-Suharto Indonesia." *Cultural Anthropology* 24, no. 1: 68–103.

Stryker, Susan. 2013. "*Kaming Mga Talyada (We Who Are Sexy)*: The Transsexual Whiteness of Christine Jorgensen in the (Post)colonial Philippines." In *The Transgender Studies Reader 2*, edited by Susan Stryker and Aren Aizura, 543–52. London: Routledge.

Suryakusuma, Julia. 1996. "The State and Sexuality in New Order Indonesia." In *Fantasizing the Feminine in Indonesia*, edited by Laurie J. Sears, 92–119. Durham, NC: Duke University Press.

Toomistu, Terje, and Kiwa. 2011. *Wariazone*. wariazone.com.

Towle, Evan B., and Lynn M. Morgan. 2002. "Romancing the Transgender Native: Rethinking the Use of the 'Third Gender' Concept." *GLQ* 8, no. 4: 469–97.

Valentine, David. 2007. *Imagining Transgender: An Ethnography of a Category*. Durham, NC: Duke University Press.

Van der Kroef, Justus M. 1992. "Transvestitism and the Religious Hermaphrodite in Indonesia." In *Asian Homosexuality*, edited by Wayne R. Dynes and Stephen Donaldson, 89–97. New York: Garland.

Wieringa, Saskia. 2007. "'If There Is No Feeling . . . ': The Dilemma between Silence and Coming Out in a Working-Class Butch/Femme Community in Jakarta." In *Love and Globalization: Transformations of Intimacy in the Contemporary World*, edited by Mark B. Padilla, Jennifer S. Hirsch, Miguel Muñoz-Laboy, Robert E. Sember, and Richard G. Parker, 70–90. Nashville, TN: Vanderbilt University Press.

Sex and Surveillance on the Highway

ANNE BALAY

Abstract Big rig work culture includes a growing population of transwomen, many of whom call themselves T-girls. Working within a dense network of company and legal rules, and reaching for the autonomy and isolation associated with the open road, these truckers find stigma, resistance, and self-respect. Many identify with the cowboy ideal of trucking and with the truck itself to both fit into, and rebel against, the changing workforce dynamics of surveillance and technology. Ethnographic data suggest that sex is one form that rebellion takes.
Keywords trans employment, working-class queers, oral history, queer ethnographic method, truck drivers

Trucking is a powerful symbol in the United States—of independence, motion, and sex. For transwomen who drive trucks, all the hardships of the job are amplified, but so is the sense of privilege and possibility and the magic of the myth: that you can have control of your life, your day's schedule, your gender . . . that you are powerful, effective, even indispensable. As their control and independence evaporate, truck drivers cling more firmly to the sex, exercising freedom where and how they can, and keeping the myth meaningful as motivation and reward in their own difficult lives. One T-girl trucker, "Leslie," used to make her sexual contacts online and then meet them when she was out driving. She put a stop to this practice when "my girlfriend got access to my messages. She is my one true love and has my heart and soul and I can't risk that for anything." Now she relies on chance encounters, which she says are not hard to find. "If somebody's looking, you can tell, that's all." Leslie would agree with "Christine," who observes that "you won't see any of these people again, so that makes you free to hook up, act crazy, be stupid. Sex on the road is what keeps you from dying of boredom, or getting too frustrated by all [the company's] impossible rules."

The situation of transwomen who drive big rigs (or T-girls, to use their term) is a microcosm of wider shifts in US culture, policy, and commerce. The web of regulations and rules that govern the interstate transportation industry

TSQ: Transgender Studies Quarterly ★ Volume 4, Number 1 ★ February 2017 **96**
DOI 10.1215/23289252-3711565 © 2017 Duke University Press

changes frequently, and drivers are subject to micromanagement and oversight. The Motor Carrier Act of 1980 essentially eliminated unionized trucking and opened freight transport up to a competitive race to the bottom.[1] Consumer goods got cheaper, truckers got paid less, and a patchwork of laws and policies began to be assembled in the attempt to keep highways safe. Drivers have to understand and comply with constantly changing policies of their company, state, and federal regulatory agencies. This level of oversight contrasts with the popular understanding of trucking as a life of freedom and independence, where you can be your own boss. Drawing on oral histories, statements by truckers online, and published research, I seek to understand connections between these laws and regulations, broad social forces, and the lived reality of truckers, especially those who are gender outlaws. Trucking deregulation corresponded with the rise in neoliberalism, so truckers were encouraged to take personal responsibility for their own choices and to blame themselves when their incomes and freedoms evaporated. This new dogma fit so well with the legendary "outlaw" status of truckers that they have had a hard time figuring out how to see and oppose it. I argue that some truckers use sex as a strategy of informal resistance to these regimes and to replace the independence and excitement the job used to offer.

Truck drivers are covered not by the US Department of Labor but by the US Department of Transportation (DOT), so regulations like the eight-hour workday do not apply, and truckers have an eleven-hour-a-day driving limit, during a fourteen-hour total workday. Imagine driving something much larger than a car, with fourteen or more gears, eleven hours a day, alone. Imagine doing this as a trans person, knowing that most states offer no antidiscrimination laws. Even when they exist, laws are largely unenforced because truckers work alone, isolated from any community from which to draw solidarity and a sense of collective power, or any structures that bring laws and their enforcement within reach. Finally, the work culture of truckers stresses independence, competition, and toughness—being exhausted, unappreciated, and stigmatized is often a source of pride, rather than an incentive to change. I conducted oral histories of eight T-girls who drive eighteen-wheelers,[2] had conversations with various other truckers, and drove a semi myself for several months in 2014. In this article I combine ethnography, participant observation, and oral history methods to explore big rig culture. I argue that recent, sweeping changes in how trucking is structured and legally regulated, combined with an increasing proportion of precarious workers driving trucks, have shifted the myth and the experience of trucking. I describe how these economic and political structures are experienced and responded to by the micro(sexual)politics of everyday transwomen workers in the industry.

T-Girl Truckers

Almost all American-born truckers are white, while immigrants are usually not, and almost all immigrant truckers work for large companies, while many white truckers are independent contractors. Though the situation for each is different, all are managed and regulated excessively, and all experience a shrinking ability to make choices or exert any control. Paradoxically, though they are forced into this job through lack of other options and understand that structures of interstate commerce are using them to maximize profit with no regard for their health and safety, they also love it and identify powerfully with its fusion of independence, rebellion, and constant motion. "Lana" came out as trans partway through her trucking career, and she told me that she was treated "pretty much exactly the same as a man. I had told them—they seen me running around with makeup and painted nails. I had told 'em all—they all knew. It wasn't like one day I showed up and was a six-foot-three woman, y'know." Several T-girls said that they were assumed to be female at work and experienced only the usual mistreatment doled out to trucking women. Some are easily identifiable as trans and face ridicule, threats, and terminations. Regardless, they report sexual interest and contact from other truckers. Rather than respond with hostility, Leslie says that truckers are more likely to ask "how I can get a T-girl, who drives a truck, and she's a big bodacious babe with big tits and blue eyes because I am a big bodacious babe with big tits and blue eyes." Collecting stories from T-girls who drive trucks not only reveals the highly surveilled conditions under which they work, with few labor guarantees and protection, but also opens up new ways to imagine embodied constraints and resistances.

There are no available statistics on transgender truckers, and only about 8 percent of truckers are identified as female. As a former trucker, and someone who did extensive fieldwork in trucking spaces, I believe that transwomen are a large and visible minority among truckers, perhaps as high as 3 percent.[3] Kristen Schilt and Matthew Wiswall (2008: 17) examine employment patterns for trans-folks, pointing out that blue-collar occupations probably select against trans-women and penalize them financially. This pattern may explain why so many of them wind up driving trucks, where they can escape from work cultures of harassment and dismissal, if only by choosing isolation. A transwoman who had driven for eight years told me, "I see a lot of T-girls out here. I think a lot of trans women choose this career because it's a place where we can work—we're by ourselves, no one's going to harass us while we're in the truck. When I worked in the printing plant I was being harassed. I couldn't go to work a single day without being harassed. I had my tires sliced, I had nails put under my tires, I had hate messages put up. One day I walked into work and saw a sign up all day, 'all fags must die.' That was in my face every single day. When I'm in the truck I don't have to deal with that. The fact that people hate me because I'm trans, well then they'll hate me but say hello to my truck." That final rhetorical flourish—drawing power from the truck as a defense against stigma—is a recurring strategy for T-girl truckers, who face not only cultural scorn but also disrespect from their employers.

Surveillance technology pervades trucking life: several large carriers have installed two-way cameras in their cabs that film both the road and the driver. They argue that this footage can protect drivers in lawsuits about accidents, but it is unclear whether such footage will prove admissible in court, and being constantly observed conflicts with every image people have about truckers. When *Overdrive* magazine asked truckers how they feel about the cameras, several threatened to drive naked as retaliation, one adding, "Then I'd chop my metformin for my blood sugar up and snort it off the electric logs."[4] Another offered to "spank my monkey for them." Most comments share outrage at invasion of privacy, which one trucker blames on "how far the trucking industry has allowed the government to go." Another trucker opines, "They dictate when I can sleep, eat, pee, etc. now!" These responses, and others in the thread, raise issues that weave through the stories I tell here: issues of health and illness, sex, nostalgia, and omnipresent technology.

Most of the truckers I interviewed live with health concerns, and few have medical insurance. "Kate" says, "They treat me like a computer, and they worry more about the freight's safety than about mine." I heard countless stories from truckers of instances where their jobs put the delivery schedule and freight over the health concerns of the trucker. Any attention to driver health is read by truckers as a thinly disguised concern for the merchandise they transport. Christine had a stroke and was put on medical leave. "I need to get back behind the wheel. I'm broke. I'm bored. But they're making me finish out my year, retest, and then they'll monitor my pressures. I may never get back out there," she worries. "Susan" expressed anxiety about her upcoming physical, repeated yearly, per DOT regulations. She is concerned that she has gained enough weight that they might test her blood pressure "or look too close at my sugars." This level of monitoring, especially of bodily function, constitutes a personal violation that most workers would resist. But somehow truckers, because they work in public space yet are invisible, are held to unfair and arbitrary standards that other drivers are not.

Sleep apnea is an industry in the world of trucking.[5] In 2014 sleepreview mag.com published an overview of truckers and sleep apnea. The article admits that some truckers "believe that government is on a witch hunt, that sleep testing and CPAP treatment is a money grab, that most trucking accidents are caused by passenger vehicles, [and] that truckers are being unjustly targeted"

(Michaelson 2014). The article describes treatments, indicators, and methods of monitoring compliance. It recommends using a CPAP machine for all sleep, every night, even though this is expensive and hard to power in a parked truck. Faced with impossibly conflicting rules, truckers are required to follow, and document, compliance with untested regulations.[6] The article acknowledges that Public Law 113-45, which regulates sleep apnea, puts an excessive burden on truckers, who "would pay out of their own pockets due to lack of medical insurance or high deductibles, forcing them to leave the profession and making it more difficult to recruit and retain drivers" (Michaelson 2014). Tests used to measure driver vigilance are discussed, but the article never asks why truckers' weight, health, and sleep are subject to such scrutiny. Truckers point out that sleep studies are requested consistently by companies that have a material interest (own sleep clinics) and that truckers are desperate enough to agree to any and all forms of government intervention because they know that they can be fired, and instantly replaced, at any time. The ubiquity of the word *compliance* in this and other trucking-related resources is enough to raise concerns.

According to Virginia Eubanks (2014), who writes about technology, poverty, and "the digital divide," poor, migrant, and marginalized communities "already live in the surveillance future." Truckers fit into that group. Their bodies are consumed by the job's structure and seen as wholly expendable and entirely available to monitoring in the interest of public safety. When truck drivers resist any form of observation, claiming a right to privacy or free speech, they are accused of having something to hide or placing their rights above concern for public safety. With no union or other protections, and none of the sense of deserving respect and autonomy that unions impart, they usually capitulate to these technologies of surveillance.[7] But this leaves them feeling as if they cannot eat or sleep without getting permission or approval, and this infantilizing structure leads many truckers to quit, and those who remain often engage in sex as a form of retaliation.

In the classic trucker movie *Convoy* (1978), the hero has sex with the truck stop waitress, and it is intimated that he has many such experiences. The comments with which I began this piece move immediately from cameras to "spanking the monkey"—sexual expression is an automatic response to excessive surveillance—an efficient and visceral way to say "fuck you" to arbitrary authority. Since trucker compliance with constant, invasive monitoring gets coerced— truckers are essentially forced to consent or forfeit their jobs—expression of sexual freedom gives voice to the frustration caused by this situation.

Christine feels constrained by a set of rules that holds her to arbitrary and impossible standards while disrespecting her humanity. She points out, "I see all these new laws about how you can't leave your dog in a parked car, but I am not allowed to idle my truck in lots of places, and I'm supposed to sleep in there in like 120 degree heat. If I were a dog, they wouldn't allow it. But I'm just a trucker, so NBD." She, and many other T-girl truckers, express their frustration at this via sexual rebellion.[8] On any given day, there are reports of highway accidents involving semitrucks. Another risk factor is being alone, in isolated — often industrial — locations, at all times of day and in all weather. After being held at gunpoint in her truck, Kate took action. "Right now I carry a Smith & Wesson with me wherever I go, pretty much. I ain't gonna be in danger. I've hurt a lot of people, but I have no regrets." Danger is a source not only of anxiety but also of pride. It is a sense of accomplishment and a visceral thrill that gives trucking and truckers' lives — vitality — sexual charge.

Being alone out there leaves truckers vulnerable, but it also makes them free, because they are free not just from coworkers and visible management but also from family observation and coercion, rigidly compartmentalized time, and urban social norms. Sex is therefore loosened from its usual context and can, to some extent, have free rein. The economist Guy Standing (2011) coined the term *precariat* to describe workers including those who may once have identified as working class, migrants, and underemployed college graduates. For Standing, one defining feature of this new class is lack of control of time; there is lots of waiting and endless bureaucracy, all with minimal guarantee of payoff. Though Standing makes only passing reference to queers, I argue that the uncertainty and marginalization that give the precariat what coherence it has also make new sexual and temporal expressions possible — even necessary. Blue-collar sexualities have consistently deviated from the binaries imposed by the mainstream and media.[9] Some of the T-girls I interviewed defined themselves as having particular sexual orientations, but on the road they said that "all bets are off." What happens when a culture of hypervigilant surveillance interacts with this culture?

Who Drives Trucks, and Why?

Esquire published a long-format piece written by a college graduate turned trucker, who notes wryly that he entered the industry in the usual way, "with a sense of complete personal abandon and lack of direction. No one enters out of high school, because they can't, so everyone goes in because something else didn't work out. Layoffs, breakups, and prison stints are popular notes of inspiration" (Langellier 2015). He does not list queers, T-girls, and immigrants specifically, but in my experience, these groups are disproportionately represented among truckers because they face so many bars to more normative employment.

Three changes intersect here: (1) queers, transfolks, women, immigrants, people with disabilities, and formerly incarcerated people make up a large and growing proportion of the trucking labor force; (2) increasing technology and systems of surveillance, and government regulations requiring their enforcement, combined with reduced pay and almost nonexistent union protection, reduce the experience of freedom and self-determination that once was trucking's main reward; and (3) a form of expression beloved by truckers that continues unsurveilled and widespread is sex: truck stops, restaurants, casinos, rest areas, sleeper cabs, all are — among many other things — spaces where sex in all its forms occurs. There is something about the flow of trucking — you do not know where you will be tomorrow, and that constant, uncontrollable motion, combined with the sense of bodily power derived from the truck itself and the expectations of unstoppable virility, makes sex seem inevitable and inconsequential.

"Chelsea" makes amateur porn films on the side and told me, "It's not that different from trucking, where you spend time with people who don't ask questions if you're willing to fuck. You don't have to be pretty. You don't have to be young. You just have to be there." Frustration caused by increased surveillance, combined with instability and diversity in the driver pool, may cause an increase in sexual experimentation. The sexual charmed circle famously described by Gayle Rubin ([1984] 2011), which generates approval for some types of sex (straight, unpaid, monogamous, vanilla, at home) by reviling others, is challenged by trucker culture at this intersection. Different prohibitions emerge, but a general sexual wildness crossing categories of gender, orientation, work, age, and race is widespread.

My informants tell endless stories about sex. Lana describes a four-wheeler (automobile driver) who drove by in the next lane, exposed her breasts, then cut in front of Lana's truck, clicked on the turn signal, and exited. Lana followed her off the highway, and they had sex. These stories are so common as to be unremarkable, and they permeate lore and scholarship as well. There is a category of people, mostly men, called truck chasers. They are attracted to truckers and hang around trucker spaces, offering sex. These people are open enough about their intentions to hold annual conventions, but secretive enough to generate concern in AIDS and HIV research circles. One set of researchers working out of Atlanta found no truckers who would admit to having sex with men on the road, but they all knew exactly where, how, and when to not do it. When the researchers interviewed truck chasers, many reported hundreds, even thousands of anonymous, male, trucker partners. According to these informants, "Fear of arrest by police and/or fear of homophobic backlash on the part of NGI [nongay identifying] truckers can enhance the excitement of the encounter, these factors simultaneously raise the level of risk" (Apostolopoulous 2007: 113).

These stories link sex and risk: the danger, the hiding, the social censure are what make the sex hot. It is because of the risk and the very real threat that sex functions as a form of rebellion against overmanagement. Remember that I began with stories about, and regulations regarding, bodily control and disability. In his ethnography of independent truck drivers, Michael Agar notes that truckers are "charged with personifying traditional American values," such as "unrestrained personal freedom," while being increasingly regulated. The contrast between the myth perpetuated in country songs, movies, and popular lore and the hyperregulated reality puts truckers in a difficult psychosocial position. Truckers' "lives are embedded in business and regulatory systems with surprisingly little personal control over choice or outcomes" (Agar 1986: 150), which clashes with the myth of the romance of the road, even as trucking becomes the last, best hope for a decent wage for an exponentially growing precariat. Living and working in the crosshairs of these competing systems means being caught between a myth of cowboy-like freedom and a micromanaged, brutally regulated reality that cannot be rejected because it has been hard wrung from a resistant market offering literally no alternatives. With this powerful regulatory panopticon trained directly on their bodies via sleep monitoring, access to bathrooms limited and public, and even constant filming of every move — the body often asserts itself via sex.

Truckers are underdogs, culturally and often sexually marginal, and excluded by temperament, location, and schedule from participation in the mainstream. And they know this, of course, and sometimes feel and express resentment. But more often, they feel pride. They frequently remind each other how important their work is — that nothing could be eaten, worn, or sold without them. Though the work is often not noticed or valued, and truckers are frequently stigmatized as disreputable, dirty, and deviant, they persist because they know the work is important, and usually, they love it. There is something addictive about the thrill, the rolling wheels, the endlessly renewed uncertainty. Truck stops are gritty, crowded, and soul killing, but also lively, communal, and affirming.

Trucker Sexuality

Carol Mason argues in *Oklahomo* that the rural Midwest had been tacitly accepting of gay and queer folks until the rest of the country projected homophobia onto it to make the coasts and cities seem liberal and accepting. She opens her last chapter with a reading of Alan Jackson's trucker anthem "Where I Come From," arguing that the trucking narrator very casually weathers sexual come-ons from a black woman, a transgender person, and a gay man, and that "his roaming ways allow him to flirt, unwittingly or not, with all of these sexual possibilities unscathed" (Mason 2015: 143). The implication is that for a trucker, or for anyone who listens to popular country music, the fact that truckers engage in trans and gay sex is not news, and that motion — constant passing through public space — is what makes this unremarkable. Sexual freedom and sexual options are what the highway offers.

Freedom and outcast status are not, after all, abstract ontological states but ways of seeing and interpreting one's experience. Truckers frequently wear cowboy clothing, embrace the Confederate flag, and engage in outlaw banter and behavior. Western shirts, cowboy boots, and cowboy hats are engineered for riding horses, not for driving an eighteen-wheeler, yet truckers frequently wear them for work and in social settings because they serve as markers for how they see themselves and wish to be perceived. This understanding of freedom as a form of self-presentation — an act of imagination — is important both because of its nostalgic force and because of how freedom and its absence are constructed in neoliberal discourse as matters of consumer choice. Sex, even when it is anonymous and public, does not escape this process. Truckers' desire to be, and to be perceived as, free and empowered even in the face of escalating regulation and control is given voice to itself through sex, which is one bodily act that the government is not constantly monitoring. If "they" tell you where, when, and how to sleep; where, when, and what to eat; where to buy fuel and how much; what route to take; how much distance to maintain from the vehicle in front of you . . . then your choice to fuck, and who and how and where, is going to be an important source of feeling free and directive that you can draw on to motivate and present yourself. Truckers, whether or not they personally indulge in any sexual wildness, can draw on its mythic presence in the discourse surrounding their job.

Chelsea is an owner-operator. Rather than work for a company that provides and maintains a truck, and assigns her freight via a dispatcher, she signed a lease on a used Volvo. She then supervised a partial overhaul and upgrade of her tractor, customized her sleeper cabin, chose a broker, and started to run freight. Truckers are paid by the mile, so any sitting, waiting, or especially bobtailing (driving the tractor without a trailer attached) as an independent is financial suicide. Chelsea, a butch, politicized T-girl with bright green hair and a snarky streak, brags, "I didn't get to be who I am by following rules and letting other people's needs define me. My dad couldn't tame my wild streak, so I'll be damned if I let a broker do it." She chose to run independent to retain her freedom. But because of the brokerage system, even that freedom is affected by dispatcher preference, prejudice, and whim. Both *freedom* and *rights* are concepts that neoliberalism offers as rewards, but that remain meaningless if material conditions limit access: they then persist as symbols that truckers use sex both to protest and to enact. As an independent, Chelsea can choose her route, decide where to buy gas, seek freight that drops her at places where she has social and sexual networks, and make more money. However, she still has to get annual DOT physical cards, which subjects her to CPAP surveillance, and according to a new federal rule (DOT 2015), she will soon need an e-log (computerized driving hours monitor) in her truck.

Chelsea is personally at the intersection that trucking is experiencing nationally. Because she is an independent, the factor that Agar calls "personalism," which is the interplay of favoritism and unconscious bias that brokers and carriers use to interact with drivers—a system in which being a T-girl and a rebel do not serve her well—butts up against the increasing surveillance by which pen and ruler record-keeping must be replaced by a computerized system demanding cyclical online updates. The added expense of this new requirement will likely force her to sign with a big company, quit, or run illegal. This dilemma helps explain truckers' antipathy for federal regulation, their frequent conservatism, and their fondness for the Confederate flag as a symbol. Changes imposed by the government make it impossible for them to continue working legally in the only job that offers them some sense of self-determination and respect, however transitory. All truckers are angry about this, and for a T-girl, especially a smartass, DIY T-girl like Chelsea, law enforcement interactions and possible arrest are more than usually threatening. Neither Chelsea nor any of my other T-girl narrators fit the model of the well-disciplined, "self-made" trans subject that Dan Irving critiques. They do not have access to medical regimes that would enable seamless transition, nor are the rights of a "properly" gendered subject of whatever sex available or desirable to them (Irving 2012: 165). They thus do not fulfill the "regulatory role" (169) within neoliberalism of transsexual subjects whose fluidity fits them for late capitalism. These women might, then, model an alternative, irreverent way to be trans. Chelsea confides: "You can imagine what happens to girls like me in holding cells or jails. That's if the cops don't get there first." So running illegal is scary yet her only real option.

Susan drove a gas truck through the upper Midwest for years, and she describes driving while trans as "like running naked through a beehive." She has driven since 1984, though she was between jobs when we spoke because she had hydroplaned during a recent storm "and tore all the plumbing out from under my truck." Susan is articulate and well informed about her rights, and urges all transwomen to go on the Equal Employment Opportunity Commission website and look around. "If somebody starts giving you shit—if they use the wrong pronouns—that's sexual harassment," she reminds me. Yet this knowledge does not do much to protect her out on the road. Recently, "I got to a refuel and some guys worked me over with fucking bats." She says most harassment comes from "Jehovah's Witnesses and black guys." She adds, "Now tell me how or why I have white privilege? I think white privilege is an environmental issue."

The risks of trucking are immense—ice, snow, darkness, speed. Trans-women experience extra risks associated with being female and with being gender outlaws. T-girls are visible, especially these working-class, tough, proud ones. They do not have insurance, so usually are pre-op. Many take hormones only sporadically and do not bother with electrolysis or vocal training. They call themselves CDs (cross dressers) or T-girls, and they typically mock what they see as the polished, rich folks who have the time and money it takes to make passing possible. But honestly, they mock everybody else, too, especially themselves and each other. They consistently use wit and humor—dirty talk and lively storytelling—to resist both the trucking and the gendering rules that impinge on them. Most of these women are identifiably trans—gender transition is not something they pass through but somewhere they inhabit, typically accompanied by sarcasm, wry humor, and alcohol. This visibility makes them easy targets in the world and certainly on the road, but Lana summarizes: "I choose this—I will not be bullied. They couldn't make me hide in my man body, so I'm sure as hell not going to hide in my woman body either. This fabulous mess is me."

For this proud visibility, Lana and others pay with harassment, frequent job loss, lower pay, and a general sense of vulnerability and fear to which they would never admit. Leslie was a T-girl for a while and told me that "anyone can get the hormones off the Internet—I'll give you the site if you want. I've been ordering from there for over ten years now, but prices are beginning to go up, and a lot of the better hormones are starting to disappear." When I next spoke to her, though, she said that she had gone off hormones, and her strength and stamina were improving. She was considering returning to her male name and identity. Leslie says that she feels lonely and unappreciated even by her friends, her relationship may be dissolving, and she just wants to give up. Add this to the danger of the job, the near-constant exhaustion, and the increased lack of control and micromanagement, and you get high levels of stress. And that is ironic, since trucking is associated with freedom and escape.

Shane Hamilton, in his book about trucking's evolution as shaped by public policy during the Wal-Mart era, links truckers to masculinity, sexual wildness, and resistance to middle-class urban norms. "The blue-collar culture of trucking cultivated a deep sense of separation from bourgeois urban society. . . . Working-class manhood, particularly in a rural context, has traditionally been defined less by whether one owns the means of production than by an ethos shaped by uncertainty and the pride of overcoming that uncertainty on one's own terms" (Hamilton 2008: 108). Attachment to uncertainty and risk are crucial here. As trucking culture continues to change, and its members are micromanaged, depersonalized, and demeaned and increasingly precarious, immigrant, and queer, attachment to uncertainty and to danger intensify in response. One surefire place to meet truckers is in casinos. And the sex that truckers have is risky, rule breaking, and anonymous. Because of their bodily identification with the power of the truck and its incessant motion, this transgressive sex has an edgy, queer, exciting quality.

The T-girls I met embrace and riff on this culture by rejecting medicalized, bourgeois transness symbolized, for them, by Caitlyn Jenner and defining themselves through their jobs, their music, their scary, fun, exciting lives, and their sexual trysts. David Valentine's exploration of the history of the category of trans as it relates to class illuminates their stance. Valentine argues that transgender became an umbrella term used to describe diverse gender variances during the 1990s, but because feminist and medical languages around gender did not agree, trans came to define male-bodied people. Working-class people who clung to old-fashioned gender roles became invisible, and their ways of doing gender reviled. This shift is why white, middle-class ways of doing gender and sex are approved and seen as political (Valentine 2007: 60). Once we understand that making a distinction between sex and gender is a choice that has causes and consequences, we can try instead to "account for the complexities of lived experience" (172) rather than explain them away. Following Valentine, I let the T-girls' flirtations with me and each other, their outrageous stories and banter, and their hesitant desire to be visible and to matter speak for themselves. Their stories of casual sex are as much about trucks as they are about gender, with "Renee" even saying, "It's the truck. Well, it's this body getting out of the truck that makes them horny." It is not about gender identity or sexual orientation really but about bodies that will not be tied down. These truckers romanticize their own lives. They repeatedly tell me that what is sexy is the road — the powerful, deadly vehicle in motion, powered by a person also in motion.

My informants report sex with women and men about equally, and they do not go into detail. What they will describe endlessly is the lead-up, or the flirtation. The sex itself is usually oral and quick, often standing and/or kneeling between two parked trucks, doors left open to create a quasi-private space between them, or in truck stop bathrooms. Corresponding to what Humphreys ([1970] 1999: 41) found in his pioneering "Tearoom Trade," they seem to be choosing what is cheap and convenient yet overlooked by police and society. Kate said, offhandedly, "If someone makes eye contact with me at the fuel island, and I'm feeling it, I go to the showers after I park, and if he's waiting there, we go in and I get right down to business." When I asked for more details, the responses were rarely about the sex itself, but more likely the place, the person, or other encounters.

Feeling free — being in control — making choices — these are important tropes for all humans, but even more important for truck drivers. Their jobs are long, hard, and dirty. Many are gone so much that they effectively do not have a home. Yet given their education, social, and class background, this job is something they are proud of and identify strongly with. Truckers get little or no respect for their hard and necessary work, and they often respond by embracing their despised status, exaggerating it, and identifying proudly with it. T-girl truckers embrace and reclaim several overlapping layers of stigma. By describing legislative changes that affect them, and how they respond, I hope both to tell their wild and powerful stories and to explore what happens when legislation limits, but does not protect, a vulnerable population. Trucking is not just a job: it is a way of life. Anyone who does it, and does it well, feels pride and a keen satisfaction. The public has an interest in making sure that truckers are well trained, confident, and rested, because they are in control of enormous deadly weapons speeding only inches from us. As the trucking workforce shifts because of globalization, changing gender norms, and decreasing options for marginalized workers, it is worth thinking about how truckers react to the structures of their labor and embodiment. Chelsea uses her bold attitude to keep her safe out there, and wears steel-toed boots and jeans when her work as a flatbedder requires it, but "I have four-inch heels, and there's days I drive in my four-inch heels. I'm sure people think I'm crazy. But I like to dress nice, and dressing nice makes me feel good." She did years of sex work after a prison sentence and can find side work at truck stops easily. The rigid Hours of Service requirements mean that she and a plurality of truckers are forced into truck stops or rest areas at night because they have run out of hours, and there is lots of waiting at shippers, receivers, and ports. "These people are bored, they have cash, they want some distraction and so do I." Sex is, then, a strategy of informal resistance to the regulation, the lack of control, and the transience of big-rig culture.

I end by foregrounding one last paradox: motion. We think of truckers as epitomizing movement, but in terms of cultural progress they seem to be standing still. Their jobs and lives have a static, nostalgic valence. By some cultural transitive property, we also think that they are going to do gender and sexuality in static, old-fashioned ways. But they always did sexuality in more fluid and interesting ways than outsiders thought they did, and they continue to do that. T-girls have fun with the gendered motion—the role playing and the sex. There is space for that fun because of the motion: T-girls might be at a fuel island fighting off baseball bat attacks one minute, doing karaoke at a bar in Indiana the next, and meeting sex partners while rolling down the highway in between. It is the physicality of the motion—bodies passing through geographic space, and gender and cultural norms crossing time and class boundaries—that works against regulatory norms of surveillance and control. Modern consumers choose surveillance and comfort (think of online shopping, Skype interviews, Facebook interactions, video sex) over the obligations of being physically present, and T-girl truckers resist that by actually going places and doing stuff. Surveillance regimes track them more aggressively, and with less choice, but their transience through time and space enables a fledgling, gorgeous resistance.

Trucks are everywhere, enormous, and indispensable. Despite this, trucks and their drivers remain somehow invisible—the regulatory systems, political economies, and technologies that govern them get little attention. I could argue that readers should care about all this because we share the road with truckers and are thus endangered by them and their surveillance networks. Instead, I argue that readers should care because truckers are people. Increasingly, trucking draws from vulnerable populations (transfolks, immigrants, women) because they are easy to exploit. Since their jobs glorify bodily freedom and rely on national mythologies of motion and commerce, I collect their stories, and respect their lives, as part of an attempt to understand how regimes of constraint can be resisted and reworked on the ground—by keeping the wheels rolling.

Anne Balay is a visiting assistant professor at Haverford College and the author of *Steel Closets: Voices of Gay, Lesbian, and Transgender Steelworkers* (2014).

Acknowledgments

I would like to thank the Penn Humanities Forum, Karen Nakamura, and Jesse Shipley for shepherding me toward ethnography, and to thank the T-girls for literally everything.

Notes

1. Government documents and industry publications give a sense of this regulatory structure, including "rules that cover everything from the number of hours a truck driver must rest to the amount of pollution a Class 8 engine emits to tests for sleep apnea. 'It is absolutely a regulatory tsunami,' says U.S. Chamber of Commerce President Thomas Donohue" (Schulz 2015).
2. To the eight T-girls I interviewed, I gave pseudonyms honoring trans icons. These oral histories were conducted in 2014 and 2015.
3. This percentage is based on the fifty truck stops I visited in the course of my research, and estimates provided to me by three truckers, each with many years of experience on the road.
4. *Overdrive* asked, "Would you drive if your carrier had a camera pointed at your face or at the road?" in a Facebook post promoting an article (Dunn 2012) reporting the proposal to film drivers. The reader comments quoted here are responses to that Facebook post, which has since been deleted. Further reader responses were reported in Dills 2012.
5. In sleep apnea, you stop breathing in your sleep, for short intervals. Obviously, this can be dangerous. Obesity and related conditions increase the odds of sleep apnea, and it is usually treated with CPAP, a machine you strap to your face that forces air down your larynx so you will breathe consistently all night. This apparatus is expensive, hard to power, and hard to keep clean.
6. The paradoxes of trucking legislation are highlighted in Veronese 2012. This article points out that 12 percent of all work-related deaths are trucker highway accidents, and that only

14 percent of truck drivers are *not* overweight or obese. Exercise is virtually impossible, as are doctor appointments, and limited food is available. Yet truckers can be fired for health reasons.

7. High pay, often touted as the reward for the danger and loss of control of truckers, and cited as the reason they do not need a union, is imaginary. Lydia DePillis (2014) ran a story in the *Washington Post* that reports decreasing wage trends. Truckers I know make more than they would in service or factory jobs, but typically between thirty thousand and fifty thousand for unceasing, brutal work schedules.

8. Chela Sandoval (2000) theorizes an "oppositional consciousness" to describe the process by which vulnerable subjects talk back to oppression.

9. I discuss the sex that male steelworkers have at work in *Steel Closets* (Balay 2014). As the twentieth century progressed, this sexual contact got defined as gay and therefore became off limits for middle class and other subjects, but remained a routine part of work life for many working-class folks.

References

Agar, Michael H. 1986. *Independents Declared: The Dilemmas of Independent Trucking.* Washington, DC: Smithsonian Institution Press.

Apostolopoulous, Yorghos, et al. 2007. "Sexual Networks of Truckers, Truckchasers, and Disease Risks." In *Twenty-First Century Sexualities: Contemporary Issues in Health, Education, and Rights*, edited by Gilbert Herdt and Cymene Howe, 112–14. New York: Routledge.

Balay, Anne. 2014. *Steel Closets: Voices of Gay, Lesbian, and Transgender Steelworkers.* Chapel Hill: University of North Carolina Press.

DePillis, Lydia. 2014. "Trucking Used to Be a Ticket to the Middle Class: Now It's Just Another Low-Wage Job." *Washington Post*, April 28. www.washingtonpost.com/news/wonk/wp /2014/04/28/trucking-used-to-be-a-ticket-to-the-middle-class-now-its-just-another-low -wage-job/.

Dills, Todd. 2012. "Reader: 'I'd Drive Naked!'—More on In-Cab Facial Video Monitoring." *Overdrive*, December 6. www.overdriveonline.com/reader-id-drive-naked-more-on-in -cab-facial-video-monitoring/.

DOT (US Department of Transportation). 2015. "Electronic Logging Devices and Hours of Service Supporting Documents." Final Rule. www.fmcsa.dot.gov/hours-service/elds/ electronic-logging-devices-and-hours-service-supporting-documents.

Dunn, Jill. 2012. "Agency Allows In-Cab Camera Monitoring to Continue." *Overdrive*, December 3. www.overdriveonline.com/agency-allows-in-cab-camera-monitoring-to-continue/.

Eubanks, Virginia. 2014. "Want to Predict the Future of Surveillance? Ask Poor Communities." *American Prospect*, January 15. prospect.org/article/want-predict-future-surveillance -ask-poor-communities.

Hamilton, Shane. 2008. *Trucking Country: The Road to America's Wal-Mart Economy.* Princeton, NJ: Princeton University Press.

Humphreys, Laud. (1970) 1999. "Tearoom Trade: Impersonal Sex in Public Places." In *Public Sex / Gay Space*, edited by William L. Leap, 29–54. New York: Columbia University Press.

Irving, Dan. 2012. "Elusive Subjects: Notes on the Relationship between Critical Political Economy and Trans Studies." In *Transfeminist Perspectives*, edited by A. Finn Enke, 153–69. Philadelphia: Temple University Press.

Langellier, Robert. 2015. "The Long Haul: One Year of Solitude on America's Highways." *Esquire*, December 7. www.esquire.com/news-politics/a40157/long-haul-year-trucking-america/.

Mason, Carol. 2015. *Oklahomo: Lessons in Unqueering America*. Albany: State University of New York Press.

Michaelson, Edward D. 2014. "Sleep Apnea and Trucking: Where Are We Now?" *Sleep Review*, October 28. www.sleepreviewmag.com/2014/10/sleep-apnea-trucking-now/.

Rubin, Gayle S. (1984) 2011. "Thinking Sex: Notes for a Radical Theory of the Politics of Sexuality." In *Deviations: A Gayle Rubin Reader*, 137–81. Durham, NC: Duke University Press.

Sandoval, Chela. 2000. *Methodology of the Oppressed*. Minneapolis: University of Minnesota Press.

Schilt, Kristen, and Matthew Wiswall. 2008. "Before and After: Gender Transitions, Human Capital, and Workplace Experiences." *B.E. Journal of Economic Analysis & Policy* 8, no. 1: Article 39.

Schulz, John D. 2015. "Trucking Regulations: Caught in a Web." *Logistics Management*, October 1. www.logisticsmgmt.com/article/trucking_regulations_caught_in_a_web.

Standing, Guy. 2011. *The Precariat: The New Dangerous Class*. London: Bloomsbury.

Valentine, David. 2007. *Imagining Transgender: An Ethnography of a Category*. Durham, NC: Duke University Press.

Veronese, Keith. 2012. "Why Truck Driving Is One of the Deadliest Jobs in America." *io9*, August 14. io9.gizmodo.com/5933246/why-truck-driving-is-one-of-the-most-unhealthy-jobs-in -america.

Staging the Trans Sex Worker

NIHILS REV and FIONA MAEVE GEIST

Abstract This article interrogates how the figure of the trans street-based sex worker is deployed to argue for positive intervention on behalf of trans individuals, in addition to how it is used at the expense of a variety of trans experiences of sex work. As a corollary, this article addresses how a nuanced account of trans sex work, responsive to these concerns, can provide the basis for a more robust conception of trans theory.
Keywords sex work, trans subjectivity, trans history, criminalization

While trans studies has gained increased recognition for its contributions as an interdisciplinary academic field (Kunzel 2014), sex work, as a topic of scholarly and literary examination, has also enjoyed significantly increased academic attention, including the development of publications aimed at explaining sex work to a lay audience (Bass 2014; Chateauvert 2014; Grant 2014). Despite this shift, even publications that trace commonalities between the histories of sex workers and that of gay liberation overwhelmingly focus on the experiences of cisgender women in sex work, to the detriment of male and noncis sex workers, as exemplified by Mattilda Bernstein Sycamore's (2014) critique of *Sex Workers Unite: A History of the Movement from Stonewall to SlutWalk*, by Mindy Chateauvert. The tendency, on the part of researchers, to position the cis female sex worker as the primary and default subject relegates the trans sex worker subject to the margins. As a consequence, the trans sex worker is an often-mentioned, complex, and titillating curiosity: positioned as both sideshow oddity and pitiable rhetorical object in much writing on sex work (Friedman 2015). While these accounts customarily allude to the latent entanglement between trans identity and trans sex work, they rarely furnish complex and situated treatments of the historical and enduring connections between trans lives and sex work as both labor and social milieux. The connection between trans embodiment and trans sex work pervades all aspects of trans existence, as is reflected in the expression "walking while trans" (Mogul et al. 2011: 61). "Walking while trans" was coined

TSQ: Transgender Studies Quarterly ★ Volume 4, Number 1 ★ February 2017
DOI 10.1215/23289252-3711577 © 2017 Duke University Press

to express how "transgender women, particularly transgender women of color, are . . . frequently perceived to be sex workers by police," to the extent that "transgender women cannot walk down the street without being stopped, harassed, verbally, sexually and physically abused and arrested, regardless of what they are doing at the time" (61). This relentless harassment on the basis that transness is conflatable with sex work projects social stigma about sex work onto the trans community. In the excavation of this stigma lies the potential for understanding and revealing the rhetorical deployment of the trans sex worker.

Vek Lewis (2010: 9) argues that "an examination of the representations of trans subjectivities and sexual identities *anywhere* is intrinsically problematic and caught up in the ethics and politics of knowledge about minorities, as well as the creation of space for minority knowledges, that resignify and contest dominant representations." It is our intention in this article to elucidate the interdependence between trans subjects and the assumption of sex work. Rather than engage in respectability arguments that abnegate trans sex work as unseemly, we engage sex work theory and trans scholarship to situate the relationship between trans identity and sex work as particular and contextual. Our initial problematic concerns the tendency among researchers, writers, and activists to assume a universal (visible) trans subject. This tendency frequently makes particularities of trans experience vanish into abstraction. By deconstructing this tendency, it is possible to discuss trans identity as material rather than metaphor, which is assisted by accounting for how the discourse of trans hypersexuality developed. Given this historical understanding we can reconstruct, to some degree, *how* the figure of the trans sex worker became near universal. Working from this understanding, we unpack how this figure circulates and becomes politically productive in different contexts. Ultimately, the political circulation of this rhetorical figure is tied to a decontextualization of trans experiences in sex work, reducing the trans sex worker to a floating signifier. By working against the tendency to abstract trans sex work from the particulars invariably bound up in such work, our aim is to articulate the basis for more politically and epistemologically incisive engagements with trans sex work.

Viviane Namaste has continuously engaged with the epistemological weakness of the abstract and monolithic trans identity and, especially, the hubris of theoretical discussions that employ trans individuals in their arguments while ignoring the content of their lives. Of particular consternation for Namaste (2000: 268) is that the "celebration of recent U.S. transgender visibility—evidenced through certain media representations, activist positions, and academic debates—does not consider the experiences of a diverse group of transsexual and transgendered people," a statement that stands to date. That is, in privileging questions of representation and identity, studies then and now have worked to erase complications such as "the presence and realities of MTF transsexual prostitutes, preferring instead to focus on questions of identity" (66). These positions that Namaste (2009) critiques were focused on questions of gender and its meanings rather than the material realities that significantly affected many trans individuals. Butler-inspired accounts, influenced by the invocation of academics prominent in queer studies and feminist criticism, inhibit understanding other categories of sex- and gender-variance due to their consanguinity with particular logics of sex and gender significance. Decontextualizing this type of analysis from the daily realities of trans individuals renders these interpretations and conclusions inadequate and, in many ways, obfuscating. Ironically, these arguments have not served to create more-nuanced understandings of trans life but have stalled discussions from moving beyond questions of identity.

Complementary to the work of Namaste, Lewis (2010: 28), in *Crossing Sex and Gender in Latin America*, engages with the problem of how contemporary criticism concerned with the "representation of *locas*, *travestis*, and *transexuales* in Latin American cinema and literature fails to question . . . the dominant views of sex- and gender-variant figures as essentially figurative and symbolic of identity composition or crisis, bypassing a deconstruction of the metaphor and a view of the possibilities of envisioning sex and gender transitivity outside its terms." This scholarship highlights that rather than an abstract and nigh-monolithic category, the performance of gender is inseparable from other cultural interpolations. Without grounding discussions of trans identity in culturally specific contexts, the labor and concerns that underwrite trans identities are subsumed into a homogenizing narrative (Aizura 2012; Valentine 2007).

While our work is somewhat divergent in concern from untangling trans existence from the cultural usage of trans individuals as metaphors for "deception, charade, crisis, risk, threat, and even political corruption" (Lewis 2010: 226), our aims are linked in attempting to move beyond reified understandings of individuals and into concrete and contextualized understandings of the issues surrounding trans identity. It is our intention to provide an explanation for the particular development of hypersexual understandings of trans identity (specifically the identity of trans women) and interrogate how, against contemporary sex-work discourse, the figure of the trans street-based sex worker is deployed to argue for positive intervention on behalf of trans individuals and is used at the expense of trans experiences *of* sex work. Next, we move into contemporary theorizing on agency and sex work before juxtaposing these insights with the deployment of trans sex work as an abject outcome. This folds into contemporary theorizing around abjection and the political currency derived from the circulation of images of abjection. Finally, we delve into what a nuanced engagement with the complex realities of trans sex work looks like, practically, before concluding by noting how such an engagement with the material realities of trans sex work is invaluable to trans studies.

Hypersexuality and Trans Identity

The metaphysical relationship connecting hypersexuality and illicit prostitution to trans identity starkly contrasts with early narratives and representations of transnormativity such as those of Christine Jorgensen, which were notably chaste and sexless. In her account, Joanne Meyerowitz (2002: 197–98) portrays trans representation in "the early 1960s . . . [when] tabloid newspapers and pulp publishers produced a stream of articles and cheap paperback books on MTFs who had worked as female impersonators, strippers, or prostitutes. They often illustrated the stories with pin-up style photos that revealed breasts, legs, and buttocks." The erotic escapades of individuals such as Hedy Jo Star, Coccinelle, and Abby Sinclair provided grist for the mill for pulp publishers looking for sensational, provocative, and sexual content.[1] Hand in hand with relaxed laws regulating obscenity, pulp publishers produced increasingly obscene and pornographic content focused on the most fantastical trans women they could find.

Later pornographic works went so far as to almost completely subsume the trans narrative. The narrative that formerly acted as at least a flimsy excuse for transgressive yet sexualized content was replaced with aggressively explicit sexual content. This fascination was not limited to the pulp presses; in 1967 the US magazine *Esquire* ran a lengthy article about transsexuality that included an interview with a former prostitute working as a topless dancer. Given the rampant mainstream sexualization and frequent use of trans women in the sex trade as spokespeople, it is no wonder that such framings persist to the present day and have proliferated beyond their origin in the popular press:

> Most popular images and impressions of trans women revolve around sexuality: from "she-male" and "chicks with dicks" pornography to media portrayals of us as sexual deceivers, prostitutes, and sex workers. And of course, there are the recurring themes of trans women who transition in order either to gain the sexual attention of men or to fulfill some kind of bizarre sex fantasy (both of which appear regularly in the media, and also in [J. Michael] Bailey and [Ray] Blanchard's model of MTF transgenderism). (Serano 2007: 134)

While the hypersexualized understanding of trans women is historically derived, the rationale for which would constitute an article in itself, the bedrock responsible for the representation of the transfeminine as hypersexual is the continued and recurrent visualization of trans women in multiple discursive sites—from pornographic literature to sexology—in relation to the notion of sexual availability.

Whatever the root cause of this conceptualization, there is a cultural logic to understanding trans women that links theories such as those of Bailey and Blanchard — which posit an understanding of trans identity as a grotesquely sexualized paraphilia (Winters 2008) — and a media both repulsed and attracted to the sexuality of trans women. This conviction, that there is a relationship between trans sex work and trans hypersexuality, is so commonplace that it finds commonsense expression in platitudes such as trans masculine porn star Buck Angel's argument that trans women participate in sex work at higher rates because "MTFs are 'men' first [therefore] they have a much higher sex drive. So it just seems natural that they would get into sex work" (quoted in Ray 2015: 317). The most obvious and visible facet of this hypersexualization, in media narratives and popular understanding, is, consequently, the figure of the trans prostitute.

FTM Experiences of Sex Work

So far we have focused on the pathologization and hypersexualization of trans women. Similarly, Henry Rubin (2003: 18) observes that in "most scholarship, FTMs are subsumed under the general study of transsexualism. It [was] only quite recently that FTMs [were] considered apart from MTFs." This scholarly tendency is apparent in Ara Wilson's *Intimate Economies of Bangkok: Tomboys, Tycoons, and Avon Ladies in the Global City*. Wilson's (2004) discussion of transactional intimacy alludes to (trans feminine) *kathoey* working alongside cis women, while (trans masculine) *toms* merit mention only as potential bouncers. While Wilson documents the erotic capital of *toms* in the media, *tom* participation in sex work remains unexamined. While trans men are often overlooked in the literature, there are differences in rates of participation in sex work. The National Transgender Discrimination Survey found that transfeminine respondents were almost twice as likely to participate in the sex trade *but* also noted that transmasculine respondents made up 26.4 percent of the participants in the sex trade. This is a significant rate of participation and obviously worth noting. While public fascination with trans feminine sexuality has been an enduring feature of trans identity, trans masculinity has never achieved the same level of notoriety. In contrast with the multiplicity of pulp publications about trans women, trans masculine narratives were more historically more limited and published much later; Mario Martino has the distinction of being the first trans man to have a published autobiography; his memoir came out in 1977. Part of this may be the limited public visibility of trans masculine individuals until fairly recently, a condition that has been attributed to a number of factors including the later widespread availability of testosterone, unsatisfying results of phalloplasty, the greater possibility for gender expression without transitioning, and the availability of identities such as stone butch (Halberstam 1998; Preciado 2013;

Rubin 2003; Stryker 2008). Obviously there is no singular explanation; however, at this point, discussions of trans sex work about trans men engaged in sex work relate to individuals such as Buck Angel or Viktor Belmont who are engaged in work far from the social fringes (Ray 2015). Regardless of relative rates of participation in the sex industry, the reality remains that for "many transgender people, the sex trade can offer greater autonomy and financial stability compared to more traditional workplaces, with few barriers to entry. However, economic insecurity and material deprivation can increase one's vulnerability to harm and decrease the ability to make self-determined choices" (Fitzgerald et al. 2015: 7). Trans identity remains—at least in a labor and material sense—overdetermined given the economically precarious position many trans people find themselves in and the discrimination to which they are subject. Trans individuals are frequently pathologized as hypersexual if not as potential sex workers despite living in different socioeconomic locations that affect rates of participation in sex work. Yet the question remains as to why this is seen as inherently stigmatizing: that is, what are the mechanisms by which sex work becomes a justification for social exclusion?

Critical Interventions in Theorizing about Sex Work

One of the critical interventions of contemporary theorizing about sex work has been to reject the models popularized by second-wave feminists such as Andrea Dworkin and Catharine MacKinnon who posited sex work, especially pornography, to be the product (and exercise) of patriarchal domination. In rejecting that model, academics have worked to not simply assume that the opposite is true—that sex work is an inherently empowering or rewarding career. Instead, they have moved to attempting to capture the complex experiences surrounding sex work. As Elizabeth Bernstein (2007: 3) articulates, it is impossible to simplify the rationale behind the entry of "women, men, and transgendered individuals into the contemporary sexual economy without situating this participation within a broader context of structural violence (i.e. conditions such as poverty, racism, homophobia, and gendered inequalities)"; rather, we also must be attuned to how overemphasis on this conception of *sex work as harm* erases whether sex work "might sometimes (or simultaneously) constitute an attempted means of escape from even more profoundly violating social conditions." Given this contemporary discourse, it is worth interrogating how even putatively radical/critical theory that is attentive to structural violence such as Dean Spade's *Normal Life: Administrative Violence, Critical Trans Politics, and the Limits of the Law* can still articulate positions that obfuscate much of this insight. This is not to rebuke the arguments Spade puts forth in *Normal Life* but to interrogate how there ends up being such a jarringly retrogressive account of trans entry into sex work given the rich history of trans sex work as a site of agency and resistance integral to the formation of trans cultures and social networks.

Trans Sex Work in Academic Literature

Spade's use of stigmatized sex work to underscore rhetorical arguments for inclusion generates accounts of exclusion that culminate in the framing of sex work as a last resort. Bianca, a case study in the introduction to *Normal Life*, is used by Spade to attune the reader to the reality of trans suffering. Positioned as typical of trans exclusion from normative institutions, Bianca is systematically denied access to vital services, which leaves her with criminalized sex work as a means to subsidize her hormones. As Spade describes her inevitable trajectory into sex work:

> When Bianca applied for welfare, she was given an assignment to attend a job center as part of participation in a workfare program. When she tried to access the job center, she was brutally harassed outside, and when she finally entered and attempted to use the women's restroom she was outed and humiliated by staff. Ultimately she felt too unsafe to return and her benefits were terminated. Bianca's total lack of income also meant that she had no access to hormone treatments she used to maintain a feminine appearance, which was emotionally necessary and kept her safe from some of the harassment and violence she faced when she was more easily identifiable as a transwoman on the street. Bianca felt her only option for finding income sufficient to pay for the hormones was to engage in criminalized sex work. At this point, she was forced to procure her hormone treatments in underground economies because it would have been cost prohibitive to obtain her medication from a doctor since Medicaid . . . would not cover the costs. This put her in further danger of police violence, arrest, and other violence. Additionally, because Bianca was accessing intravenously injected hormones through street economies, she was at greater risk of HIV, hepatitis, and other communicable diseases. (Spade 2011: 10)

In the narrative provided by Spade, trans sex work stands in for a variety of institutional rejections experienced by trans individuals that culminate in entry into criminalized labor. Additionally, Spade implicitly traces a logical connection between trans abjection and trans sex work. Bianca is, ultimately, patronizingly used as a symbol of the social rejection of trans individuals and the difficult lives they must lead because of this rejection. Spade's work undertakes the challenge of prioritizing the structural reality trans people face in confronting institutions, public policy, and the reigning social climate rather than privileging personal identity. Yet in his instrumentation of the cases of such trans sex workers in order to speak more generally about how the exclusion of trans people is produced institutionally, Spade obliterates any sense of agency contra Bernstein's argument that sex work should be viewed in terms of its relationality to other social factors. Spade outlines a life shaped by institutional rejection where criminalized sex work is presented as a consequence of rejection rather than a potential solution to it. Additionally, Bianca, despite Spade's attentiveness to structural issues, is presented as an individual with absolutely no community whether by way of other trans individuals, other sex workers, or both. Yet this seems discordant with the accounts of trans sex recorded by Tor Fletcher in "Trans Sex Workers: Negotiating Sex, Gender, and Non-Normative Desire" (2013), for example. As one respondent reported, "The only community that existed for trans women was the sex-working community and at the time it was a way of survival and . . . the scene was very vibrant with clubbing, dancing, and partying" (Fletcher 2013: 70). Fletcher's interview subjects also reported experiencing discrimination and stigma but were not solely defined as victims. While Spade's reductionist approach to trans sex work may reflect his attempt to increase the concern for trans individuals, his introduction pivots on the social recognition of trans prostitution as absolute abjection.

Critical Interventions on Marginalization

In contrast to Spade, the following critiques are concerned with inadequate and reductionist accounts of trans sex work. The first, Laura Agustín's *Sex at the Margins: Migration, Labour Markets, and the Rescue Industry* (2007), critiques the rescue industry by examining related attempts to abolish, reform, or curtail sex work, in addition to the assumptions underpinning such interventions. Agustín focuses on the construction of anti–sex work discourse and, furthermore, the ways in which organizations concerned with "saving" sex workers from their jobs produce and perpetuate demeaning and patronizing assumptions about those they serve. Likewise, in "Trans Necropolitics: A Transnational Reflection on Violence, Death, and the Trans of Color Afterlife" (2013), C. Riley Snorton and Jin Haritaworn critique the use of violent trans persons of color deaths around the globe in the name of benefiting, at best, the tangential political goals of white gay demagogues in the United States. The fusion of these two critiques situates our understanding of the sociopolitical milieu of the trans sex worker and thus that of transness itself.

Agustín's work is constructed around interrogating the assumptions that govern the relationships between NGOs and sex workers. Specifically, Agustín concentrates on how NGOs understand sex work discourse and their attendant demeaning and patronizing assumptions about sex workers, particularly migrant sex workers. For Agustín (2007: 135), the concerns of NGOs are centered on how to "control prostitution," [while] unpredictable local toleration predominates, police abuse is endemic, commercial sex is blamed for spreading sexually transmitted diseases, thriving networks facilitate workers' mobility and entrance into commercial sex, which pays far better than any other job available to women, male and transgender workers are overlooked, and research focuses repeatedly on individual motivations for buying and selling sex.

That is, undue focus is given to the question of how prostitution can be regulated or why individuals either purchase sex or sell it without an attentiveness to the structural factors that regulate the sex industry and the lived experiences of sex workers in that industry. Epidemiologically, NGOs are invested in reducing the harms associated with prostitution. NGOs situate themselves either as heroic saviors, self-appointed experts on the "rescue" of sex workers, or as moral authorities amid an understanding of prostitution as an individual choice born of particular social factors. By ignoring the large-scale structural factors that shape prostitution (hence Agustín's sobriquet, the "rescue industry," characterizing this so-called activism), and by missing the multiplicity of experience and circumstance among the heterogeneous group *sex workers*, rescue industry NGOs misunderstand even the simplest needs of sex workers. While many of these organizations use feminist principles that seek to look at the collective social violence of patriarchy as a motivating factor in engaging in sex work, this more often spreads misleading portrayals of sex work. Agustín explores the "passive victim" and "exploitive pimp," roles often depicted as a certainty, and which she argues are unhelpful for understanding the dynamic realities of sex work.

In this instance Agustín (2007: 39) argues that "the roles of 'perpetrator' and 'victim' are treated as *identities* rather than temporary conditions. But services that want victims to become 'survivors' sometimes reinforce passivity, particularly in therapeutic contexts, diagnosing syndromes and disorders and emphasising damage over coping." The category of victim becomes so ingrained in this process that, as Agustín cautions, organizations become so invested in producing the category of victim that the "helpers themselves [become] disturbingly important figures" (8). This turns back on our earlier discussion of Spade's writing on trans prostitution as a metaphor for social death —or at least the necropolitical management of trans life by forced integration into the criminal economy. For Spade's rhetorical usage to work, trans individuals must be the passive victims of the machinations of administrative systems. While the explicitly gendered nature of social welfare is a bleak situation faced by trans individuals, this sort of victim discourse is predicated on "the abject victim subject who seeks rights, primarily because she is the one who has had the worst happen to her" (Kapur 2002: 5). While this makes for a distressing image of the indifference of the state to trans suffering, it also casts trans individuals and particularly trans sex workers as passive victims lacking in agency, as previously noted, but, most important, as bereft of the capacity for meaningful choice.

This perspective is in line with critiques launched by scholars such as Snorton, Haritaworn, and Sarah Lamble regarding the construction of trans victimhood as political currency. Specifically, for all three theorists, the question is *who* utilizes the bodies of brutalized and dead trans persons of color and to what end. Alternately phrased, how are the deaths of marginalized trans persons, especially trans women, they ask, made productive? Lamble, a legal scholar, addresses this in the politicized mourning undertaken on Trans Day of Remembrance (TDOR). Lamble points out that much TDOR rhetoric concentrates on transphobia and homophobia, neglecting the equally, if not more, relevant issues surrounding transmisogyny, racism, and the global impact to date of settler colonialism. Furthermore, violent acts are often framed as individual rather than systemic, or self-perpetuating and often ignoring the pattern of deaths and violence as perpetrated mainly against trans women, nonwhite individuals, many of whom are sex workers, and many located outside the United States. As Lamble (2013: 31) maintains, TDOR fails to contextualize these "incidents of violence within their specific time and place, thus obscuring the ways in which hierarchies of race, class, and sexuality situate and constitute such acts. In the process, transgender bodies are universalized along a singular identity plane of victimhood and rendered visible primarily through the violence that is acted upon them." By saying this, Lamble is claiming not that transphobia is irrelevant in all cases but that lumping all trans death together as the product of transphobia works to erase the contexts that produce violence in addition to noncisgender identity itself. TDOR does not verify that individuals were killed because they were trans and in fact counts as victims of transphobia trans persons murdered for reasons completely unrelated to being trans. Lamble draws our attention to the listing of Deanna/Thomas Wilkinson, Shawn Keagan, and Grace Baxter as victims of transphobic violence when their murders were because of their involvement in sex work, as their killers were unaware of their trans status. The public spectacle of mourning over slain trans persons involves abstracting the victims of violence from the many reasons that they were subjected to violence. Contrary to the generalized conception of transphobia underlying events like TDOR, the fatal violence experienced by gender-variant people is particular and situational. The political currency in this instance, by Lamble's estimation, is not to address the variety of identity factors that contribute to experiencing this violence but to unmoor trans bodies (especially trans bodies of color and the bodies of trans sex workers) from their particularity in the construction of *why* they experienced violence. Such decontextualized understandings of trans suffering erase the complex lives of trans individuals until all that remains is their experience of individualized violence.

Snorton and Haritaworn argue that this unified sense of victimhood is the alchemy by which value is extracted from the deaths of trans persons of color. Consonant with Lamble's argument that trans death is stripped of its particularities to establish political legitimacy for the projects of more socially valorized trans persons, Snorton and Haritaworn engage in a complementary critique of the circulation of trans suffering for political value. That is, Snorton and Haritaworn (2013: 71) aim to "provide an example of how trans women of color act as resources—both literally and metaphorically—for the articulation and visibility of a more privileged transgender subject." What is intriguing about Haritaworn and Snorton's argument is their attentiveness to the different sorts of bodies that circulate and how they accrue value. What Snorton and Haritaworn articulate are the different ways in which particular queer and trans lives find their expression of political "value." In Snorton's discussion, the complex afterlife of Tyra Hunter is unpacked, while for Haritaworn the focus is on how antimigrant rhetoric becomes married to the development of transphobia as a state-sponsored discourse. Yet what is telling in Haritaworn's description of the "Smash Transphobia" action at Berlin's Frobenstrasse is both the historical disinterest in the suffering of trans individuals engaged in sex work in the area and the erasure of their particularity, for the sake of engineering a racialized anti-immigrant rhetoric to "protect" trans individuals. Echoing through the concerns of their essay is how, instead of "those most in need of survival, the circulation of trans people of color in their afterlife accrues value to a newly professionalizing and institutionalizing class of experts whose lives could not be further removed from those they are professing to help. Immobilized in life, and barred from spaces designated as white . . . it is in their death that poor and sex working trans people are invited back in; it is in death that they suddenly come to matter" (Snorton and Haritaworn 2013: 74). That is, generating respectable trans subjects in need of state protection is implicitly tied to the exploitation of violence against the more marginalized. In this sense, the violence and death faced by marginalized trans subjects is the key to admission into social tolerance for the less marginalized under the aegis of "protection." Once more, trans sex workers and the complex experiences of violence and death are abstracted to particular, political purposes, and the very textures of being a trans woman involved in the industry become erased as possible sites of meaning and action.

Practical Considerations on Trans Sex Work
There is a continuity between the logic of abstracting trans suffering from its context and the use of the rhetorical figure of the trans sex worker. Such a figure is conceptualized less as a human being in a social context than as a continuation of

the murdered trans body theorized by Lamble, Haritaworn, and Snorton, albeit less dramatic in presentation. That is, the depiction of trans sex workers in terms of poverty, exclusion, and suffering, as previously argued, works to strip away their agency. What, on the other hand, would an account that neither sugarcoated real harms experienced by trans sex workers nor treated them as passive victims of systematic violence look like? If we remove the figure of the trans sex worker from abstraction and instead sensitively interrogate the particularities of trans sex work in context, what do we gain? A sterling example of this sort of research is Marcia Ochoa's *Queen for a Day:* Transformistas, *Beauty Queens, and the Performance of Femininity in Venezuela.* To be sure, Ochoa is not exclusively concerned with *transformistas* or prostitution. She also tackles the production of femininity in Venezuela, which allows her to interrogate the continuity between the spectacular performance of runway beauty for which Venezuela is famous and the prostitution of *transformistas.*

Ochoa (2014: 89) argues that "glamour, beauty, and femininity are technologies with specific practices that result in social legibility, intimate power, and, potentially, physical survival in a hostile environment." The performance of the above is mediated by a history of colonization, racialization, and emergent modernity along with the social scripts embedded in Venezuela. Relevant to this discussion, Ochoa's attempt to explain the performance or accomplishment of femininity in modern Venezuela focuses on how "a *transformista* . . . body does not make sense without an understanding of the social forces acting on it" (160). In terms of the *transformista* body, these social forces are conceptions of femininity drawn from beauty pageant ideals celebrated as a contribution of Venezuela to the world at large and articulated in the face of experiences of daily violence and ubiquitous participation in the sex trade. However, Ochoa is attentive also to the uniqueness of the *transformista* experience, noting that contrary to the notion of Western transition and transsexuality as "changing the state of the body to concur with the gender identity that resides in the mind[,] . . . for *transformistas,* gender is always already in their bodies. The task of a *transformista* is to enable its emergence" (161). For *transformistas,* this emergence is mediated by their use of medical technologies and by their participation in sex work, which structures their visibility and identity.

For *transformistas,* sex work occurs on the Avenida Libertador, in the business district of Venezuela's capital, Caracas. The visibility of *transformistas* on the Avenida Libertador is integral to their commercialized sexual exchanges, and this visibility is strategically integrated into the material structure of the Avenida. The *pasarelas,* walkways "designed to facilitate foot traffic between the north and south sides of the Avenida," provide a tactical barrier between *transformistas* and the police and allow *transformistas* to solicit clients, although they do not signal the passing cars but "just stand on the end of the *pasarela* in a sort of pose and make eye contact with a driver when a car slows down" (Ochoa 2014: 148). Additionally, the *pasarela* serves as a runway, mimicking those used by Venezuelan beauty queens (the *misses* juxtaposed with the *transformistas* in Ochoa's elucidation of Venezuelan femininity). Ochoa explicitly draws out this parallel, noting that this makeshift runway

> makes *transformistas* immediately legible as glamorous women to passerby. While it is common knowledge that the glamorous ladies of Avenida Libertador are *transformistas* this stance normalizes their visibility within the Venezuelan aesthetic of beauty and femininity, if even from a distance. . . . In addition to runway walking, *transformistas* also often stand still and pose. Occasionally, in these poses, some *transformistas* will open their shirts up to bare their hormone- or surgically enhanced breasts. Sometimes a *transformista* will remove her top altogether and go bare breasted. . . . Ostensibly, this stance is used to market the commodity that *transformistas* are selling—their bodies. It is also a display of one visual sign that marks them as women (not just feminine appearing, but physically, carnally female), and thus reinforces *transformistas*' authenticity as women. . . . By directly flaunting the local ordinances in a highly visible way, *transformistas* are asserting that they are in charge of the space—that they can stand calmly and display themselves and police can't do anything about it. (Ochoa 2014: 150, 151)

Ochoa's attentiveness to the practices of *transformistas* "selling themselves" on the Avenida illuminates both their abject social position and their defiance and self-actualization. Contrary to simplistic "poverty porn" that pathologizes the lives and bodies of trans sex workers, Ochoa's account acknowledges the immense systematic violence and marginalization faced by *transformistas* while also acknowledging their agency. Notably, for our purposes, this account also engages with the particularities of *transformista* identity and how it informs *transformistas*' engagement with sex work, rather than attempt to account for their engagement with sex work as merely a product of social marginalization, even as the two are related.

Realities of the Trans Sex Worker

There is a great need for adopting nuanced and particular studies on these complex yet crucial topics in trans studies, sex work studies, and ultimately both gender and feminist studies. This is in concordance with Lewis's (2006: 88) argument that often the purpose or effect of research is to "impose the researcher's point of view, prioritising abstract theory over subjective knowledge, utilising subjects as exemplar of currently fashionable intellectual paradigms or positioning them as curiosities meant to intrigue." By interrogating the biases structuring academic forays into the sociology of Latin American trans identities, Lewis deconstructs how "outside" perspectives, rather than writing in sympathy with their subjects, instead use them for theoretical purposes. Similarly, it is our attempt to foster an understanding of trans identity structured by proximity to sex work but where the ubiquity of trans sex work is used fruitfully rather than punitively. This requires deconstructing and rejecting the poverty porn narrative that frames trans sex work in terms of trans victimhood. Sex work is a variegated experience including, but not limited to, "escorting, street-based sex work, massage, prostitution, dance, pornography acting/performing, professional domination and submission, fetish and phone sex work" (Van der Meulen et al. 2013: 2). So much of the academic discourse on trans sex work focuses on limited aspects of the varieties of sex work performed by trans persons. Yet this also raises the possibility of work engaging with all the varieties of trans sex work, trans sex workers (past and present), how they are influenced by the complex negotiations of trans identities, and furthermore how trans identity and embodiment are shaped by the ubiquity of trans sex work. This is aligned with theoretical innovations that view trans identity through the complex lens of political economy, rejecting narratives of simple self-fashioning but looking at the complex interactions between policy, technology, law, and identity as expressed through neoliberal modernity (Irving 2012). Taking trans sex work seriously, therefore, involves illuminating the connections between sexuality, commerce, legality, nation, race, and gender and attentiveness to their particularity rather than dwelling on narratives rooted in pathology, criminality, and decay, which posit trans sex workers as metaphors for wider social concerns. It requires that we start from a different point: treating them as agents navigating complex identities.

Nihils Rev is an independent scholar in Northampton, Massachusetts. They work in local community organizing on queer and trans issues. Their research interests include gender philosophy, sex work, and impossible subjectivities. They are coauthoring a book on theories of disgust, transsexuality, and transsexuality.

Fiona Maeve Geist is a PhD candidate in the philosophy, interpretation and culture program at SUNY Binghamton. Her dissertation is located at the intersection of genealogy, the history of sex work, medical discourses, endocrinology, and plastic surgery, and the impact of colonialism on sexuality and gender.

Note

1.   Susana Vargas Cervantes (2014) similarly traces the complex mappings of gender, sexuality, class, and race as reflected in popular periodicals in Mexico.

References

Agustín, Laura María. 2007. *Sex at the Margins: Migration, Labour Markets, and the Rescue Industry*. London: Zed Books.

Aizura, Aren. 2012. "Transnational Transgender Rights and Immigration Law." In *Transfeminist Perspectives in and beyond Transgender and Gender Studies*, edited by Anne Enke, 133–50. Philadelphia: Temple University Press.

Bass, Alison. 2014. *Getting Screwed: Sex Workers and the Law*. Brooklyn, NY: Verso.

Bernstein, Elizabeth. 2007. *Temporarily Yours: Intimacy, Authenticity, and the Commerce of Sex*. Chicago: University of Chicago Press.

Chateauvert, Melinda. 2014. *Sex Workers Unite: A History of the Movement from Stonewall to SlutWalk*. Boston: Beacon.

Fitzgerald, Erin, Sarah Elspeth, Darby Hickey, Cherno Biko, and Harper Tobin. 2015. *Meaningful Work: Transgender Experiences in the Sex Trade*. National Center for Transgender Equality.

Fletcher, Tor. 2013. "Trans Sex Workers: Negotiating Sex, Gender, and Non-Normative Desire." In *Selling Sex: Experience, Advocacy, and Research on Sex Work in Canada*, edited by Emily Van der Meulen, Elya M. Durisin, and Victoria Love, 65–73. Vancouver: University of British Columbia Press.

Friedman, Mack. 2015. "Epidemic of Neglect: Trans Women Sex Workers and HIV." In *$PREAD: The Best of the Magazine That Illuminated the Sex Industry and Started a Media Revolution*, edited by Rachel Aimee, Eliyanna Kaiser, and Audacia Ray, 235–43. New York: Feminist Press.

Grant, Melissa Gira. 2014. *Playing the Whore: The Work of Sex Work*. London: Verso.

Halberstam, Jack. 1998. *Female Masculinity*. Durham, NC: Duke University Press.

Irving, Dan. 2012. "Elusive Subjects: Notes on the Relationship between Critical Political Economy and Trans Studies." In *Transfeminist Perspectives in and beyond Transgender and Gender Studies*, edited by Anne Enke, 153–69. Philadelphia: Temple University Press.

Kapur, Ratna. 2002. "The Tragedy of Victimization Rhetoric: Resurrecting the 'Native' Subject in International/Post-Colonial Feminist Legal Politics." *Harvard Human Rights Journal* 15, no. 1: 1–37.

Kunzel, R. 2014. "The Flourishing of Transgender Studies." *TSQ* 1, nos. 1–2: 285–97.

Lamble, Sarah. 2013. "Retelling Racialized Violence, Remaking White Innocence: The Politics of Interlocking Oppressions in Transgender Day of Remembrance." In *The Transgender Studies Reader 2*, edited by Susan Stryker and Aren Z. Aizura, 30–45. New York: Routledge.

Lewis, Vek. 2006. "Sociological Work on Transgender in Latin America: Some Considerations." *Journal of Iberian and Latin American Research* 12, no. 2: 77–89.

———. 2010. *Crossing Sex and Gender in Latin America*. New York: Palgrave.

Mogul, Joey L., Andrea J. Ritchie, and Kay Whitlock. 2011. *Queer (In)justice: The Criminalization of LGBT People in the United States*. Boston: Beacon.

Namaste, Viviane K. 2000. *Invisible Lives: The Erasure of Transsexual and Transgendered People*. Chicago: University of Chicago Press.

———. 2009. "Undoing Theory: The 'Transgender Question' and the Epistemic Violence of Anglo-American Feminist Theory." *Hypatia* 24, no. 3: 11–32.

Ochoa, Marcia. 2014. *Queen for a Day: Transformistas, Beauty Queens, and the Performance of Femininity in Venezuela*. Durham, NC: Duke University Press.

Preciado, Paul B. 2013. *Testo Junkie: Sex, Drugs, and Biopolitics in the Pharmacopornographic Era*. New York: Feminist Press.

Ray, Audacia. 2015. "Up in Buck's Business: An Interview with Buck Angel." In *$PREAD: The Best of the Magazine That Illuminated the Sex Industry and Started a Media Revolution*, edited by Rachel Aimee, Eliyanna Kaiser, and Audacia Ray, 315–21. New York: Feminist Press.

Rubin, Henry. 2003. *Self-Made Men: Identity and Embodiment among Transsexual Men*. Nashville: Vanderbilt University Press.

Serano, Julia. 2007. *Whipping Girl: A Transsexual Woman on Sexism and the Scapegoating of Femininity*. Seattle: Seal.

Snorton, C. Riley, and Jin Haritaworn. 2013. "Trans Necropolitics: A Transnational Reflection on Violence, Death, and the Trans of Color Afterlife." In *The Transgender Studies Reader 2*, edited by Susan Stryker and Aren Z. Aizura, 66–76. New York: Routledge.

Spade, Dean. 2011. *Normal Life: Administrative Violence, Critical Trans Politics, and the Limits of Law*. Brooklyn, NY: South End.

Stryker, Susan. 2008. *Transgender History*. Seattle: Seal.

Sycamore, Mattilda Bernstein. 2014. "'Sex Workers Unite,' by Melinda Chateauvert." *SFGate*, January 10. www.sfgate.com/books/article/Sex-Workers-Unite-by-Melinda-Chateauvert -5132503.php.

Valentine, David. 2007. *Imagining Transgender: An Ethnography of a Category*. Durham, NC: Duke University Press.

Van der Meulen, Emily, Elya M. Durisin, and Victoria Love. 2013. Introduction to *Selling Sex: Experience, Advocacy, and Research on Sex Work in Canada*, edited by Emily Van der Meulen, Elya M. Durisin, and Victoria Love, 1–25. Vancouver: University of British Columbia Press.

Vargas Cervantes, Susana. 2014. *Mujercitos*. Barcelona: RM Verlag.

Wilson, Ara. 2004. *The Intimate Economies of Bangkok: Tomboys, Tycoons, and Avon Ladies in the Global City*. Berkeley: University of California Press.

Winters, Kelly. 2008. *Gender Madness in American Psychiatry: Essay from the Struggle for Dignity (Text Revision)*. Dillon, CO: GID Reform Advocates.

Drag Race to the Bottom?

*Updated Notes on the Aesthetic
and Political Economy of* RuPaul's Drag Race

CORY G. COLLINS

Abstract *RuPaul's Drag Race* (*RPDR*) is a reality television competition program for drag queens that has continued to expand its popularity, both in the LGBT population and in wider audiences. Drag queens and their highlighting of performativity have long been notable for scholars of gender, while *RPDR* itself has steadily gained scholarly attention. Much of the literature, while acknowledging the potential for subversiveness, takes issue with its reproduction of hegemonic stereotypes. I review season 7, as well as the show's relation to some of the political economic elements of the drag industry, and suggest that the "policing" of drag, identified by Sarah Tucker Jenkins, may be eroding. In essence, *RPDR* has shown a decisive trend toward more stylistic liberty. This includes the liberty to break previously established rules around gender norms in performance. The show's greater popularity and profitability may enable this liberty.
Keywords: gender, performativity, drag queen, television

*R*uPaul's Drag Race (*RPDR*) is the reality television competition show for drag queens that has aired on Logo since 2009 and began its eighth season this year. It has expanded the visibility of drag in hitherto unfathomable ways and is a dominant way in which the cultural mainstream has come to understand performativity. The program has also played a notable role in creating a popular understanding of LGBTQ history and has stood out for a self-referential approach that parodies and queers reality television itself. While there is a range of past scholarly attention to the program, some of it finds fault with elements that preserve dominant conceptions of gender, class, sexuality, and race, despite an overarching quality of subversiveness. *RPDR*'s frayed history with the trans community has also been highlighted (Duffy 2015). And there are particular patterns of ownership, distribution, and wealth inequality on which the program is unsurprisingly mostly silent, themselves intertwined in a somewhat narrow vision of drag that is circumscribed for television. Nevertheless, recent seasons

TSQ: Transgender Studies Quarterly ∗ Volume 4, Number 1 ∗ February 2017   **128**
DOI 10.1215/23289252-3711589   © 2017 Duke University Press

have continued to expand and challenge some boundaries that have previously been identified as problematic by scholarship.

RPDR is structured similarly to *Project Runway*, another reality show whose fashion designers and models compete for $100,000 and other prizes and are gradually eliminated. *RPDR* contains much more than fashion-based challenges, however; its contestants must also perform stand-up comedy, dance, act, lip-sync, construct crafts, and apply makeup. It also emphasizes *reading* and *shade*, the practices of artfully pointed or cleverly veiled insult, respectively, that will be familiar to audiences of Jennie Livingston's *Paris Is Burning* (1991).

Prior to *RPDR*, Livingston's documentary was perhaps the best-known cultural text to portray drag. Its nuanced, novel exploration of the New York "ballroom" cultures has been cited as an organizing tool for queer youth as much as a resource for the cultural memory of drag queens. The film, itself criticized at times for exploiting its subjects, is known to have influenced RuPaul himself, and *RPDR*'s highly citational nature makes great use of the film's phrases, gestures, and names (Levitt 2013).

RPDR shows contestants interviewing and socializing as males, in addition to their transformation into female impersonators. Contestants engage in various challenges — celebrity impersonation, musical performance, stand-up comedy — to determine their standing for the judges, who also assess their performance and fashion on a given episode's runway presentation. The worst two contestants per episode must face off in a lip-sync showdown, and the loser will "sashay away" until only three contestants remain, one of whom is crowned America's Next Drag Superstar. Throughout each episode confessional interviews provide the queens' private commentary.

The palette of fashion and makeup on offer is aesthetically broad and often highly sophisticated. In keeping with the standards of drag, it is more exaggerated, thematic, and directly stimulating than what is found in the world of mainstream fashion design. Over eight seasons, the queens have channeled postapocalyptic science fiction and countrified Americana; dressed up in the clothing styles of inaugural balls, the Tony Awards, thrift shops, and Spanish *telenovelas*; and imitated the likes of Little Edie, Queen Amidala, Judge Judy, Klaus Nomi, and Imelda Marcos. They have made gowns from curtains, cotton candy, Saran Wrap, and other unusual materials — and almost always in ways more inventive and satisfying than those found on *Project Runway*.

To be sure, the camp, the morbid, the regal, and much of what lies in between all find some representation. But it does not occur in equal measure. The victory of season 4's ghoulish Sharon Needles, for example, was often taken as a win for the more underground styles of drag that have sometimes been excluded in the past, even if Needles represented them only by implication. But there remains a constructed, perhaps self-imposed divide between kitschy comedy queens and high fashion–conscious "pageant queens," who often participate in a highly developed, expensive system of national pageants. This axis, acknowledged and reinforced by archetypes in a season 6 performance challenge ("Shade: The Rusical"), probably creates boundaries that more transgressive styles of drag may not cross.

Previous Scholarship

RPDR is fascinating in its own right for the complex and unusual aesthetics of its contestants. In playing with gender, drag makes visible the prism of influences that refract and define performativity. When executed creatively, the resulting looks are uncommonly fierce. But *RPDR* has also been of interest to scholars of media, gender, and sexuality for its reproduction of hegemonic stereotypes. Its treatment of trans contestants, race, language, and, broadly, its policing of queer subjects have been objects of significant concern.

The most extensive works of scholarship that have engaged with *RPDR* include Sarah Tucker Jenkins's (2013) intersectional feminist analysis and the volume edited by Jim Daems (2015). Jenkins examines hegemonic conceptions of gender, race, class, and sexuality in great detail from the first through the fourth seasons. She and other authors tend to find that, despite subversive elements, the program ultimately strengthens hegemonic stereotypes.

Matthew Goldmark (2013), for example, examines the use of language in the show's first season and problematizes its lack of critical engagement with language proficiency and class as barriers to social mobility. Like Jenkins, Eir-Anne Edgar (2011: 143) takes issue with the exclusionary, singularly feminine form of drag that is rewarded, but the analysis relies only on season 1, before a variety of instances where the show's judges grow to accept and celebrate, if unevenly, the "queerness of mixing gender norms." Benny LeMaster (2015) reaches similar conclusions, focusing on the spinoff series *Drag U*'s neoliberal ideas of competition and narcissism, as well as its reinforcement of homonormative and gender-normative constraints. Sabrina Strings and Long T. Bui (2015) explore racial politics in the third season.

Jenkins is among those who find that the program reinforces harmful hegemonic stereotypes. Importantly, however, Jenkins also diagnoses a problematic "policing" of drag in which styles outside fairly well-defined boundaries are excluded, marginalized, or mocked. But there are signs, albeit tentative ones, that this policing of drag is becoming less harsh. And though RuPaul himself has been personally dismissive of concerns around transphobic language, the program has abandoned and apologized for its previous use of words such as *tranny* and *she-male* (D'Addario 2014; Daems 2015: 4).

A Drag Race to the Bottom?

Though season 8's Chi Chi DeVayne finally brought the issue of class into focus, the stories of personal growth and dramatic conflict on *RPDR* tell us surprisingly little about the material and economic life of drag queens. *RPDR* has undoubtedly, in the words of one contestant, Latrice Royale, "changed the world of drag forever." This certainly includes its economics. *RPDR* is both a cause and a symptom of the ability of many more drag queens to live from and gain recognition for an art that was once much more marginal. And certainly, the program draws significant and profit-making audiences to Logo and has no direct competitors in the same genre. Contestants have unprecedented opportunity for exposure from the program, and *RPDR* can be a pathway to the commanding heights of the industry. But there is also great opportunity for risk and loss, with contestants going on to face markedly differing careers. Certainly, *RPDR*'s contestants are no less immune to the disillusionment and pain that can follow national exposure on reality television.

Above all, at the level of individual practitioners (or, as it were, producers), the soaring interest in drag is a double-edged sword. It creates new markets but also new competitors. There are perhaps no reliable public data on this point, save for anecdotal or autobiographical accounts. But a range of inequalities structures the political economy that *RPDR* both produces and sustains.

For example, the fees an individual queen can command appear to vary greatly by geographic location. "Big huge cities like New York and Miami, they don't pay very good," said Florida queen Misty Eyez (2011), going on to cite Key West and South Beach as other low-paying markets. Eyez was advising a queen returning to the industry after several years who wondered whether declining compensation was a national trend. Eyez also appeared to suggest that some past *RPDR* contestants are commanding fees as low as $25 and as high as $1,500 for a single booking (a set of three to five songs). She goes on to state that it is normal for most queens to work for free or for tips only for years until they establish a reputation. Whether *RPDR* has helped exacerbate this precarity remains unclear, as the contemporary economics of drag institutions are mostly uncharted.

Season 7

Season 7 of *RPDR* was marked by a somewhat more mixed reception compared with other recent seasons. The winner, Violet Chachki, had a sizable online following and well-developed fashions but was also scrutinized for a "condescending attitude [and an] unwavering belief in her own superiority" (Shepherd 2015). In contrast, Katya, the season's Miss Congeniality, found empathy with viewers through her struggle to retain confidence and sobriety. But she was also a notable curiosity for her resurrection of the Soviet aesthetic within the US imaginary. Her opening costume was directly inspired by the Red Banner and is emblazoned with the hammer and sickle on an ushanka-style fur cap. In a challenge where contestants had to reinvent themselves as Hello Kitty's new best friend using a full-body doll suit, "Hello Katya" presented as a Siberian smoker in a kerchief whose "socialist side will balance out Hello Kitty's decadent capitalism" (*RPDR* 2015).

Other contestants, such as Max and Miss Fame, also displayed richly executed looks that showed drag in its most elevated form, while Jaidynn Diore Fierce's performance of Ariana Grande's "Break Free" was one of the most memorable lip-syncs of the series. But while the seventh season of *RPDR* had high ratings, it is often viewed as a flop with its core audience. The high number of younger and perhaps less-experienced queens has sometimes been highlighted as a potential cause. Nevertheless, if individual personalities seemed less alluring to fans, the season and its immediate predecessors saw some queens and challenges break previously well-established molds of style. There are many arenas where the "policing" of drag that Jenkins described appears to be softening.

For example, season 7 included a runway presentation theme of bearded drag. Significantly, past queens have been scolded or eliminated for using a beard or otherwise presenting in "boy" drag. The use of a beard by Milk in season 5 is the most notable instance, but cocompetitor Alaska Thunderfuck was also criticized for appearing as a man. As well, Jenkins (2013) highlights the rejection of androgynous drag chosen by season 4's Milan and season 1's Ongina as a significant part of *RPDR*'s narrow policing of drag. While queens since season 4 have still been scrutinized for nontraditional choices, there are signs that a trajectory toward more stylistic liberty may be forming. Milk also appeared as a male RuPaul Charles on the runway, something unfathomable in the social milieu of past seasons, while also donning other looks that rely more on spectacle than gender illusion, such as a pregnant Phyllis Diller look-alike sporting an AIDS ribbon. In season 7, the judges respond positively to an array of bearded looks. And even if the use of bearded drag was circumscribed to a particular episode, its appearance remains pathbreaking given the past hostility to androgynous aesthetics.

Perhaps surprisingly, earlier seasons have witnessed what Jenkins describes as the devaluing of femininity in specific contestants. That is, some contestants, in the eyes of their competitors, presented as too "real," too feminine, and too convincing—as lacking the exaggerated style that typifies much drag. The gender ambiguity of certain contestants is singled out and marked with suspicion. But this line of criticism appears to have receded, at least to behind the camera. Season 6's Monica Beverly Hillz came out as a transgender woman during an episode of the show and faced no detectable policing. The devaluing of femininity did not appear to surface in season 7, or at least not in the overt manner described by Jenkins.

More broadly, the artistic significance of drag on *RPDR* continues to expand, and the modes of style permitted within its boundaries are steadily growing in number, however tentatively. Drag continues to be a sometimes-marginal repertoire from which more mainstream art tends to draw, however contentiously, while repurposing and queering a pastiche of influences from folk art, high art, and mass culture. *RPDR* will continue to co-constitute and frame this repurposing, albeit from a position of previously unknown dominance in the industry. Pendulum swings in the broader culture probably broadly configure what is permitted in drag and its forays into television. Indeed, RuPaul Charles himself has cast punk-inspired genderfuck drag as a reaction to the homophobic Reagan years, the window of time that permitted his initial success as coextensive with Bill Clinton's election, and the current milieu of acceptance as reflecting a cultural openness signaled by the Obama presidency (Houston PBS 2011).

It may be that a particular economic structure—a single profitable television program for a specialized audience of mostly gay men and heterosexual women—does sometimes facilitate a homogenized, McDrag type of product. But gradual comfort with the styles on offer may prime the public for greater openness to and more appetite for the androgynous, animalistic, genderfuck, and other subaltern styles that have mostly just been hinted at on *RPDR*. Simultaneously, the program's escalating popularity may open up a space for risk and experimentation that did not exist when the series debuted with nine queens, used transphobic slurs with cavalier disregard, and offered only $25,000 in prize money. Most recently and significantly, Kim Chi and "hybrid" queen Acid Betty appeared on season 8. Despite the specter of self-censorship, the presence of these queens, with their more expansive and transgressive artistry, seems to represent an erosion of the policing of drag and a step toward a fuller diversity of styles—and an indication that a trend toward stylistic liberty and expanded definitions of drag will only continue.

Cory G. Collins is a PhD student in sociology at Memorial University of Newfoundland.

References

D'Addario, Daniel. 2015. "RuPaul's Aggressive Tirade in Defense of the Term 'Tranny.'" *Salon*, May 27. www.salon.com/2014/05/27/rupauls_aggressive_tirade_in_defense_of_the_term_tranny/.

Daems, Jim. 2015. *The Makeup of RuPaul's Drag Race*. Jefferson, NC: McFarland.

Duffy, Nick. 2015. "RuPaul's Drag Race Axes 'You've Got She-Mail' Catchphrase." *Pink News*, March 2. www.pinknews.co.uk/2015/03/02/rupauls-drag-race-axes-youve-got-she-mail-catchphrase/.

Edgar, Eir-Anne. 2011. "*Xtravaganza!* Drag Representation and Articulation in *RuPaul's Drag Race*." *Studies in Popular Culture* 34, no. 1: 133–46.

Goldmark, Matthew. 2013. "National Drag: The Language of Inclusion in RuPaul's Drag Race." *GLQ* 21, no. 4: 501–20.

Houston PBS. 2011. "RuPaul on InnerVIEWS with Ernie Manouse." YouTube video, 26:48. March 17. www.youtube.com/watch?v=hgbcnlRN158.

Jenkins, Sarah Tucker. 2013. "Hegemonic 'Realness'? An Intersectional Feminist Analysis of RuPaul's Drag Race." MA diss., Florida Atlantic University.

LeMaster, Benny. 2015. "Discontents of Being and Becoming Fabulous on RuPaul's Drag U: Queer Criticism in Neoliberal Times." *Women's Studies in Communication* 38, no. 2: 167–86.

Levitt, Lauren. 2013. "Reality Realness: *Paris Is Burning* and *RuPaul's Drag Race*." *Interventions* 3, no. 1. interventionsjournal.net/2013/11/07/reality-realness-paris-is-burning-and-rupauls -drag-race/.

Livingston, Jennie. 1991. *Paris Is Burning*. DVD. Miramax Home Entertainment.

Misty Eyez. 2011. "Ask Misty: How Much Money Do Girls Make." YouTube video, 3:54. April 18. www.youtube.com/watch?v=Oz9Se8ufxEA.

Shepherd, Julianne Escobedo. 2015. "What the Hell Happened on *RuPaul's Drag Race?*" *The Muse* (blog), June 3. themuse.jezebel.com/what-the-hell-happened-on-rupauls-drag-race-1708 447405.

Strings, Sabrina, and Long T. Bui. 2014. "'She Is Not Acting, She Is': The Conflict between Gender and Racial Realness on RuPaul's Drag Race." *Feminist Media Studies* 14, no. 5: 822–36.

The Dallas Buyers Club

Who's Buying It?

AKKADIA FORD

Abstract The representation of transgender lives on film is of increasing thematic concern within both mainstream and independent cinema. The ways in which filmmakers represent and depict trans* people communicate to audiences certain views about transgender lives and concerns. Production and exhibition of a film provokes engagement with the subject, inviting reading, interpretation, and misinterpretation. *Dallas Buyers Club* (dir. Jean-Marc Vallee, 2013) sits uneasily with contemporary transliterate (Ford 2014, 2016) audiences. The trans* body is misrepresented through a narrative of negative affect and economic precarity and as a trope erased in cinematic time, through the central character Rayon (Jared Leto), a trans* woman, and the establishment of an HIV medication "buyers club" in the mid-1980s.
Keywords: trans representation, films, Rayon, *Dallas Buyers Club*

> Incredible . . . so proud to share this journey with you . . . this is for the 36 million
> people who have lost the battle to AIDS. To those of you out there who have ever
> felt injustice because of who you are, or who you love, tonight I stand here in front
> of the world with you.
> —Jared Leto, Academy Award acceptance speech

W hen Jared Leto took the stage to receive the screen industry's highest accolade, an Academy Award, for Best Performance by an Actor in a Supporting Role, the audience stood in ovation for what was a popular win with Hollywood. Significantly, though awarded for his depiction of the trans* woman Rayon in *Dallas Buyers Club* (dir. Jean-Marc Vallee, 2013), Leto failed to mention the words *transgender* or *transsexual* in his acceptance speech, nor did he acknowledge the many transgender people whom he had publicly stated that he had based his performance on (Criswell 2014).

TSQ: Transgender Studies Quarterly ∗ Volume 4, Number 1 ∗ February 2017 **135**
DOI 10.1215/23289252-3711601 © 2017 Duke University Press

Dallas Buyers Club (*DBC*) is a feature film, classed as "Biography/Drama/History" (IMDB 2013), using traditional Hollywood genre conventions, fictional narrative structures, and filming styles to convey the life story of Ron Woodroof, depicted as a heterosexual rodeo cowboy, who establishes an HIV medication "buyers club" after receiving a positive diagnosis of AIDS and given a bleak thirty days to live. While the title of *DBC* literally positions the film as a narrative concerned with commodification and transactional exchanges between "buyers," the film fails to communicate the central role of Rayon in the narrative of a club. Rayon is the connection point for Ron between the subcultural buyers and the hegemonic authority "suppliers" of HIV medications, but Rayon is also a depressing contemporary example of a sacrificial female character, a fallen-woman type redirected and transposed onto the trans* body.

The film is set in 1985, an era of conservative economic policies called "Reaganomics" and substantial economic turbulence (Niskanen 2002). It was a time of openly homophobic American politics, when mainstream media had just begun to report on the virus already recognized for six years, and when AIDS denial was the order of the day and considered a "laughing matter" in the White House (Kinsella 1989: 3). Access to AIDS medication was strictly controlled and at the early, experimental stages of development under the control of the Food and Drug Administration (FDA). After inadequate prior testing, human trials of AZT were approved, positioning humans as experimental specimens for both the FDA and Barrow Wilkem in the film, a thinly fictionalized name for Burroughs Wellcome, the actual company that manufactured AZT in 1985. In *DBC* the virus is callously noted as being a "unique opportunity" financially, justifying the rushed human trials, with the hospital and administering physicians to be "very well compensated."

In defiance of the prognosis and lack of access to treatments, Woodroof finds an alternate way to source medications, across the border in Mexico. The theoretical terrain of borderlands (Anzaldúa 1987) as a transitional space (Cotten 2012) and "crossing the border" is present in the text in multiple forms, with the Mexico-US borderlands a theoretically and physically fraught terrain often cited simplistically (Lewis 2012: 34). These include the borderland economies of recreational drug use and street sex work. As a "Fallen Woman" (Jacobs 1997), Rayon's story arc is compressed within these borderlands: her characterization follows a sacrificial narrative of being expelled from the domestic space of the family, living on the streets, sexually unshackled, and dying before the story ends. This narrative treatment of Rayon's life and body also illustrate what Michelle O'Brian (2013) calls the "invisible" trans* body in hegemonic society. This invisibility and exclusion leads to—and necessitates—participation in border-land economies, especially in connection to accessing medications. The establishment and work of the buyers club is also in the economic borderland between officially sanctioned medical practices that restricted access to legal medication through experimental drug trials and "illegal" access. Following successful models of buyers clubs established by gay activists across the country and in order to gain access to potential buyers of the drugs in the trans* and gay community, Ron partners with Rayon, whom he meets in hospital. Rayon is participating in the hospital's AZT trial and, because of the scarcity of medication, has made an arrangement to help a friend also access the medication. This is by paying Rayon to "split my dose with him. That way we'll both get some" (Borten and Wallack 2012: 25). Ron hears this and immediately asks, "How much is he paying you?" Rayon replies, "Five grand . . . I coulda charged him twenty" (25). That Rayon accesses AZT during the trial in hospital and then "splits" the dose with a friend parallels the way in which many trans* people are reduced to accessing and sharing vital medications on the streets (O'Brien 2013).

This scene, about thirty minutes into the narrative, establishes the basis of the relationship between Ron and Rayon. The commodification of the body, as a site of AIDS drug trial testing and the economic power of the pharmaceutical company running the AZT trial, establishes the economic necessity for Ron and Rayon to engage in subversive entrepreneurial activities in order to obtain the medicines they need to stay alive. This sets the stage for establishing the buyers club, in which a monthly membership fee is exchanged for medications and vitamins.

The economics of filmmaking, the business end of "show business," is significant in this production and raises multiple issues of the commodification and fictionalization of trans* lives in cinema and the Hollywood box office, which profits from these stories. While the initial production was classed as an independent film, produced for a "low" budget by Hollywood standards, the subsequent box office reception and the major screen industry accolades for the film mainstreamed the text (IMDB 2013). This is a stark contrast to the economically deprived circumstances in which the majority of independent trans* filmmakers live and produce work.

While in 2014 the film received all the highest awards, including from the Academy, Golden Globe, and Screen Actors Guild (IMDB 2013), the text was simultaneously heavily criticized from within the international trans* community for the stereotypical and negative depiction of Rayon, which has been described as "antitrans*." Casting a nontrans* actor/actress as Rayon was criticized, raising comparisons with now-rejected cinematic practices including "blackfacing," a practice common throughout Hollywood and early cinema. "It is no longer acceptable to cast cross-racially, so why is it acceptable to cast someone who is not transgender in a transgender role?" asks Susan Rohwer (2013). The characterization of Ron as a heterosexual rodeo cowboy has also become one of the central criticisms of the text and has been challenged by people who knew him (Minutaglio 1992).

In particular, the fictitious narrative of Rayon was burdened with what was a terminal illness in 1985 and with societal stigmas around HIV that continue to resonate in the mainstream. While it is acknowledged that in the twenty-first century, with retroviral medications, HIV is no longer officially considered a terminal illness in developed countries, the situation remains bleak for people in economically deprived circumstances, for those incarcerated, and for people living with HIV in countries without affordable access to retrovirals (such as sub-Saharan Africa and parts of Southeast Asia).

The film perpetuates damaging narratives and reflects the hegemonic views of society, which marginalizes, shadows, and criminalizes participation in street economies, particularly those related to recreational drug use and adult industry work. Through gesture, clothing, mannerisms, and textual references, Rayon is positioned as a street sex worker. The narrative depiction of Rayon as a patient continues the disenfranchising and misleading trope that transgender and transsexual people are "ill" in some way, needing medication and hospitalization, and also places the character of Rayon under the control of authority figures, including doctors, hospital, pharmaceutical company, and the FDA, which were in control of the drug trials and approval or nonapproval of AZT.

The writers of *Dallas Buyers Club* wielded a weighted pen against Rayon and created her character in a way that mainstream audiences would not relate to—except as an outsider. The negative story arc of Rayon includes hostile treatment by her family. Gender normativity and heteronormativity are reinforced through the character of Rayon's father. Toward the end of the film, Rayon visits him at work in a large corner office at the bank, only to find her picture strategically excluded from the family photos on display. He then speaks pejoratively to Rayon, stating, "I suppose I should thank you for wearing men's clothes and not embarrassing me." As a bank manager, he sits at the apex of the economic structures of society, literally in control of money. In contrast, Rayon is portrayed as economically disempowered and vulnerable, on the streets, engaged in street cash economies, but ultimately needing to have the economic power of her father's position to "save" the buyers club (by facilitating the cashing in of Rayon's life insurance policy).

Despite the huge successes of the club, Rayon receives no narrative praise or recognition for her work from Woodroof when she hands over the contents of her life insurance policy, which she has cashed out to continue the club's work. The writers use the powerful metaphor of money and the respectability of an insurance policy to gain audience empathy for Rayon, but then disempower the moment by Ron saying, "Where'd you get that? . . . Did you sell your ass?" to which Rayon retorts, "Just a simple fuckin' thank-you would do." Rayon is subsequently depicted as dying alone, in hospital, returning her to the setting where audiences first met her. This scene presents a devastating contrast to the recognition that Woodroof receives in the film for establishing the buyers club and the heroic finale for his character, who is depicted as "20 pounds heavier, looking healthier" riding out on a bull in the rodeo ring to a cheering crowd. This completely overrides the text that appears onscreen stating, "Ronald Woodroof died on September 12, 1992, seven years after he was diagnosed." Clearly, the point of the narrative is the "redemption" of Woodroof, the homophobic male-identified character; Rayon, the female-identified character, is the sacrifice that enables this.

Transgender activists and scholars have stridently pointed to the damaging and incorrect stereotypes that portrayals such as the fictitious character of Rayon perpetuate in the mainstream and have worked for decades to eliminate this form of thinking from the public sphere. In the words of Susan Stryker (2006: 2), "I'm not going to listen to you say that about me, or people like me, any more." With the upsurge of public recognition for trans* people and the social justice imperatives of human rights, trans* film scholars and, increasingly, audiences are refusing to accept the transphobic writing and depictions that films such as *Dallas Buyers Club* offer to the public. We are just not buying these story lines anymore.

Akkadia Ford has a PhD in cultural studies from the School of Arts and Social Sciences at Southern Cross University, Australia, focusing on the Trans New Wave and transliteracy as an original theoretical approach to reading gender-diverse cinema. Akkadia is a trained filmmaker, establishing and working as festival director of Queer Fruits Film Festival (2009–12). Recent publications include "Regional and Queer: Refusing to Be Invisible, Creating Queer Space in a Non-Queer World" (*Géographies des sexualités/Geographies of Sexualities*, 2016) and "Transliteracy and the Trans New Wave: Developing a New Canon of Cinematic Representations of Gender Diversity and Sexuality" (*Journal of Communication and Media Studies*, 2016).

References

Anzaldúa, Gloria E. 1987. *Borderlands/La Frontera: The New Mestiza*. San Francisco: Aunt Lute.

Borten, Craig, and Melisa Wallack. 2012. "Dallas Buyers Club." Script, 5th rev. December 2. www .focusguilds2013.com/workspace/media/dbc_final-script_-12.02.12-.pdf.

Cotten, Trystan T. 2012. *Transgender Migrations: The Bodies, Borders, and Politics of Transition*. New York: Routledge.

Criswell, Luke. 2014. "Jared Leto Talks Playing Transgender in 'Dallas Buyers Club.'" *Los Angeles Confidential Magazine*, April 17. la-confidential-magazine.com/jared-leto-talks-dallas -buyers-club-and-thirty-seconds-to-mars.

IMDB (International Movie Data Base). 2013. "Dallas Buyers Club." www.imdb.com/title/tt0790636/ (accessed January 4, 2016).

Jacobs, Lea. 1997. *The Wages of Sin: Censorship and the Fallen Woman Film, 1928–1942*. Berkeley: University of California Press.

Kinsella, James. 1989. *Covering the Plague: AIDS and the American Media*. New Brunswick, NJ: Rutgers University Press.

Leto, Jared. 2014. Academy Award acceptance speech. March 2. www.youtube.com/watch ?v=VCtch3DzLRs.

Lewis, Vek. 2012. "Forging 'Moral Geographies': Law, Sexual Minorities, and Internal Tensions in Northern Mexico Border Towns." In *Transgender Migrations: Bodies, Borders, and the Politics of Transition*, edited by Trystan Cotten, 32–56. New York: Routledge.

Minutaglio, Bill. 1992. "Buying Time: World Traveler Ron Woodroof Smuggles Drugs— and Hope—for People with AIDS." *Dallas Morning News*, August 9; republished November 1, 2013. www.dallasnews.com/news/news/1992/08/09/buying-time-world-traveler -ron-woodroof-smuggles-drugs–and-hope–for-people-with-aids.

Niskanen, William A. 2002. "Reagonomics." In *The Concise Encyclopedia of Economics*. www .econlib.org/library/Enc1/Reaganomics.html (accessed January 24, 2015).

O'Brien, Michelle. 2013. "Tracing This Body: Transsexuality, Pharmaceuticals, and Capitalism." In *The Transgender Studies Reader 2*, edited by Susan Stryker and Aren Z. Aizura, 56–65. New York: Routledge.

Rohwer, Susan. 2013. "Jared Leto a 'Revelation' in 'Dallas Buyer's Club': But the Role Should've Gone to a Trans Actor." *Los Angeles Times*, November 1. www.articles.latimes.com/2013 /nov/01/news/la-ol-dallas-buyers-club-jared-leto-transgender-actors-20131101.

Stryker, Susan. 2006. "(De)Subjugated Knowledges: An Introduction to Transgender Studies." In *The Transgender Studies Reader*, edited by Susan Stryker and Stephen Whittle, 1–17. New York: Routledge.

The Wrong Wrong Body

Notes on Trans Phenomenology

ANDREA LONG CHU

Trans: A Memoir
Juliet Jacques
London: Verso Books, 2015. 320 pp.

Assuming a Body: Transgender and Rhetorics of Materiality
Gayle Salamon
New York: Columbia University Press, 2010. 240 pp. 3 illustrations.

Second Skins: The Body Narratives of Transsexuality
Jay Prosser
New York: Columbia University Press, 1998. 288 pp. 31 photos.

From 2010 to 2012, Juliet Jacques penned an immensely popular autobiographical column for the *Guardian* while transitioning from male to female. With *Trans: A Memoir*, Jacques reworks and expands on her earlier work with biting wit and brutal intimacy. But as Sandy Stone (1991) pointed out over two decades ago, transsexuality is just as much an issue of *genre* as of gender, and Jacques remains deeply suspicious of the transition memoir. Her wryly generic title, far from announcing the book's allegiance to genre conventions developed to court a prurient public interest and satisfy medical gatekeepers, registers Jacques's uneasy and often recalcitrant navigation of the memoir form. A number of the book's chapters end, therefore, as if in protest, with short critical essays explicitly devoted to, say, trans representation in film or the origins of transgender theory. Much of the book is in fact a memoir *about* a memoir, and Jacques's ethical and political reflections on her original *Guardian* column, in which she explicitly engages with a broad tradition of trans autobiographical writing, quickly come to stand in for

TSQ: Transgender Studies Quarterly ★ Volume 4, Number 1 ★ February 2017 **141**
DOI 10.1215/23289252-3711613   © 2017 Duke University Press

the concerns underlying the writing and publication of *Trans* itself. As Jacques puts it in the epilogue: "Having written my life story once already, I found it incredibly frustrating that if I wanted to be a literary writer and journalist, I had to cannibalise myself a second time before I could do anything else. Initially, I wanted to write a wider history of trans people in Britain, as well as short stories, but all I could get publishers to consider was a personal story" (299).

In other words, *Trans: A Memoir* is a book trapped in the wrong genre. Jacques begins by reprinting the account of her surgery originally published by the *Guardian* in 2012, in a move dislodging, if not totally dispensing with, sex reassignment surgery (SRS) as the transition memoir's structuring desideratum—the "be-all and end-all," as Jacques says (252). The effect is to open up a kind of breathing room for Jacques's poignant ability to render everyday life in prose without compromising its unremarkableness. If the author duly includes certain staples of trans autobiographical writing—coming out, changing names, hormone therapy, street harassment—the reader is just as likely to encounter Jacques's involvement in Manchester's postpunk music scene, her rotation through temp jobs punctuated by the odd freelance-writing gig, or her melancholic attachment to a collection of short stories about trans life whose writing she is forced to endlessly defer. Indeed, if *Trans* passes as a memoir about transition, then it is equally, if not principally, a document of precarity, depression, and the low, slow sizzle of bureaucratic life. Not only does Jacques take readers on a Kafkaesque tour of the National Health Service's gender reassignment process— at one point Jacques had considered titling her book *The Process* in a nod to Kafka's *The Trial* (*Der Prozess* in the original German)—but also, in a stroke of grim irony, Jacques actually works for the NHS in various administrative positions for the bulk of the book, including a post at the very hospital where her surgery has been performed. Transition for Jacques is not some "mythical hero's journey," as the media would usually have it, but "a bunch of hoops to jump through while working in boring jobs" (294).

Perhaps Jacques's book will be remembered (and it surely should be) as the first transition memoir to have succeeded in making transition *boring*. Jacques's writing, of course, is anything but: brisk, cutting, unpretentious, sometimes graphically vulnerable, with a bone-dry sense of humor. But the book's greatest strength lies in the kind of overwhelmingly underwhelming ordinariness that Jacques skillfully captures in print—what Martin Heidegger (1962) might call "everydayness," what Beth Povinelli (2006) might call "thick life," and what Jacques does call "the minutiae of existence" (118). Jacques has written a phenomenology of real-life experience—and, more specifically, Real Life Experience, that long march through the clinics during which a pre-op trans person must demonstrate that transition will not disturb their or anyone else's social productivity—and she proves herself a street-and-pub phenomenologist of formidable rank and resolve. For above all, *Trans* is a study in waiting: waiting for hormones, waiting for the *Guardian* to start her column, waiting for her temp agency to call back, waiting for the privilege to wait for surgery, all while shuttling between editors, psychiatrists, therapists, administrators. Jacques's is a thick present like Edmund Husserl (1964) never imagined, an abeyance, a holding pattern over the unextraordinary.

Indeed, one gets the sense that the governing affect of transition is not that of going places—compare Jan Morris's (1974) exotic trip to Casablanca for her surgery—but of going nowhere, slow. Jacques's name for this is being "burnt out" (294). Jacques lives transition not as a narrative passage from wrong to right, dysphoria to alignment, but as something akin to Lauren Berlant's (2011: 199) *impasse*, "a space of time lived without a narrative genre" endemic to the circulation of precarity in neoliberal times. This is not to downplay the real material, psychic, and affective benefits of Jacques's transition. (The American reader, moreover, cannot help but marvel at the miracle of socialized medicine, no matter how bureaucratic.) But it is to suggest that the ethics of getting by that Jacques develops for herself over the course of the memoir operates without the guarantees of a phantasmatic future anterior; hers is an ethics, in Povinelli's (2008: 511) words, that is "radically present tense." As Jacques herself tells her therapist after her operation, transitioning has no necessary relationship to stable employment, affordable housing, or psychic well-being: "And that's just fixing *my* stuff. I can have as many operations as I like, David Cameron is still prime minister" (280).

This is the context in which I take Jacques's line that she felt "not trapped in the wrong body but trapped in the wrong society" (305). Compare Morris's (1974: 3) first line in *Conundrum*, later to be plastered on the cover of the 2012 reprint: "I was three or perhaps four years old when I realized that I had been born into the wrong body, and should really be a girl." Jacques writes early on in *Trans* that the wrong-body narrative "had never quite spoken to me" (75), and she often implies that her book, like *Transgender Journey* before it, is intended to "get beyond the 'wrong body' clichés I'd always seen in newspaper articles" (180). Indeed, on these grounds it would be easy to take *Trans* as a fresher, more critical, farther-left update of Morris's approach, mercifully purged of identity politics and hence more digestible for feminist and queer theorists raised on Judith Butler. Witness, for instance, the radical imprint of Verso Books. (No doubt Verso is looking to continue to expand its less-than-stellar offerings in the gender and sexuality department—subjects too touchy-feely, one suspects, for the traditional socialist crowd, to whom Verso's recent republication of several classic texts in socialist feminism must have seemed a tolerable compromise. One recalls as well that Verso, too, independent radical press that it is, must have been among those publishers that told Jacques they were only interested in a personal story.) But if Jacques is critical of the wrong-body narrative, she is also ambivalent about it, and she relies on its rhetorics throughout the book: "male in body but female in spirit" (118), "finally be comfortable in my body" (159), "my body was catching up with my mind" (225), "the anatomy I always wanted" (272), "re-launching the symbiotic relationship between my body and my mind from a starting point that felt right" (306).

In fact it would be presumptive, I think, to say that Jacques "relies" on the narrative, as if the wrong body were, for those trans folks who *do* take it up, at best a strategy deployed under politically compromised and compromising circumstances, a kind of calculated last resort in the face of cis ignorance, abhorrence, or prurience. To be sure, the wrong-body narrative (alongside the before and after photographs) has long served as the reigning mode of sensationalization of trans life, from Christine Jorgensen all the way to Caitlyn Jenner. But it is precisely the sensationalizing character of the wrong-body narrative—rather than its "essentialism," as we used to call it in the nineties (or "essentialism," as we call it in the twenty-teens)—with which Jacques takes issue: think Jorgensen in 1952 or Jenner in 2015, all made up for the cameras and the magazines, as if transsexualism were some curious condition in which *extraordinarily beautiful women* became trapped in men's bodies. Jacques (2016), trans phenomenologist, repudiates this: "It was very important to include daily experiences in this book, partly as a counter to the glamorisation, the sensationalisation of trans lives. I wanted to show being trans within an everyday context, within boring jobs."

On the essentialist question, in fact, Jacques is quite content to remain agnostic. When her friends or coworkers ask her *why* she feels uncomfortable in her pretransition body, she has "no answer. . . . I didn't think too much about nature and nurture when I was worrying about the possibility of having my head kicked in if I answered back to any of the people who yelled at me in the street" (185). When it is a matter of improvising modes of survival in the ordinary, and when that ordinary has become "a landfill for overwhelming and impending crises of life-building and expectation" (Berlant 2011: 3), the essentialist question is quite simply beside the point. What does it matter whether bodies exist outside discourse or not when yours is under low, slow siege, not just by the threat of physical assault but also by bureaucracy, depression, anxiety, and precarity? So when Jacques writes that she "felt trapped not by my body but [by] a society that didn't want me to modify it" (76), she is directing us to what it means to survive in a society where the only *right* kind of wrong body is the sensationalized wrong body, extradited from the ordinary and airlifted out of the everyday. What such a society forecloses is the possibility of a trans phenomenology in which the ordinary body, wrong or otherwise, is given pride of place: "It's easy to forget how important the body is, especially for trans people. Before I get to the city, street, house or bedroom I live in, I spend more time in my body than anywhere else, and if that's not right then I can't do much else" (308). What's important—*what's essential*—is "to live in a body that is right for you. Or is as good as you can get it" (Jacques 2016).

Of course a phenomenology like Jacques's would not be unheard-of where the thinking of trans life is concerned. One of trans studies' founding documents, Harold Garfinkel's (1967) classic study of the (putatively) transgender woman he identifies as "Agnes," adopts a phenomenological approach to sex status as achieved through organized everyday practices. More recently, Henry Rubin (1998) has advocated for the phenomenologies of Jean-Paul Sartre and Maurice Merleau-Ponty as useful complements to the Foucauldian discourse analysis then (and arguably still) hegemonic in feminist and queer studies. For phenomenology, Rubin writes, "bodies are the ultimate point of view" (268). As such, phenomenology directs us toward "the circumscribed agency of embodied subjects" (271), thus enabling trans studies "to theorize transsexual and transgender experience on its own terms" (279). But as Rubin's work is sociologically oriented, I set it aside here. In the wake of Jacques's new book, I am most interested in revisiting two other works of trans phenomenology, more literary in persuasion: Jay Prosser's *Second Skins: The Body Narratives of Transsexuality* (1998) and Gayle Salamon's *Assuming a Body: Transgender and Rhetorics of Materiality* (2010). Both works draw (to different extents) on an archive of memoirs as primary documents for theorizing trans life while managing to come to almost diametrically opposed conclusions about the trans body. My reading of *Trans: A Memoir* owes a great deal to each of these texts; at the same time, both trans phenomenologies ultimately miscarry, I think, in ways I hope to show by reconnecting them with a number of thinkers in the phenomenological tradition and finally with Jacques herself.

Let me begin with Salamon. *Assuming a Body* draws on phenomenology, psychoanalysis, and queer theory to combat what Salamon sees as trans studies' temptation to rely on a fantasy of unmediated access to the materiality of the body. In the book's first half, Salamon insists that phenomenology and social construction are complementary enterprises, and trans studies will require both in order to give an account of gender nonnormative embodiment unleashed from the fetters of *the real*, "a phrase that, it seems to me, can never quite shed its normativizing and disciplinary dimensions" (3). In subsequent chapters, engaging a range of cultural materials (films, photographs, newspaper articles), she critiques trans theorists who are wary of social construction (including Prosser) and feminist theorists and women's studies scholars uneasy with the entrance of trans theory into their fields and departments. Later sections take a compelling speculative turn, in which Salamon, perhaps surprisingly, turns to Luce Irigaray's work to ask if a conception of sexual difference without sexual dimorphism would be useful for trans studies. The book ends with a reading of Morris's *Conundrum* alongside legal and bureaucratic issues facing trans people, especially those who are transitioning.

As Susan Stryker's blurb on the back cover suggests, Salamon's theoretical concerns often lead her to reopen "the field's fiery formative decade in the 1990s," and in this conflict her loyalties lie first and foremost with Judith Butler, who receives the first thanks in the acknowledgments. Like Butler, Salamon is made ethically and politically anxious by claims of realness or materiality (call it "sex") anterior to all signification; for her, such claims are ultimately of a piece with the essentialist logic that grounds, for instance, the transphobic police state (for instance, the so-called bathroom bill passed by the North Carolina state legislature in 2016). In the first chapters Salamon pursues this critique by arguing that the psychoanalytic bodily ego and the phenomenological body image both describe a "felt sense" of the body that is never continuous with the so-called physical body but through which the latter is always already psychically and socially mediated and vested with meaning. Again like Butler, Salamon tends to blur the lines between *signification*, in a structuralist sense; *discourse*, in a Foucauldian sense; *the social*, in a constructionist sense; and *the imaginary* and *the symbolic*, in a psychoanalytic sense. Salamon's understanding of felt sense thus takes shape along lines familiar to any student of the hermeneutics of suspicion: "The very feelings of embodiment that would seem to be the most personal, most individual, and most immune to regulatory injunction," she claims, are actually *effects* of psychic investments and discursive sedimentations (77).

As a result, Salamon must square the phenomenological circle. "One can contend," she contends, "both that a body is socially constructed and that its felt sense is undeniable"; what is crucial is that we tarry with the "tension between the historicity of the body and the immediacy of its felt sense." But Salamon is often tempted to resolve this tension, as when she confronts readers with a familiar distinction that subtly profits from a certain semantic overdetermination of the verb *to feel*: "Claiming that the body feels natural is not the same as claiming that it is natural" (77). To be sure, in everyday life, not only am I unaware of "the forces that have shaped and continue to shape my body," but indeed, "bodily life would grind to a halt were such awareness required." Yet to defend a theory of social construction, Salamon must insist that this "simple givenness," this unproblematic availability of the phenomenological body, "is a fiction, albeit a necessary one" (78) — even though only two pages earlier she assures readers that "to claim that our experiences of our sexed and gendered bodies are socially constructed is not to claim that our experiences are fictive" (76). Here the phenomenological account is absorbed into the social constructionist account, and the felt sense of the body Salamon wants so much to affirm is revealed as, at best, an ontologically indefensible but pragmatically necessary—call it *strategic*—essentialism and, at worst, a perverse kind of ideology that it is nevertheless impossible, at the risk of total phenomenological gridlock, to demystify.

Now my aim here is not to catch Salamon in a logical contradiction or to discount the tremendous resources afforded by theories of social construction. My point is simply that phenomenology and social construction are reconciled nowhere near as readily as Salamon suggests. Phenomenology begins with the notion that the givenness *of* experience *to* experience *as* experience cannot be explained (away) as the effect of some underlying reality. So when Salamon interprets Husserl's famous slogan "Back to the things themselves!" as a call for "understanding things as they are and not merely as they appear" (89), she has got things exactly backward. On the contrary, as Husserl (1982: 44) writes in *Ideas I*, this slogan expresses phenomenology's "principle of principles," namely, "that everything that offers itself originarily to us in intuition (in its fleshly actuality, so to speak) must be accepted simply as it gives itself" (translation modified). Or as he later puts it, "Nothing shall interest us but precisely the subjective alteration of manners of givenness, of manners of appearing" (Husserl 1970: 146). In other words, phenomenology is first and foremost about *phenomena*, that is, what appears, what manifests, what is given to experience. Its task is not, therefore, to unearth the invisible "substratum of history" by which the phenomenon is "always subtended," precisely because, as Salamon herself admits, "that history is invisible in the more mundane course of everyday life" (78). Rather, phenomenology asks how what *does* appear comes to appear in the first place, as well as what that which appears even "is." From this perspective, the givenness of phenomenality as such—how and why what is experienced is experienced as experience—is no more elucidated by social construction or historical materialism than it is by biochemistry or particle physics.

Now if this smacks of a little naïveté, for Salamon it would be the doomsday scenario, courtesy of the Lacanian Real, "that domain of plenitude and fullness that not only exists outside of language, but, indeed, is fundamentally incompossible with subjectivity itself[,] . . . outside of language, outside of meaning, outside of the symbolic, outside of relation, outside of desire[,] . . . a motionless and meaningless stasis equated with radical abjection and death" (41). This, indeed, is her opinion of Prosser's *Second Skins* (1998). Prosser, like Salamon, takes phenomenology and psychoanalysis as points of departure for considering the feeling of trans embodiment, but his conclusions are very different. Prosser begins his book with a ruthless and exhaustive critique of how queer theory in the 1990s (his primary target is Butler) both arrogated and disavowed trans subjects by transforming them into sigils of gender performativity through which "queer can sustain its very queerness" (58). (Think of Jack Halberstam's [1994] pomo refrain: "We are all transsexuals.") For Prosser, the queer annexation of trans occludes "the *narrative* of becoming a biological man or a biological woman (as opposed to the performative of effecting one)" that is essential, for better or worse, to understanding transsexual life (32). Transsexuality's irreducible narrativity—what Prosser calls *body narratives*, chief among them the wrong-body narrative—leads Prosser to a series of readings of an archive of trans memoirs, Radclyffe Hall's *Well of Loneliness*, Leslie Feinberg's *Stone Butch Blues*, and autobiographical photographs (including, on the book's final page, a photo of the author himself). Throughout *Second Skins*, Prosser is most concerned not with debunking or deconstructing transsexual narratives of gender authenticity but with how theory is to make itself responsible to such claims. In this sense Prosser seems to have quite deliberately gone against the grain of paranoid reading long before it became fashionable to do so (see Sedgwick 2003).

Hence Prosser, unlike Salamon, demonstrates little anxiety over the status of a "felt sense" of the body, especially when it comes to wrong embodiment. Prosser duly notes that the wrong-body narrative is a "powerful medicodiscursive sign" that has been deployed by researchers and researched alike—often, in the latter case, as a strategy for obtaining surgery or hormones. But to assume in advance that this narrative is always already a technology of power through which transsexuals are interpellated into gender normativity would be to foreclose the sincerely held convictions of many transsexuals themselves. At the end of the day, "transsexuals continue to deploy the image of wrong embodiment because being trapped in the wrong body is *simply what transsexuality feels like*" (69; emphasis mine). Prosser's term for this is "the literal"—an openly polemical choice given the "fear of the literal" (13) that grips many feminist and queer theorists, who routinely evaluate their critical objects "on the basis of whether they reveal ('good': antiessentialist) or conceal ('bad': essentialist) their constructedness" (15). Thus flouting the protocols of 1990s theory, Prosser asks us to attend to the literal and ontological senses of transsexual embodiment.

Prosser quickly clarifies, however, that this embodiment "is just as much about feeling one inhabits material flesh as the flesh itself." This distinction sets the stage for what Prosser, like Salamon, calls a "body image." Even as he cautions us against aligning the body image with "the imaginary," Prosser claims that the body image, although it "clearly already has material force for transsexuals," is nonetheless "radically split off from the material body" (7, 69). So when Salamon contends, contra Prosser (she thinks), that "the usefulness of the body image for theorizing gendered embodiment is precisely not that the body image is material" (38), she is in fact only echoing Prosser's earlier claim that the body image is "radically non-coincident with the material body" (85). What might more rightly distinguish their positions is that Prosser understands this felt sense as demanding to be literalized, most prototypically through surgical intervention. Reading a procedure like SRS as a "recovery of what was not," Prosser compares the longed-for post-op body to the "phantom limb" of neuroscientific fame, describing it as a "prior phantomization of sex, which is not to undermine but to underline the felt presence of transsex precisely in the very space of its physical absence." This "felt imaginary" summons its own literalization, "its externalization, its substantiation, in material flesh" (84–86).

Yet it seems to me that despite his best efforts Prosser ends up putting literality, as it were, on the wrong side of the equation. Prosser's literal is fundamentally a literal-to-come, linked to an imagined, idealized, or phantasmatic future where the "imaginary or phantomized signifieds" of the transsexual body image will be—one day, some day—reunited with their "corporeal referents" (86). I should be clear here that I am taking issue not with Prosser's faith in the referent but with the way that this faith again displaces the body's literality into a projected future anterior where surgically enabled transition will have finally been "completed." This seems to be largely in keeping with Prosser's perhaps worrying tendency to privilege SRS as "*the* definitive transsexual experience" (89). What's left behind by this narrative is another body, one that Prosser calls "physical" or "material," the present, preoperative (or indeed, *non*-operative) body—that is to say, the wrong body itself, in the flesh. (For the record, this same thing quietly transpires in Salamon's text in her passing references to a "literal body" or "blunt materiality" [25, 88].) What are the stakes of Prosser's alignment of the literal not with the wrong body of the present but with the right body of the future? As Halberstam (1998: 172) asks, who specifically "can afford to dream of a right body," especially when rightness "may as easily depend on whiteness or class privilege as it does on being regendered"? Isn't the whole point of the naked phenomenality of "felt sense" that the very thing that feels itself to be trapped in the wrong body *is nothing other than the wrong body itself*?

What I am getting at here is how ironic it is that Prosser should win literality for the post-transition transsexual body only through the dereliction of the literality of the wrong body itself—what Heidegger would call *facticity*, the way that finite beings find themselves thrown into the world and dispersed into the specific possibilities of everyday life. This is not to say that the wrong body is not undesirable, irritating, constraining, even unbearable. On the contrary, the wrong body is literally, nakedly wrong. But it is only through the wrong body's *already being there*—its "naked 'that it is and has to be'" (Heidegger 1962: 173)—that the very wrongness of that body comes to be disclosed in the first place. I am therefore inclined to read certain trans folks' "felt sense" of themselves less as body images and more as what I would call, paraphrasing Eve Sedgwick (1990), "nonce ontologies."[1] A nonce ontology is an irreducibly phenomenological improvisation on the relationship between thinking and being that has always already taken root in an ethical and political being-in-the-middle-of-some-thing—what Fred Moten calls "sharing before origin" (2008: 73). At a moment when the hermeneutics of suspicion has become all but synonymous with reading *tout court*, when the work of the critic all too often turns out to be either the relentless reproach of a text for collaborating with the enemy or the painstaking selection of an object that will consent to behave just like the critic herself, nonce ontologies call us to a phenomenological reengagement with what is naive, sincere, uncomplicated, unironic, uncritical, unstrategic, or just plain ordinary about everyday being in the world—a "return," as Husserl (1970: 59) once put it, "to the naïveté of life."

So when Prosser writes that "transition often proves a barely livable zone" (1998: 12), the keyword here is *barely*: to say that transition is barely livable must already be to say that transition *is livable*, no matter how bare this life gets. This is where Jacques comes back in. I do not wish to engage, however, in that crude lit-crit exercise of imagining how Prosser and Salamon would have each read *Trans: A Memoir* had it been available to them. (I would find it far more interesting, if just as crude, to imagine how Jacques would read *them*; perhaps one day she will indulge me.) Instead, let me offer a kind of inexact parallel, by way of Cat Fitz-patrick's (2015) review of *Trans: A Memoir* published in the *Lambda Literary Review*. Fitzpatrick praises Jacques for her "clear-eyed and evocative" storytelling, but finds *Trans* limited by the formal constraints of its genre, which is "structured, between sensationalism and exclusion, to preclude any real discussion of the mundane realities of what it is like to actually be a trans person, either before or after transition." Given the histories that Salamon, Prosser, and Jacques herself describe, it is hard to disagree.

But I do not think it follows, as Fitzpatrick does, that a book like *Trans* "may well do a lot to further the conversations cis people have about trans people, but it can do little to further our conversations with each other"—if only because, as Jacques's nonce ontology teaches us, the very "mundane realities" the trans memoir ought to formally occlude have nowhere else to unfold but in the thick of a trans ordinary entangled in without being reducible to its cisnormative conditions. To conclude that authentic trans writing, "not just by us but actually for us," will not become possible until some vaguely postrevolutionary moment when trans people will "control the means of distribution" is to imagine that trans lives, bodies, and their many modes of survival, getting by, and making ends meet are already determined by an omnipotent cisnormative present. It is to have mistaken cisnormativity's fantasy of itself as a sovereign enclosure for how things actually are on the ground, at the office, in the streets, at the pub, in the existential minutiae of the trans ordinary. This, indeed, is the whole point of *Trans: A Memoir*. It is about the livability of the dead-end, the survivability of what's wrong — whether that is the wrong body, the wrong society, or the wrong genre — even as the wrongness of what is given is equiprimordial, as Heidegger would say, with givenness itself. It is to say that abjection, unlivability, and their attendant modes of spectacularization are not the only possible grounds for making ethical and political claims. It is about getting by, getting along, getting a body as good as you can get it. If it is about holding out for what is right, this is only because it is already about holding out in what is wrong, even if that is the wrong kind of wrong to hold on to. In the end, Jacques writes, "I was just trying to *live*" (162).

Andrea Long Chu is a PhD student in comparative literature at New York University, where she works on black studies, trans/feminist/queer theories, affect theory, and phenomenology.

Note

1.   Sedgwick's famous phrase is "nonce taxonomies," which she uses to describe the plural, shifting, and often contradictory ways in which gender or sexual subcultures name and classify their own modes of being, living, desiring, and practicing.

References

Berlant, Lauren. 2011. *Cruel Optimism*. Durham, NC: Duke University Press.

Fitzpatrick, Cat. 2015. Review of *Trans: A Memoir*, by Juliet Jacques. *Lambda Literary*, November 3. www.lambdaliterary.org/reviews/11/03/trans-by-juliet-jacques/.

Garfinkel, Harold. 1967. *Studies in Ethnomethodology*. Englewood Cliffs, NJ: Prentice-Hall.

Halberstam, Judith. 1994. "F2M: The Making of Female Masculinity." In *The Lesbian Postmodern*, edited by Laura L. Doan, 210–28. New York: Columbia University Press.

———. 1998. *Female Masculinity*. Durham, NC: Duke University Press.

Heidegger, Martin. 1962. *Being and Time*. Translated by John Macquarrie and Edward Robinson. New York: Harper and Row.

Husserl, Edmund. 1964. *The Phenomenology of Internal Time-Consciousness*. Edited by Martin Heidegger. Translated by James S. Churchill. Bloomington: University of Indiana Press.

———. 1970. *The Crisis of the European Sciences and Transcendental Phenomenology: An Introduction to Phenomenological Philosophy*. Translated by David Carr. Evanston, IL: Northwestern University Press.

———. 1982. *Ideas Pertaining to a Pure Phenomenology and to a Phenomenological Philosophy. First Book. General Introduction to a Pure Phenomenology*. Translated by Fred Kersten. The Hague: Martinus Nijhoff.

Jacques, Juliet. 2016. Interview by Beatrice Wilford. *Five Books*, January 8. fivebooks.com/interview /juliet-jacques-autofiction/.

Morris, Jan. 1974. *Conundrum*. New York: Harcourt Brace Jovanovich.

Moten, Fred. 2008. *Hughson's Tavern*. Providence, RI: Leon Works.

Povinelli, Elizabeth A. 2006. *The Empire of Love: Toward a Theory of Intimacy, Genealogy, and Carnality*. Durham, NC: Duke University Press.

———. 2008. "The Child in the Broom Closet: States of Killing and Letting Die." *South Atlantic Quarterly* 107, no. 3: 509–30.

Rubin, Henry S. 1998. "Phenomenology as Method in Trans Studies." *GLQ* 4, no. 2: 263–81.

Sedgwick, Eve Kosofsky. 1990. *Epistemology of the Closet*. Berkeley: University of California Press.

———. 2003. "Paranoid Reading and Reparative Reading, or, You're So Paranoid You Probably Think This Essay Is about You." In *Touching Feeling: Affect, Pedagogy, Performativity*, 123–51. Durham, NC: Duke University Press.

Stone, Sandy. 1991. "The *Empire* Strikes Back: A Posttranssexual Manifesto." In *Body Guards: The Cultural Politics of Gender Ambiguity*, 280–304. New York: Routledge.

Broadcasts of Betweenity

OLIVER BENDORF

Last Psalm at Sea Level
Meg Day
New York City: Barrow Street Press, 2014. 72 pp.

"How noisy everything grows": This quotation by Karl Kraus serves as epigraph for Walter Benjamin's essay "Karl Kraus" (2005: 433), a profile of the journalist in which Benjamin advances his own theory on eros, modernity, and the circulation of information. This essay was published in 1931, five years before "The Work of Art in the Age of Mechanical Reproduction" (Benjamin 1968), where Benjamin's triangulation of sensory perception, aesthetics, and the political really converge. This is one way to understand what is at stake in Meg Day's award-winning book of poems *Last Psalm at Sea Level*, which offers the reader a new relationship to the relational and political possibilities of sound, through psalms of grief, psalms of optimism, psalms of distress and rescue, of kinship, gender, and the body. Deceptively pastoral, these poems in fact can be read as a kind of theory of modern communication, through lyric and formal explorations of the ways we seek to hear and be heard, such as prayer, radio, and the gendered tenor that our own voice carries. In these poems, gender is a technology of the body, and the body is a technology of sound.

> My father never taught me how to half-way; betweenity
> merely broadcasts unfinished business.
> (Day 20, "When all you have is a hammer, everything looks like a nail")

Sometimes, gender is a sound, but sound is not merely something to be heard. Day's book begins with an epigraph on loneliness and pulses with the pathos of desire for belonging. Yet if it is redemptive, it is through sound and its technologies, connections to "the world's tin can," and I am reminded of Fred Moten's (2015: 13) work on the sociality of sound, also set forth in the imperative mode: "Do something with the sound like it's your friend," Moten exhorts us, in a section of "hand up to your ear," itself full of directives. For Day as for Moten, listening is an act that need not be aural; sound is not merely something to be heard but to be social with, intimate with. Moten writes, "You might be someone that needs listening to."

Last Psalm at Sea Level is necessarily synesthetic, then, in a way reminiscent of Anne Carson's lyric blurring of color, shape, sound, and feeling in *Autobiography of Red*. But the synesthesia takes on a practical bent here, where listening is often a visual process:

> At five, I knew my name only as a chestbeat-thumped M,
> as three letters scratched in crayon, knew my momma's call
> from down the aisle at church—the quick flick of wrists
> visible only in periphery.
> (Day 22, "Sit on the Floor with Me")

Identity is often discursively something that we *read* or are *read* as, in David Valentine's (2007: 111) *Imagining Transgender: An Ethnography of a Category*, in which he writes, about trying to determine who should get safer-sex kits he was handing out in the Meat Market, "Sorry, I said, they're only for the girls, invoking my instructions that the kits only be distributed to those I could read as 'transgender.'" (Perhaps this tendency is an outgrowth of the reaches of literary interpretation, in which everything can be a text.) What Day offers us is the seemingly radical notion that identity is not necessarily something that we *read* but something for which we *listen*. What becomes possible when we experience identity—subjectivity—not as a text but as a sound, or the absence thereof?

This book is not *about* sound, not exactly. It is more that it is of and with sound—of listening, pleading, commanding, asking questions, answering other questions, voice, humility. The radio is often an object of eros in these poems, and what is striking is the way it becomes a technology not of, but with, the body, in a cybernetic loop, human and machine. Take a look here:

> At five, I pressed my lips to the grate of my grandmother's
> Crosley, let broadcasts buzz into the pipe of my jawbone
> & learned to listen with my tongue, a flick-thin string
> that carried sound from the world's tin can to mine.
> (Day 22, "Sit on the Floor with Me")

This intimacy between identity and audio technology is a thread that continues throughout the book. We can see it again here:

> Unbuttoning his nightshirt, two sizes too big & monogrammed
> at the pocket with the initials *FTM*, he pulls the radio
> to his bare torso, the antennae tucked under one arm.
> (Day 37, "Broadcast among the Other Skeletons")

In this poem, FTM is a name, an initial, something stitched onto a garment that does not even quite fit, but is donned anyway. Again, the radio appears against the skin, and this time the antennae — another flick-thin technology meant to carry sound from the world to us — are tucked, held close. For most people reading this, "FTM" will unambiguously signal "female-to-male." Sometimes, though, as I have learned through Internet searches, the acronym also stands for "first-time mother." That double entendre, in which the two meanings are seemingly incongruous, is in fact crucial to how these poems upend the predictability of gendered experiences and roles.

If *Last Psalm at Sea Level* is a book of trans experience, it troubles the narrative of agency and instead suggests that the feedback loop goes both ways. Sometimes, through circumstances of death or illness memory or the perception of strangers, roles are thrust on us: daughter, son, husband, wife, mother, father. Kinship is queered. Breasts are taken out by cancer. Sometimes, a child is thrust into the role of an adult. Sometimes we bereave too soon. Elsewhere, the speaker imagines what becomes possible by thrusting oneself into roles. In the poem "On nights when I am Brandon Teena," Day uses sound to transmit an identification with Teena, a trans man murdered in landlocked Nebraska in 1993, imagining the "sharp squeal of the screen door" and "that first heavy boot" — sounds that foretell a violence enacted to punish betweenity. How noisy everything grows, in some moments of distress.

In its earliest uses, radio allowed ships to maintain contact with each other while out at sea. Not yet able to transmit speech, these radios worked by Morse code, with ships tapping out messages to each other and to stations on land. These radios allowed sinking ships to call for help in a continuous sequence of three dits, three dahs, and three dits, all run together without letterspacing. SOS, the universal distress signal: Save our ship.

"Save our ship": the imperative, the plea, is a mode impossible to ignore throughout *Last Psalm at Sea Level*. Psalms, after all, assume the efficacy of prayer: "Listen to my words, Lord, consider my lament," goes Psalm 5:1. These sacred songs of Day's are full of the imperative:

> Why have you made me
> know the sea?
> Make me a bird, Lord;
> make me a man.
> (Day 5, "Hymn to a Landlocked God")

Another example is the stunning English-to-English translation of John Donne's Holy Sonnet 14, "Batter my heart, three person'd God," which Day rewrites as "Batter My Heart, Transgender'd God."

The German government first adopted SOS, now the international Morse distress signal, in radio regulations effective in 1905. During World War I, both sides used radio to relay messages, and after the war's end, broadcasting began in the United States and in Europe, 1922 in France and 1923 in Germany. Radio was an exciting new medium, but tightly controlled in France at the time. Between 1927 and 1933, Benjamin wrote and presented around eighty radio broadcasts. In 1933 he went into exile in Paris. What I am trying to say is that Day's notion of sound as political has precedent.

In these poems, when it comes to sound, the personal is political. In an interview I conducted in 2013, Day told me, "I feel less invested in talking about myself these days . . . I'd much rather talk about sound. I'd much rather have a conversation about why young Deaf folks are being oralized as hearing college students fulfill their 'foreign language' requirement with American Sign Language. I'd much rather engage on the topic of spoken word as having its roots, yes, in hiphop, but also in political evangelism and pulpit-pounding and advertising." Day's other work, including the chapbook *We Can't Read This*, displays sign-language diagrams alongside poem text, in what Cathy Park Hong describes as "a how-to on re-imagining the body and language when one is denied the instruments of voice and hearing" (blurb for Day 2013). This triangulation between sensory perception, the aesthetic, and the political is why I think it is so fruitful to read *Last Psalm at Sea Level* in conversation with "Art in the Age."

In a poem toward the middle of the book, Day writes, "When they took my breasts, I dreamt of Icarus." In the book's first part, flying is a desired method of being in the world. Flying is salvation. "Make me a bird, Lord." Later, though, it is not flying, it is standing, as with this strikingly succinct and relevant comment on using one's body as a political technology:

> There is a reason we stand in ovation. There is a reason
> we stand for something.
> (Day 58, "To My Student, Who Asked, "Since When Does a Bunch of Normal
>   People Standing Around Actually Change Anything?"")

The act of listening is political, and so is the act of standing. Lord, make me an instrument. I cannot help but think of recent acts of protest, including in my then residence of Madison, Wisconsin, for Tony Robinson, black, eighteen, shot and killed by police, and for whom I joined in several marches. Day's lines on standing helped me to a new understanding of what it is we do when we stand. This connection is explicit, too, as Day writes about state violence not from afar but from as close as it comes, as in two poems, appearing side by side, "During the Ricochet of the Bullet from His Taser," for Oscar Grant, black, twenty-two, shot and killed by police, and "During the Ricochet of the Bullet from Your Taser," for Johannes Mehserle, the police officer who shot Grant in Oakland. The body is an instrument, yes, but it is also a fragile blur of skin and bone and a pumping heart and rage and love. Grief finds its way to the body, and what is the audio output of that? Sometimes we who do have voices have a moral imperative to make noise for those who do not. Day's rigor is matched with generosity in showing us our inextricable human relations through sound, and why those matter for what kind of world we want to live in.

One thing about sea level is that it is not a static place or measure; it creeps around in geological time and has been rising. *Last Psalm at Sea Level* is a book of immense grief and cautious optimism, of "angels once, or at least the sound of them" (Day 6, "Ghazal for Finally Leaving What Has Already Left"). Day is a poet who knows that not only are there two ways to leave sea level—go up or go down—but also that, often, we do both. Neil Armstrong and his moonwalk, and then his return to our blue planet. Amelia Earhart's flight and her disappearance into the Pacific. These transmissions, these psalms, from a poet for whom the coastline is home, are coming in loud and clear.

Oliver Bendorf is the author of *The Spectral Wilderness* (2015), which won the Wick Poetry Prize. His writing and art have been published in *Adirondack Review, Alaska Quarterly Review, jubilat, Rumpus, Troubling the Line: Trans and Genderqueer Poetry and Poetics*, and elsewhere. He holds an MFA and an MLIS from the University of Wisconsin–Madison.

References

Benjamin, Walter. 1968. "The Work of Art in the Age of Mechanical Reproduction." In *Illuminations*, edited by Hannah Arendt, 217–52. New York: Harcourt, Brace.

———. 2005. "Karl Kraus." In *Walter Benjamin, Selected Writings*, vol. 2, pt. 2, *1931–1934*, edited by Michael W. Jennings, Howard Eiland, and Gary Smith, 433–58. Cambridge, MA: Belknap Press of Harvard University Press.

Day, Meg. 2013. *We Can't Read This*. Fairfax, VA: Gazing Grain.

Moten, Fred. 2015. *The Little Edges*. Middletown, CT: Wesleyan University Press.

Valentine, David. 2007. *Imagining Transgender: An Ethnography of a Category*. Durham, NC: Duke University Press.

Printed and bound by CPI Group (UK) Ltd, Croydon, CR0 4YY

13/04/2025

14656484-0003